EUROPEAN STUDIES SERIES

General Editors   Colin Jones
                    Richard Overy

Series Advisers   Joe Bergin
                    John Breuilly
                    Ruth Harris

This series marks a major initiative in European history publishing aimed primarily, though not exclusively, at an undergraduate audience. It will encompass a wide variety of books on aspects of European history since 1500, with particular emphasis on France and Germany, although no country will be excluded and a special effort will be made to cover previously neglected areas, such as Scandinavia, Eastern Europe and Southern Europe.

The series will include political accounts and broad thematic treatments, both of a comparative kind and studies of a single country, and will lay particular emphasis on social and cultural history where this opens up fruitful new ways of examining the past. The aim of the series is to make available a wide range of titles in areas where there is now an obvious gap or where the existing historical literature is out of date or narrowly focused. The series will also include translations of important books published elsewhere in Europe.

Interest in European affairs and history has never been greater; *European Studies* will help make that European heritage closer, richer and more comprehensible.

EUROPEAN STUDIES SERIES

Titles in the series

More titles in preparation

Early Modern Germany, 1477–1806

MICHAEL HUGHES

MACMILLAN

First published 1992 by
MACMILLAN EDUCATION LTD
Houndmills, Basingstoke, Hampshire RG21 2XS
and London
Companies and representatives
throughout the world

ISBN 0–333–53773–4 hardcover
ISBN 0–333–53774–2 paperback

A catalogue record for this book is available
from the British Library.

Typeset by LBJ Enterprises Limited
of Chilcompton and Tadley
Printed in Hong Kong

For Yvonne

Contents

Preface

This is a study of Germany in the Early Modern period. It is a story of the failure of a feudal Empire to find unity, except in the loosest of federations, and the failure of a nation to create a state for itself. The basic aim of the book is to investigate the survival of the idea of Germanness, or German national feeling, during a period when, according to traditional accounts, Germany as a state had virtually ceased to exist. The element of continuity in Germany's development will also be examined in an attempt to discover how far back in Germany's past it is necessary to go to find the roots of the "German problem", the Germans' search for a political expression of their strongly developed awareness of cultural unity, which was to have important consequences for the rest of Europe in the late nineteenth and twentieth centuries. It is not a collective history of individual German states but an attempt to show that an all-German dimension persisted until the end of the Holy Roman Empire in 1806. Only then did Germany cease to exist, except as a geographical expression and an idea in men's minds, until its re-creation in the Confederation of 1815.

The Germans were themselves responsible for the long neglect of the Holy Roman Empire, the first *Reich*, the German political organization in the Early Modern period, is a traditionally state-centred historiography. For nineteenth- and early twentieth-century historians, progress in German history meant progress towards national unity. The Empire was seen as the embodiment of division and weakness and seemed to lack all the essential characteristics of a real state. Viewed with hindsight the Empire for a long time seemed exotic and too often it was remembered in the aphorisms of critics like Pufendorf and Voltaire. Understandably perhaps, after 1945 views of

Germany's past seemed to be overshadowed by recent events and there was a tendency to scour German history to discover the roots of the events of 1933 to 1945. This has produced a concentration on nineteenth- and twentieth-century history and contributed to a pessimistic interpretation of that history derived from the underlying assumption that Germany's problems stemmed from her arrested development and divergence from the rest of Western Europe. Germany's slide into disunity and impotence in the Early Modern period was compared with the simultaneous rise of powerful unified states, like France and England. Germany was rather to be compared to Poland and escaped a similar fate, partition and extinction, only through a combination of fortunate circumstances. This was echoed in the traditional German view, taught in German schools until 1945, which attributed Germany's division and weakness and all that flowed from them to the Thirty Years' War and the treaties of Westphalia. After 1919 it was very convenient to link this to the Treaty of Versailles and blame all Germany's problems on foreigners.

Any attempt to present a manageable account of German history after 1648 runs up against serious problems. The German equivalent of the Whig theory of history — a concentration on state-building combined with a belief that Germany after 1648 was no longer a state but a collection of states — has produced a fragmentary approach. The concept of the state was identified almost exclusively with the nineteenth-century power state (*Machtstaat*) or institutional state (*Anstaltstaat*). In traditional historiography there are large "blank" areas between the important events like the Reformation, the Thirty Years' War, the Seven Years' War and the French Revolution. During these intervals of "stagnation", such as the periods 1555 to 1600 and 1648 to 1740, nothing of note seemed to be happening. "Germany" apparently disappeared, to be replaced by states like Prussia, Austria and, a long way behind, Saxony, Bavaria and the Palatinate. Substantial areas of Germany and all-German history were ignored. In the same way those groups which apparently stood in the way of state-building, for example the parliamentary Estates, were written out of German history. It is the object of this book to examine some of these blanks. An alternative to the all-German approach in the past was to study what is essentially local history, the developments in the individual little states. Not only is this extremely complex but it also involves the risk of sliding into a narrow antiquarianism. In the same way study of the daily lives of "ordinary" Germans can become folkloric. Too many traditional histories of "Germany" tended to deal only with developments in Prussia and, when written by Austrian historians, in Austria, as the real "growth points" in German history. One problem was that a separate Austrian "national" historiography developed early and reflected the long-standing ambivalent relationship between Austria and Germany.

There has been particular concentration on Prussia, a result of the development of the so-called Borussian legend in the nineteenth century, the notion that it was Prussia's manifest destiny from the seventeenth century to lead and unite Germany. The Borussian legend is remarkably tenacious in popular views of German history. One example among many will serve to illustrate the distorting effect of this. Between 1907 and 1909 a commission of thirty-two historians of the Württemberg Historical and Antiquarian Society published a large and sumptuous two-volume study of Duke Charles Eugene of Württemberg (1744–93) and his times. The introductory chapter praised Frederick II of Prussia to the skies, portraying him as the pioneer of a new and creative state idea and the founder of a state which acted as a beacon for the whole German nation. Among the king's manifold achievements one in particular was highlighted: Frederick prevented the creation of a German-Austrian great power and began the process of excluding Austria from German affairs.

There has been some change in approach in recent years. The significance of the Empire is increasingly recognized in recent historiography, which has taken a much more favourable view of it than used to be the case. In recent years, when the whole future shape of Germany has again become the subject of debate and the search for a new *Modell Deutschland* has become current, there has been a new interest in the old *Reich*. The tradition of federalism in German history, long neglected, is again the object of serious study. It is now recognized that, though pre-modern in essence, the *Reich* did show evidence of growth, vitality and progress and can no longer be seen as a nation in aspic. The looseness of the German constitution provided opportunities for a great variety of different evolutions and there was nothing inevitable about developments. Perhaps the pendulum has swung too far: there is some danger now of a new form of anachronism, a new *Reichsromantik* or *Reichspathos*, with the Holy Roman Empire being portrayed as a combination of the European Court of Human Rights, the United Nations and the EEC. The fact that the Empire was, at least in part, devoted to peace, freedom and justice derived as much from external factors as from a conscious choice of its inhabitants. This idealization of the old *Reich* is itself part of the "new nationalism" seen recently in Germany.

It is now possible to trace some trends which affected the whole of Germany (though there are always exceptions to any generalization). It is the object of this study to describe these trends and to attempt to provide a genuine history of Germany as a whole in the last century and a half of the Holy Roman Empire. The experience of individual states will be used to illustrate general developments but it will very quickly become clear that there was no typical German state. One of the most striking characteristics of the Empire was its enormous complexity and the great variety of developments within its component parts. There is a widespread but mistaken belief that everything was more simple in earlier centuries and that things have become more complicated as a result of industrialization and the dawning of the mass age. In reality the opposite is the case: uniformity and standardization are characteristics of the modern age. The Holy Roman Empire was a system which sheltered a very wide variety of political systems, local self-government, clerical rule, urban republicanism, parliamentary government, limited monarchy and absolute monarchy. Traditional interpretations can be misleading in other ways. The Empire was not uniformly stagnant. Modernization took place within it although there were great differences between developments in the individual states. The period was not dominated by the rise of absolutism and religious antagonism.

Throughout the period studied foreign influence was of great importance in Germany's development. The "German question" was always also a European question. At the beginning Germany was involved in the rivalry between the Habsburgs and the Valois and at the end French influence and control became paramount. Germany's involvement in European affairs will be an important element in this study.

The keynote of this period in German history is the interplay between dualities, between unity and diversity in politics, in economic and social development and in culture, between the Empire and the states, the Emperor and the princes, rulers and their subjects, after the Reformation between two faiths and from the later eighteenth century between Prussia and Austria. While Germany as a whole did not progress from a feudal collection of provinces to a centrally administered total state (*Gesamtstaat*), individual German states progressed a long way along that road. State-building in the individual states prevented state-building in the Empire but the fact that the Empire retained some state-like functions prevented the states from exercising total sovereignty.

The approach adopted in the book is chronological and it employs a mixture of narrative and analysis. It is written with sixth-form and undergraduate students of history and general readers wanting to understand the background of the "German question" in mind. It is primarily a political history which concentrates on key developments producing substantial change within a remarkably stable constitutional framework established in the late fifteenth and early sixteenth centuries. Economic and social developments will be introduced only as background to analysis of the political situation; artistic, musical and literary aspects are not covered. A case will be made for the legitimacy of writing about "Germany" even when it was deeply fragmented. A political Germany existed in the *Reich*, much more important than used to be thought. There was no economic Germany but there was no economic France either. A spiritual or intellectual Germany was always there, as was a Germany of the mind. Germany as an employment common market also continued to exist, even if it was weakened by the confessionalization of life which followed the Reformation.

I must thank all those who have contributed to the writing of this book. I am particularly grateful to the University College of Wales for leave of absence and financial help, to the U.C.W. Hugh Owen Library and the library of the German Historical Institute, London, to Dr Jeremy Black of the University of Durham, Mr M. D. Hughes and Dr and Mrs J. Marek.

Michael Hughes

List of Abbreviations

AmHR	American Historical Review
CEH	Central European History
EcHR	Economic History Review
EHR	English Historical Review
EHQ	European History Quarterly
ESR	European Studies Review
HJ	Historical Journal
JCH	Journal of Contemporary History
JEcH	Journal of Economic History
JMH	Journal of Modern History
PandP	Past and Present
TRHS	Transactions of the Royal Historical Society

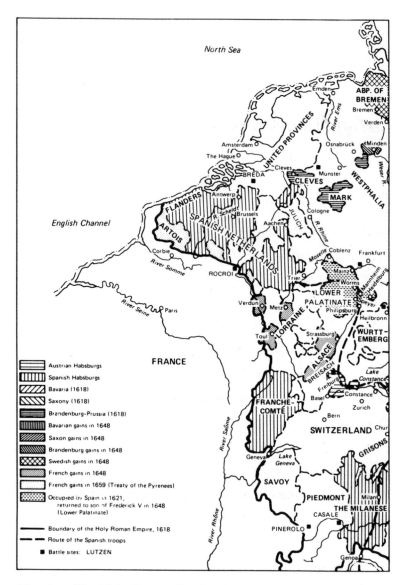

Map 1   The Holy Roman Empire during the Thirty Years' War

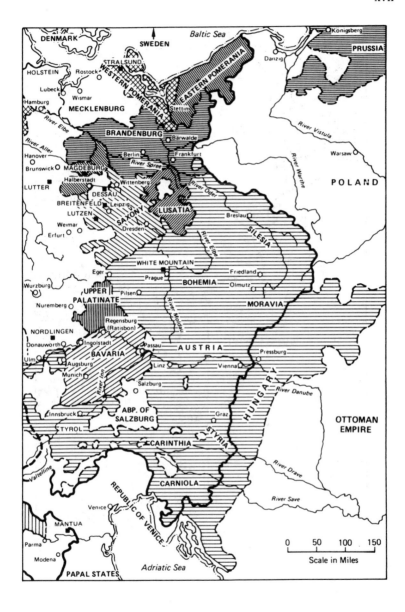

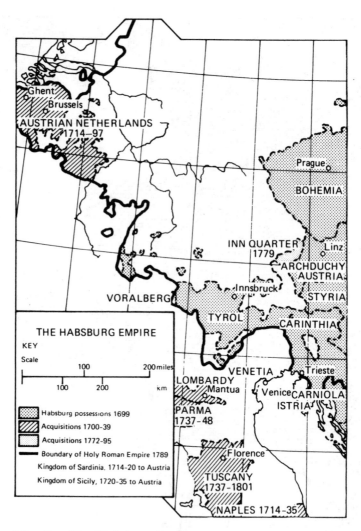

Map 2   The Habsburg Empire

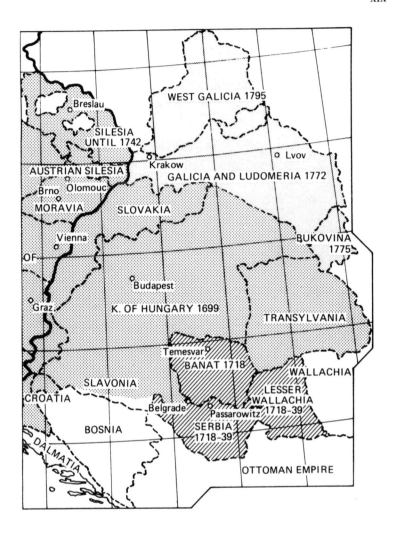

1 *Introduction*

On 21 April 1477 in the Brabant city of Malines Maximilian of Habsburg, son of the Holy Roman Emperor Frederick III, married by proxy, Mary, sole heiress to the Burgundian territories, including the Netherlands and the county of Burgundy, after the death of her father Charles the Bold, Duke of Burgundy. The Habsburgs had only recently taken a great step forward when, through the marriage of Albert of Austria, Frederick III's predecessor, to the daughter of the Luxemburg Emperor Sigismund, they acquired a claim to Hungary and Bohemia. This second marriage opened for them the marvellous prospect of a huge new territorial base from which to strike at their main dynastic rival, the King of France, and to launch a bid to strengthen their position in Germany. The marriage coincided with a growing popular campaign within Germany for a revival or renewal of the Holy Roman Empire (*renovatio imperii*) as a means of solving Germany's many problems. Both hopes, dynastic and national, were destined to be cruelly disappointed.

This study begins with an examination of Germany on the eve of the Protestant Reformation. The most striking feature of the country at that time was its fragmentation into the famous patchwork quilt of states, which is probably the best-remembered aspect of the Holy Roman Empire. In order to understand the conditions of the time, it is necessary to make a quick tour of earlier German history. [1] Between the tenth and twelfth centuries there were signs of the growth of national self-consciousness in the German lands, associated with a revival of the Holy Roman Empire, which suggested that the first European national state might be emerging there. The Empire was the centre of gravity in Europe and the Emperor shared with the ruler of Byzantium the great prestige associated with the inheritance of imperial Rome and the Frankish empire of Charlemagne. During the eleventh, twelfth and thirteenth centuries Germany really mattered in Europe. Under the greatest emperors of the Middle Ages, Frederick I Barbarossa and his grandson Frederick II, both from the House of Hohenstaufen, Germany seemed united and strong. It was economically vital and had a large population. It enjoyed a fortunate geographical position astride the major European trade routes at a time when the bulk of trade was carried by road or on navigable waterways. Germany was a more urban society than most areas of Europe. Urban growth and the social mobility associated with it were particularly marked and there were strong concentrations of powerful and prosperous towns in the Baltic region, the Rhine valley and the south. It is estimated that on the eve of the Reformation ten per cent of the population lived in towns.

The early promise was not fulfilled. The first signs of decline began to appear in the fourteenth century, and then in the fifteenth Germany seemed to enter a long period of economic, political and social decay, which lasted until the early nineteenth century. For some five hundred years Germany was to be a negative quantity in Europe, which had things done to it but which was able to achieve little. It became the anvil when it should have been the hammer.

In reality the political cohesion and strength of Germany in the Middle Ages were illusory. The Hohenstaufen period, especially the reign of Frederick Barbarossa (1155–90), is traditionally regarded as the zenith of medieval German power. In fact apparent success only masked a number of well-established and damaging trends in Germany's political development. With the death of the last Hohenstaufen, Conrad IV, in 1254, these trends resumed. The Great Interregnum, "the terrible time without an Emperor", followed until 1273 and then there was a succession of weak rulers, minorities and double elections. These accelerated certain constitutional developments visible from the beginning of the thirteenth century, as a result of which Germany began to diverge increasingly from many of her neighbours. While elsewhere rulers were beginning the process of subordinating their great feudatories, depriving them of their semi-independent status, the German nobility began to take powers from their king. A number of acts marked Germany's progress down this road — for example in 1231–2 Frederick II issued the Statute in Favour of the Princes — though these were only the early steps in a long process. Later Henry VII (1308–13) deliberately gave away many important royal rights to the great nobles in order to buy their support for his campaigns in Italy. He also had hopes of persuading them to agree to the ending of the elective nature of the German crown by making concessions but they rejected this, instinctively sensing the danger an hereditary monarchy represented to their position.

Some of the reasons for Germany's problems were obvious and, while they help to explain what happened, they do not tell the whole story, as many of the same factors were present in other countries without producing the same results. Germany was big, sprawling and dislocated. As a result the monarchy, which initially relied on rule through personal contacts, was unable to penetrate into some parts. Germany lacked geographical unity and natural frontiers. The relics of an older tribal consciousness were also present in the "tribal" or "stem" duchies (*Stammherzogtümer*) Swabia, Franconia, Saxony, Bavaria and Austria, whose dukes had earlier elected one of their number as German king. More important, the medieval kings and emperors (the latter title was taken by the rulers crowned by the pope) were unable to establish strong and effective government. The reasons for this were many. There were frequent changes of dynasty as the German crown remained elective. The Saxon dynasty ruled from 919 to 1024, the Salians from 1024 to 1125 and the Staufer or Hohenstaufen from 1138 to 1254. The absence of an hereditary German royal dynasty meant that German national consciousness lacked a point of focus around which it could coalesce.

There is no simple explanation as to why the elective monarchy persisted in Germany. Among the factors must be listed the already mentioned survival of tribal consciousness and its associated tradition of elected leaders. The long drawn-out conflict between the papacy and the German crown in the eleventh century, known as the Investiture Contest, also played an important part. In 1076 the pope excommunicated Henry IV, giving the king's political opponents in Germany an excuse to elect another king. By the mid-thirteenth century the electoral system had solidified to the extent that seven hereditary electorates had emerged and it was accepted that their consent was required for a valid election.

There is dispute concerning the basis of the special status of the seven electors. The three ecclesiastics, the Archbishops of Mainz, Trier and Cologne, were the senior prelates of the German Church. It has been suggested that the four lay electors, Saxony, Bohemia, Brandenburg and the Palatinate, owed their status to descent from the daughters of Emperor Otto I or to the fact that they were political allies of the Emperor Charles IV, in whose reign the Golden Bull, which finalised electoral arrangements, was issued.[2] Previously the right to participate in royal elections had been undefined and varied from time to time. Some of the other great nobles continued to claim a say in elections and confusion continued until the whole process was systematized in great detail in the Golden Bull of 1356, which, after the election of King Sigismund in 1410, remained in force until the end of the Empire. The superior status of the electors was symbolized by recognition that the lands of the four lay rulers were indivisible primogenitures and by the grant to each of the seven of a special ceremonial function at the coronation of the king/Emperor. Details of this were also laid down in the Bull. The towns were forbidden to accept the electors' subjects as citizens. The Bull also proposed annual meetings of the electors to share the government of the Empire with the king/Emperor, but such a permanent council did not come into existence in the form envisaged.

In order to secure election, candidates for the German crown had to make concessions to the electors. This aggravated the second inherent weakness of the German crown, its inability to control its own nominal servants. The size of Germany and the many threats to its borders made it essential for the kings to delegate power but a combination of circumstances made it possible for men originally commissioned as royal officials to turn their territories into hereditary fiefs, especially when they coincided with the older tribal dukedoms (*Stammherzogtümer*). The offices of count (*Graf*) and imperial steward (*Reichsvogt*), established as instruments of royal control, were easily turned into hereditary territorial possessions. This feudalization led to the emergence of a group of intermediate rulers between the king/Emperor and the mass of Germans, who became only indirect subjects of their monarch. These rulers, usually for convenience described as "the princes", were able gradually to pare away more and more royal rights and royal lands, especially the major accumulation of the Hohenstaufens in the south west and Franconia, either by seizing them or as a result of grants from the crown, until they became as good as sovereign in their own territories.

There were very heavy losses during the Interregnum, which lasted from 1256 until 1273. As a result of losses the German monarchs became dependent on their nominal inferiors and the overmighty subject became permanently institutionalized in German political life. A wide gulf therefore opened between the king/Emperor's claims to enjoy the plenitude of power of the Roman Caesars and the real and manifest weakness of his position. The power of the German princes became institutionalized not only in the elective monarchy but also in the imperial diet (*Hoftag* later *Reichstag*). Its form was becoming systematized by the thirteenth century, though its membership and composition were not finally fixed until the seventeenth. It was accepted early that the consent of the *Reichstag* was essential for legislation: Germany became a dualistic state in which power was shared between the crown and the nobility, with the balance shifting increasingly in favour of the latter. The same process was to become apparent in many of the individual German states with the rise of parliamentary Estates, though in the great majority the crown eventually emasculated the Estates, the exact opposite of the all-German situation. Some German monarchs did make efforts to reverse this process but in vain.

Unlike many of the fellow rulers, the German monarchs were unable to make use of a policy of divide and rule to strengthen their position. In the Middle Ages German kings and Emperors, in order to achieve short-term aims, too readily abandoned groups who might have been their natural allies. Too many were, for example, obsessed with the recovery of shadowy imperial authority in Italy, which was richer than Germany, had a more pleasant climate and contained Rome, and were prepared to sacrifice their German interests. Germany was seen as no more than a source of men and money and the nobility were best able to provide both. Frederick II, known as the Wonder of the World and a great German ruler, spent all of his time and effort in Italy. Only in the later thirteenth century did these Italian ambitions gradually become less important though non-German affairs continued to occupy the attention of German rulers. The damaging Investiture Contest arose from papal fear of a revival of imperial power in Italy, which led successive popes to support the Emperor's enemies in Germany. It also deprived the Emperors of the support of the clergy, elsewhere often useful allies of the monarchy. The German Church became feudalized and its higher offices, bishoprics, great abbeys and their chapters, a near monopoly of the nobility.

Another such group were the *ministeriales*, a class of royal servants which became part of the nobility in the course of the twelfth century. At that time there was a fluid situation within the German aristocracy with plenty of opportunities to rise. New families were elbowing their way up while others were falling or dying out. By the sixteenth century the whole system had settled down and very few new major ruling families emerged thereafter.

The towns, whose growth was at first encouraged by German rulers as a counterweight to the nobility and a vital source of revenues, were completely sacrificed for the kings' Italian ambitions. For example, in the Statute in Favour of the Princes, Frederick II gave the princes the right of chartering towns. Great towns like Cologne, Strasburg, Augsburg, Nuremberg and Lübeck were powerful enough to retain their autonomy but the majority were very vulnerable. In the course of the fifteenth century many previously self-governing towns fell under the control of neighbouring rulers, such as Mainz and Erfurt, and the process continued into the sixteenth century.

Some kings deliberately weakened the crown. There was a substantial loss of royal power under Charles IV (1346–78), later to be seen as a brilliant ruler. In fact he concentrated on furthering the interests of Bohemia, which became a great power under him, and of his Luxemburg dynasty. In the process Germany was seriously damaged. Within thirty years of his death the Great Schism split Christendom and the Hussite conflict, religious and ethnic civil wars, ravaged Bohemia. Charles also made the financial problems of the German crown much worse. Before his reign royal lands and rights had been gradually alienated to reward followers or to raise ready cash. Often the land was leased but it proved very difficult for the crown to recover land at the termination of the lease, as shown by the proverb *Pfand gibt oft Land* (roughly, "a lease often gives ownership"). The Hohenstaufen plan to create a belt of imperial territory across Germany as the basis for a revival of royal power came to nothing. There was no imperial treasury; at a time when individual states were beginning to rationalize their financial administrations, the *Reich* did not. During his reign Charles IV gave away large amounts of land and rights. His motive was buy votes for his son's election and deliberately to impoverish the German crown in order to make the title hereditary in the House of Luxemburg, enriched by the silver of Bohemia. No potential rival would, he calculated, have the resources to sustain the imperial dignity.

The desire to secure the election of his son Wenceslas was a major motive behind the issue of the Golden Bull. He failed to create an hereditary monarchy. His plans for the creation of a powerful state came to nothing: he partitioned his lands among his five sons and nephews and all died without male heirs. His son Wenceslas was deposed by the German rulers in 1400 as incompetent and five years later the League of Marbach declared the right of the princes to share the Emperor's power and to depose an Emperor they disapproved of.

Charles had effectively deprived later emperors of anything but very scant revenues from the Empire. Emperors were forced to draw on the resources of their own personal possessions, if they were available, to fund imperial policies in Germany.

As a consequence of their lack of resources German monarchs were unable to fulfil the basic functions of government, strong administration and the maintenance of law and order. This led in the fourteenth century to bouts of anarchy and petty wars, which damaged the economy. Serious damage was caused by chronic rivalry between the Habsburg, Wittelsbach and Luxemburg families, all ambitious for more land and the royal title. As a result Germany entered a vicious circle: the weakness of the central government forced the substantial local nobles to take over more functions of government themselves, further weakening central authority. The local nobles needed more money to sustain their governments and therefore they took over more imperial revenues and rights. In the fifteenth century another period of prolonged anarchy led the towns of the south west to form leagues to protect themselves and their commerce. They acted nominally as the agents of the Emperor but in reality the self-help strategy embodied in these leagues symbolized imperial weakness. The first Swabian League was established in 1376 as a defensive organization and was a sign of growing friction between the towns and the nobility. The greatest league was the Swabian League of 1488 to 1534, made up of towns and small and ecclesiastical states. It was very powerful and a source of serious concern to the German nobility. It eventually broke up as a result of religious disputes. Its collapse destroyed another institution which might have balanced the power of the princes or prevented their total victory. The leagues were temporary as it was impossible to establish permanent cohesion between the towns.

In addition to the above factors, certain basic divisions within Germany were well-established before the fifteenth century. The survival of regionalism has already been mentioned. There were broad differences between north and south, separated by the Main river, in geography and agriculture. One reason for this was the absence of navigable waterways, on which bulk goods were moved, linking north and south. The main south German rivers, the Main and the Danube, flowed west and east. There were marked differences in the German spoken in the two regions. The Teutonic Order began to disintegrate, among other factors, because of rivalry between speakers of High and Low German.

The social and economic differences between east and west, divided by the Elbe river, were also growing. [3] The east gradually diverged from the west and remained backward in its development. There is some danger in over-emphasizing the contrast in the period before the fifteenth century. In the twelfth and early thirteenth centuries Germany, along with the rest of Western Europe, experienced a population rise and the peasants lost their bargaining power. As a result, serfdom became established by 1200. The continuing population rise and a desire to escape serfdom led to a great migration of Germans eastwards into sparsely populated areas. Recruiters known as *locatores* collected settlers from as far west as Flanders and assembled great German wagon trains, which rolled eastwards. The native Slav populations were driven out or Germanized. This became combined with a Christianizing mission among the heathen Slavs organized first by the Cistercians and later the Teutonic Knights, the Knights of St Mary's Hospital in Jerusalem, who were thrown out of the Holy Land by the Moslems and eventually set up their new headquarters in Königsberg. They subsequently moved to the great fortress of Marienburg in Prussia, where they were given large areas of land to subdue and settle. Many new towns were established with German municipal law and a high degree of self-government. They also became centres of Germanization. German commercial power, embodied most spectacularly in the Hanseatic League, stretched out, with German towns, along the Baltic coast and southwards into Poland, Bohemia and Hungary, though German dominance in the last areas became weaker from the fifteenth century as natives began to displace the former German urban ruling class. New German states emerged from this eastwards expansion, including Mecklenburg, Brandenburg, Pomerania and Silesia. In contrast to the west, the east was markedly free. By the mid-fourteenth century the east was still thinly populated and labourers, a rare commodity, were able to retain their freedom. There was little or no feudalization, village and town self-government through popular assemblies was common and most peasants held their land as free tenants or in return for light labour services.

Circumstances began to change with the coming of the Black Death in Western Europe from the mid-fourteenth to the fifteenth century. This precipitated an agrarian crisis caused by a sudden population fall, made worse by earlier emigration. In the west the epidemic caused the decay of feudalism: the fifteenth century was the Golden Age of the western peasant, with rising living standards. It also produced the lord-tenant system known as *Grundherrschaft*, under which the lords left the farming of the bulk of the land to tenants in return for payments. In the east *Gutsherrschaft* became predominant. Under that system the lords farmed most of the land directly to produce a surplus, using the labour of unfree tenants who were allowed a small plot from which to feed their families. Landlords, including the Teutonic Order, responded to the labour shortage with a new policy, the imposition of unfreedom on their tenants, taking advantage of weak rulers to do so. Serfdom began to become established in the east and was further strengthened in the sixteenth and seventeenth centuries with the emergence of a class of noble capitalist farmers, the *Junkers*, who made themselves rich by selling surplus grain to Western Europe. They were able to make themselves politically dominant over their rulers, to destroy the great majority of the towns and to exact high labour services from their serfs. Serfdom lingered on in the east into the nineteenth century. As industry developed in the west, Eastern Europe, including Germany east of the Elbe, was organized to feed the growing urban centres of the Netherlands, north eastern France and south eastern England. Danzig developed as a great centre for the shipment of grain drawn to it from the Vistula river basin. The cultivation of the grain was based on serf labour. There was therefore no market in the east for imported manufactures except luxuries for the landowners. Industry was restricted to the nobles' estates. In the absence of a developed urban class, the nobles remained economically and socially dominant. The distinction between east and west was to remain politically significant in Germany into the twentieth century.

2 Germany on the Eve of the Reformation

In the late fifteenth century the Holy Roman Empire was changing in two important ways.[1] First it was shedding its international or supranational image and becoming more self-consciously German in character. Secondly, it was entering a prolonged period of political, social, religious and economic unrest which coincided with growing threats from outside. These problems reached a crisis point simultaneously in the years around 1500.

In the late fifteenth century Germany entered a period of chronic instability which produced a wave of millenarianism, an expectation that the end of the world was approaching. Turkish attacks on Europe were viewed as part of a pattern of divine punishment for men's sins. There was an excited and restless spirit abroad. The times seemed "out of joint" and there was a real fear of imminent catastrophe. Among the symptoms of this were serious social divisions, growing violence, including frequent rioting and rampant anti-Semitism, and more extreme religious observance. Men's need for reassurance about the availability of salvation and the rush to achieve it, if possible by a short-cut, took many forms, traditional and new, including a frenzy of charitable works, the spread of superstitious practices, frantic efforts to see as many holy relics as possible, pilgrimages and the emergence of wild preachers. The last was seen especially in overpopulated areas like Bohemia, Westphalia and the Netherlands, where they gained a following among groups on the margins of society. Such an excess of religion was easily explained: pictorial representations of religious themes were everywhere in churches, in paintings, sculptures and stained-glass windows, which were used during services to point up the religious message. Wood-block prints containing religious themes were very popular.

These problems were made worse by the absence of a strong central authority in Germany and there were fears that the weakness of the Empire threatened the stability of the individual German states. In the fifteenth century many anonymous pamphlets appeared calling for a fundamental reform of the Empire and often for social and economic reforms, including secularization of Church property, the abolition of the nobility, a married clergy and the fixing of fair prices. This overlapping of political, social and spiritual grievances, the blending of anti-clericalism, anti-noble sentiments and an idealization of the Empire, was typical. Some predicted the emergence of a messianic leader from the lower orders to head a movement to restore the Emperor to all his powers as a strict but just father of his people. Revolutionary and reactionary sentiments were often mixed: a social, political and religious revolution was envisaged, a violent overturning of society portrayed as the gateway to a new Golden Age. At the same time there was a yearning for a return to the society of the past, the memory of which was gilded by remoteness and myth. Anger against innovations and talk of the "good old days" were frequent.

Economic problems played a major part in all this. Germany was, on the surface, still enjoying the prosperity seen in the later Middle Ages but some parts of the economy were finding it hard to adapt to new methods and new circumstances and strains were beginning to show. The effects were patchy but certain trends were clear. The whole economic structure of Europe was changing to Germany's disadvantage in the first third of the sixteenth century. The Hanseatic League, after reaching the peak of its prosperity in the fifteenth century, began to decline as powerful foreign interests, in particular the rising Scandinavian states, England and the Netherlands, encroached in the Baltic. The lack of German fleet and natural accidents like the migration of the herring shoals from the Baltic into the North Sea compounded the situation. Germany also experienced a relative decline in population in comparison with her neighbours, especially France. The Mediterranean and Baltic were beginning to lose their economic primacy, on which Germany, due to its central position, had grown prosperous, and the rise of the "Atlantic economy" was beginning to move the centres of European economic activity decisively away from Germany to cities like Antwerp, Seville and Lisbon. The movement of goods on the great land and river routes across the continent declined after reaching a peak around 1500.

The overall economic picture was very mixed, with examples of growth and expansion alongside stagnation and decline. Some

German towns saw their predominance beginning to disappear, as silver mines became exhausted and foreign competitors began to undercut them. In the sixteenth century, as if to illustrate the decline in enterprise, many of the south German cities, previously centres of commerce and manufacturing, became financial centres. Popular mentalities remained rooted in a pre-capitalist age in medieval notions of a moral economy; monopolies and "usury" remained the object of considerable popular hostility, seen in many complaints against them in the *Reichstag*. The falling behind of Germany was made worse by the political fragmentation of the country and the emergence of distinct and self-centred state economies. The ability of the *Reich* to regulate the all-German economy, if it had ever existed, was disappearing.

The population of Germany rose between the late fifteenth and the early seventeenth centuries, though estimates of the figures vary between 12 and 18 millions in 1500 and 16 and 21 millions in 1618. There were clear local variations within the overall picture: growth was strongest in the west and south. Growing demand for food pushed up prices and this, combined with the injection into the European economy of large quantities of silver from South America, produced the unprecedented price inflation known as the Price Revolution, which lasted from the 1470s to the 1620s. Initially, while it was mild, the inflation stimulated production and Germany benefited.

Towns were the main beneficiaries. There were about 4000 towns and cities in Germany at the beginning of the sixteenth century. "Towns" were defined by a special legal status rather than economic activities; the majority were in reality walled villages dependent on the agricultural production of land outside the walls but some were more. The largest towns were commercial centres like Cologne, Nuremberg, Strasburg, Augsburg, Vienna, Lübeck and Magdeburg. The early sixteenth century saw a boom in the Hanseatic cities and the great manufacturing centres of the south and central Germany, whose capitalist enterprises in banking, long-distance trade, textiles, metalwork and mining did very well. The growth of centres like Hamburg, Prague, Nuremberg and the Saxon mining towns was revealed in sharp rises in their populations, reflecting both their attractiveness to immigrants and growing demographic pressures in the rural areas. Individual entrepreneurs, many of them former guild members, made fortunes producing cheap textiles and other items of mass consumption. Augsburg, seat of the huge Fugger enterprise, was a major textile centre until the early seventeenth century and its prosperity spread far beyond its walls as a result of the employment of substantial numbers of out-workers in the countryside to spin and weave. This was symbolized most splendidly in the person of Jacob Fugger, known as the Rich, who died in 1525. In the Harz, Thuringia and the Alps new methods enabled previously inaccessible veins of lead, copper and silver ore to be worked. Such enterprises needed substantial capital and were vulnerable to changes in demand. With the arrival of substantial imports from South America, Germany lost its position as the major source of silver in Europe. Capital generated by mining and manufacturing funded an expanding financial business in Germany, toppling the Italians from their earlier dominant position. Houses like the Fuggers used their immense financial power to obtain trade monopolies and other favours. Charles V, notoriously, owed his ability to bribe the German electors to vote for him as Emperor to massive loans from the Fuggers. The great south German finance houses such as the Fuggers and Welsers at first joined in the growing colonial trade with bases in southern Spain. In the early 1520s there were plans for a great German investment in South American trade and manufacturing but it came to nothing. Major rivals appeared. By the middle of the sixteenth century the Germans had been ousted and first Antwerp and later Amsterdam supplanted them. By about the middle of the sixteenth century the Dutch had overtaken the Hanseatic League in Baltic trade. Only towns which were able to maintain links with centres of the Atlantic economy remained buoyant. Hamburg and Frankfurt benefited from the talents of refugees they welcomed within their walls, such as Sephardic Jews from Spain and Portugal and people from the Netherlands.

Demographic and economic changes promoted growing social mobility, with enhanced opportunities to rise and fall. Within each social class there was a widening gulf between the rich, who seemed to be growing richer, and the poor, whose conditions seemed to be worsening, leading to serious social tension. The situation was made worse by visible displays of luxury and conspicuous consumption on the part of the new rich. From about 1530 the price inflation was to become obvious and added substantially to the crisis mentality. It was beyond the comprehension of most men and there seemed no way of dealing with it. Real incomes for the majority were falling but government efforts to deal with the problem had no effect because governments were as ignorant of the real causes as the masses. The rise of the money economy was another cause of instability. It was said that only monopolists and usurers were flourishing. It seemed everything was for sale. Even the Church was not immune, being seen as riddled with simony and nothing more than a great bureaucratic money-making machine. Hostility to early manifestations of the market economy and economic individualism were subsumed in a general attack on "monopoly", a shorthand term for a whole range of objectionable economic practices. They were frequently attacked in the imperial diet and on his election as Emperor Charles V had to promise to bring them to a stop. It was easy to blame everything on divine wrath or wicked men.

In particular the peasants in many parts of the country felt themselves under pressure. Agriculture and forestry were the overwhelmingly dominant sectors of the economy in terms of employment and as sources of revenue for governments, the Church and the nobility, of capital and of food, fuel, building materials and commodities used in manufactures. In the fourteenth and fifteenth centuries landlords and governments suffered increasing financial difficulties and this led to a large-scale conversion of labour services into money rents. A very complex system of tenures, based on mutual rights and obligations of lords and tenants, emerged, the balance of which changed according to circumstances. Serfdom survived in most parts of western Germany only in the form of relics but even these were seen as increasingly burdensome by the peasantry. From about 1500 the sharp population rise contributed to new economic and social difficulties. Some parts of Germany saw mounting land hunger. At first this was partly relieved by various methods of making extra land available for cultivation, such as using mountain pastures or reclaiming land from the sea, but, apart from a few favoured areas like the Tyrol and East Frisia, this was a solution with limited possibilities. Subdivision of existing holdings was another short-term answer.

A fundamental problem was the inflexibility of agriculture. Yields in the bulk of German agriculture were very low, giving, typically, a return of about 5:1 of the sowing, and it was very hard to convert from subsistence farming to production for the market. Where growing market opportunities appeared, for example from the expansion of town populations, attempts to exploit them often added to conflicts between lords and tenants and between different groups of tenants. The divisions between peasants with substantial holdings (*Vollbauer*), and those with smaller plots or with no land at all, known by a variety of names (*Halbbauer, Insten, Gärtner, Kossäten*), became deeper. Only the more fortunate peasants were able to cash in on the price rise but in most cases the landlords, the nobles, the Church, townsmen or the state were the main beneficiaries. The position of the lower nobility was ambivalent. Some could benefit from new opportunities offered by economic change and were able to retain social and political power but this opportunity was available to few. The social, economic and political trends of the time seemed to be undermining the status of the free imperial knights. In the medieval period, as heavy armoured cavalry, they had formed the core of armies and their castles, of which there were an estimated 10 000 in Germany, had given them power. By 1500 they were clearly outdated, their military uselessness having been revealed by massed archers, the Hussite and Swiss peasant armies and Italian professional mercenaries. The increasing use of mercenaries rather than semi-amateur armies was one of the reasons why states faced growing economic problems. The rise of powerful states led, in most parts of Germany, to the destruction of their castles and to steady encroachments on their rights. Subordination to the rising princely states, voluntary or enforced, meant an end to their autonomy. Many knights were losing their land as they were forced to pledge it and many found the only answer to their problems lay in placing higher burdens on their tenants, adding to peasant discontent. Social barriers hardened visibly in the late fifteenth century, especially the distinction between nobles and non-nobles. The nobility began to close ranks as the sources of their status disappeared. For example, inter-class marriages, which had become common earlier, especially between noble men and the daughters of rich citizens, were frowned on.

As their military role disappeared, many knights, suffering from an identity crisis, turned to organized crime to sustain them, especially in the west and south west, where the states were weak, and this added to the serious law and order problem in the later fifteenth century. This culminated in the great rebellion of the knights in 1522, led by Ulrich von Hutten and Franz von Sickingen. It arose from a mixture of enthusiasm for the Lutheran religion — many knights, including Hutten and Sickingen introduced the new faith on their lands early — and an attempt to regain lost status. It began in August 1522 with a meeting of some six hundred knights at Landau, at which a fraternal union was established for six years. Sickingen then attacked the Archbishop of Trier with the stated aim of secularizing the see. The knights' hostility was focused against the higher clergy and against those knights who had capitulated and become servants of the rising states. The leaders appealed to German national sentiment in stirring up resentment against Rome's supposed plundering of German treasure and urged Luther to join them in a campaign to liberate the fatherland. They had a Utopian vision of a decentralized political and ecclesiastical system, which would restore the knights' usefulness. The rising was largely restricted to the south west but there was a real fear that it would spread and infect the nobilities of other states.

Sickingen held out in his castle against Hessian and Palatinate armies until April 1523. He was killed in the fighting while Hutten died later the same year in Switzerland. The collapse of the revolt was followed by a systematic razing of knightly castles. Thereafter the majority of the free knights lost their political power. In 1542 an institutional structure of three circles (*Ritterkreise*) was created for them in return for payments to the Emperor and some 1500 knightly families kept their status but they had to seek employment in the Church or in imperial or princely service. The larger states, including Austria, continued their attempts to subordinate the knights, using a variety of techniques, until the end of the Empire. Had it not been for the protection of the imperial courts, they would have disappeared as a distinct class much sooner.

The towns were also experiencing growing social and political tensions. In the early sixteenth century many saw a growing influx of new inhabitants from rural areas. The newcomers were usually denied citizenship and formed a voiceless urban proletariat and a large reservoir of discontent when economic activity declined. During periods of recession towns also stopped immigration, which in turn added to discontent in rural areas. Most German cities were governed by small groups of patricians, often guild masters or substantial traders. These tended to be unchanging circles of families; in the prosperous towns there was not the same pressure as elsewhere to become landed gentlemen. Only in a few cities, usually the seat of state governments, did a "new" middle class in the form of educated administrators, lawyers and teachers become significant. Friction between groups was endemic in some towns, for example between those who were *ratsfähig*, eligible for membership of the town council, or those who were *Bürger* and had the rights of citizenship and the rest. Some cities in the south and in Switzerland ruled substantial territories outside their walls and the magistracies often imitated princely rulers in seeking to increase their powers over their subjects. The fourteenth and fifteenth centuries saw many violent risings in towns, often with the object of forcing a clique of council families to admit "new men" to a share of power. From the late

fourteenth to the early sixteenth century there were a number of
rebellions by town dwellers excluded from the charmed circle of city
government but expected to contribute with their money and lives to the
defence of the city.[2]

Growing political tensions were also appearing in many states.
Constitutional battles arose from attempts by rulers to lay the foundations of the state by equipping themselves with standing armies and
trained professional bureaucracies. Among the leaders in this process
were Trier, the lands of the Teutonic Order, Bohemia and Württemberg. In the fourteenth and fifteenth centuries there was a gradual
evolution of feudal lordships into something recognizable as the modern
state. Many princes were trying to consolidate their lands and take an
essential step in state-building by imitating the electors in introducing
primogeniture and ending the practices of division and appanage-
creation. This was achieved in Württemberg in 1482 and Bavaria in
1506. New methods of government were appearing, with the use of
written records and procedures and the employment of professional
administrators. A new class of literate legally trained middle-class
officials was appearing, a product of the universities of Prague,
Heidelberg, Vienna or Leipzig, the last set up to cater for Germans
thrown out of Prague during the Hussite troubles.

One of the most spectacular signs of the rise of the professional
administrator was the great expansion in universities in Germany before
the Reformation. Five universities existed before 1400, Prague, Vienna,
Heidelberg, Cologne and Erfurt, and eight were added in the fifteenth
century. In the fifteenth and early sixteenth centuries Germans continued to study at Italian and French universities but this was changing
quickly. Although the Reformation increased the output of universities,
such experts were scarce and the salaries available were very generous.
The rise of the expert lawyer and administrator was seen as part of a
general assault on traditional structures. Viewed with the same suspicion
was the gradual intrusion of Roman Law. Justinian's code, glossed or
amended in the Italian universities, undermined legal particularism. It
replaced or existed alongside the traditional unwritten customary law
and led to the creation of an apparatus of state courts alongside and
gradually replacing the traditional noble and town tribunals.

Roman Law emphasized authority and enjoyed enormous prestige
because of Renaissance admiration for the Ancient World and it was
increasingly looked to when common and customary law did not provide
an answer. It involved the new concept that law was not simply
remembered but could be made and it increased the ability of govern-

ments to shape the future by issuing regulations. Ironically the initial demand for the reception of Roman Law did not usually come from rulers but from the educated laity, who wanted a more orderly judicial system — the reception of Roman Law was an expression rather than a cause of the crisis mentality of the time — but it contributed to the strengthening of the state and added to the professionalism of government. The impact of Roman Law was patchy and some areas, such as Saxony, were not touched by it but its piecemeal acceptance added to the feeling that the good old world was being swept away in a tide of innovation. The most practical manifestation was in the production of written law codes for cities and states (for example in Nuremberg in 1484 and Bavaria 1485–95), which was becoming common in the sixteenth century. In 1501 a corpus of imperial laws was published. Such codification was seen by some as a means of improving efficiency and achieving standardization. It was also seen by others as a cause of problems: in contrast to the good old days when there was only one law and everyone was happy, there were now dozens of laws and thousands of lawyers and everyone was miserable.

Alongside the beginnings of modern administration some states saw the simultaneous rise of parliamentary Estates (*Landstände* or *Landschaft*), claiming to share power with the princes.[3] The Estates originated in the feudal relationship: in return for the protection of the lord, subjects owed a duty to advise and aid him. Their role was strengthened by a thirteenth-century imperial law which obliged rulers to seek the consent of their nobility if they were planning to make substantial changes in their fiefs. In the later Middle Ages many became powerful, administering the prince's finances, guaranteeing loans, recruiting and maintaining troops bound to them by oath and pursuing diplomatic relations with other Estates and even with German and foreign rulers. The causes of the growing power of the Estates included shortage of money and rulers' inability to exist on their traditional incomes, divisions of territory, succession disputes and rulers' desire to associate the influential sections of their subjects with their actions. The financial needs of states were becoming very pressing and this acted as an important motor of change. An attempt was made to modernize the medieval obligation of feudatories to aid and advise the overlord in the form of regular taxation and an increase in the number of tolls, dues and fees. In many cases the Estates saw themselves as custodians of traditional modes of government.

Changes were also taking place in the shape of Germany. By the end of the fifteenth century it was again contracting as pieces around the periphery began to fall away. In 1460 Schleswig passed to Denmark and the Burgundian lands, Switzerland and the Netherlands drifted away over a number of years. People who had earlier been German were becoming Swiss, Dutch or Flemish. A number of imperial cities like Basle joined the Swiss confederation and many seriously considered joining. Schaffhausen became Swiss as late as 1501. From 1471 the Swiss did not attend the imperial diet and from 1495 they claimed exemption from the jurisdiction of the imperial courts. This was accepted *de facto* in 1499.

In 1410 the Teutonic Knights lost the battle of Tannenberg against the Poles, after which the Polish crown took sovereignty over Prussia and Danzig. In 1466 in the second Treaty of Thorn the Order had to cede the bulk of its territories to Poland. German power retreated further as the eastern Baltic became a battleground between Russia, Poland, Denmark and Sweden.

In Bohemia during the fifteenth century the Hussite heresy appeared as part of a national reaction by the Czechs against domination by a Latin German Empire. It brought to a temporary end German immigration into the region. There was a strong nationalist element in the German "crusades" against the Hussites between 1421 and 1430. The 1422 *Reichstag* at Nuremberg agreed to levy a common tax on the whole Empire to fund the war against the Hussites, the first imperial tax. After 1491 Bohemia was temporarily detached from the Empire when it passed into the hands of the Polish royal house. The Empire's influence in Italy also declined, though claims to authority there were maintained. This loss of non-German areas was symbolized in 1486 when the title of the Empire was formally changed to the Holy Roman Empire *of the German Nation*. Earlier its title had also included the *Welsch*, i.e. Italian, nation. By the middle of the fourteenth century the use of the phrase "German lands" to describe the Empire had become common.

What Germany lost were primarily non-German areas and this had some beneficial effects. The Empire acquired clearer boundaries and became more German in character, though it still contained substantial non-German minorities. There was a strong wave of German sentiment in the 1470s against Burgundian power, which was encroaching on the western borders of the *Reich*. German national feeling was also fostered by developments during the Renaissance, which promoted a new interest in German history and study of "German" heroes of the past. The German Renaissance, centred in the prosperous cities of the south west and Alsace, produced a new German culture, which was not a pale copy of Italian models. The Emperor Maximilian I supported a number of humanist writers like Konrad Celtis and Sebastian Brant, who also contributed to the growth of German national feeling.[4] Interest in figures like Arminius, or Hermann, the Germanic chieftain who had destroyed several Roman legions, and Charlemagne grew. In 1497 a German edition of Tacitus' *Germania* appeared. The idea of *translatio imperii*, the belief that the sceptre of imperial power had been transferred from the Romans to the Germans, was revived.

As the political cohesion of Germany began visibly to weaken and as her neighbours, particularly France, began to overtake her, a psychology of decline set in. Some Germans sought to compensate by adopting a grossly romanticized view of their own past, with great emphasis on the innate superiority of the Germans. The idea arose that the Germans were the *Urvolk*, the original people of Europe who had retained their "pure" blood and who spoke the original language of humanity, the *Ursprache*, as spoken by Adam and Eve. Much was made of the superior virtues of the Germans, their loyalty and honesty, which made them such an easy prey for foxy and devious Latins like the French. Such ideas fuelled anti- foreign sentiment, always a strong element in German national feeling. In the absence of a real all-German monarch on whom to focus their emotions, the Germans tended to focus their hatred against someone outside. In the fifteenth and sixteenth centuries the Italians and the Spaniards became the targets for such feelings. Anti-Italian feeling turned easily into anti-papal sentiment, expressed in the claim that the pope was robbing Germany, as was to become clear during the Reformation. From the seventeenth to the twentieth centuries the same role was filled by the French; the France of Louis XIV was to be seen as a rapacious thief of German land.

In the last decades of the fifteenth century this essentially negative nationalism was reinforced by more positive developments. The *Reich* began belatedly to acquire the common institutions of a state. There was also an increase in enthusiasm for the Empire, which developed from a revival of interest in Classical Rome, of which many Germans saw the Empire as the spiritual heir, and from growing discontent. The symbols of the Empire, eagles, the imperial crown and various coats of arms, were in widespread use. Groups such as the smaller nobility, the peasants and the urban poor, victims of change, looked to a revival of imperial power to protect them against their oppressors, landlords, guild masters, a greedy immoral clergy and princes beginning to make themselves absolute and depriving localities of their long-held rights. Emperors like Maximilian I and Charles V were seen by many as new messiahs leading a rebirth of the German nation and the Habsburgs employed propagandists to foster this idea.

The reign of Emperor Maximilian I (1493–1519) saw the culmination of many of these developments. He has been labelled the last medieval Emperor — others reserve this title for his successor, Charles V — responsible for the last serious attempt to rescue the Empire from the decline which was staring it in the face. His skilful propaganda contributed to the growth of a very romanticized view of his role. He was certainly similar to many of his predecessors in that he placed German affairs low in his order of priorities and devoted himself to the pursuit of dynastic interests in many parts of Europe, especially in Italy, which brought him into chronic conflict with the French. Maximilian's reign also saw a major political battle over reform of the structure of the Empire.

Discussion of the imperial constitution and calls for reform of the Empire had been growing in intensity among German rulers and intellectuals from the early fifteenth century on. In the course of that century a number of reform schemes were put forward. Some of these were by noted philosophers, such as Nicholas of Kues' *Concordantia Catholica* (1433), and some were anonymous, such as the *Reformation of the Emperor Sigismund* (dated 1439–1441). Cardinal Nicholas of Kues was Bishop of Brixen in the Tyrol. He travelled widely in Germany as papal legate between 1450 and 1452 and found a great deal wrong with the Church. These reform plans were part of the prevailing universalist spirit of the times and contained a common core of proposals, including regular meetings of the imperial diet, a permanent council of German rulers to share power with the Emperor, the creation of an effective peace-keeping apparatus in the *Reich*, a proper legal system, a standing imperial army maintained by regular taxation of all the states and an organized imperial civil service. Early attempts were made to bring in such reforms at the imperial diets of 1434 and 1437 and the Emperor Sigismund tried to strengthen his powers by creating a lasting alliance with the German cities but nothing came of these proposals as they met strong resistance from the electors. There were deep divisions between the crown and the princes on the type of reform needed and too many vested interests opposed to it. From the middle years of the century the initiative came increasingly from princes anxious to place more restrictions on the power of the crown as part of a reform package, in order to make it impossible for future emperors to recover their authority.

The country's territorial losses and growing internal lawlessness were seen as signs of obvious flaws caused by the weakness, especially in finances, of the monarchy. There were serious deficiencies in the coinage system and there was no organized imperial government or army to maintain law and order. The failure of monarchs to create an effective peace-keeping apparatus had serious effects on German political and economic life. The failure of King Wenceslas to maintain order was used to justify his deposition in 1400. There was a growing fear that the imperial title might pass to a foreign ruler and be lost to the German nation. Imperial justice was very weak, as reflected in the prevalence of private wars to settle differences under the graphically named *Faustrecht*, the law of the fist, the activities of self-appointed free courts, the *Fehmgerichte*, and the formation of leagues of cities, nobles and rulers to maintain order and settle disputes in their areas. Papal mediation was often more effective in ending disputes between the states than imperial jurisdiction. The towns were especially deeply concerned about public order. In 1488 a new league was set up in Swabia in the south west to resist encroachments by more powerful neighbouring states, especially Bavaria. This and other leagues were retrospectively authorized by the Emperor and were potentially a powerful vehicle for a revival of imperial power in south western Germany.

In the early fifteenth century attempts were made to re-establish an aulic court (*Hofgericht*) or a royal chamber court (*Kammergericht*), staffed with qualified jurists, as a supreme court for the whole Empire but they only lasted for a short time and their competence was limited by the general weakness of the crown. The aulic court worked only for brief periods, for example in the years 1470–5, when it was leased to the Elector of Mainz. The chamber court also functioned occasionally at Rottweil in Swabia. Recent research has gone some way to rehabilitating these courts, showing that they were not as totally ineffective as once thought. Although Frederick III made much of his jurisdiction, in reality it did not exist for the majority of his reign. The imperial diet met only infrequently against the opposition of the princes, who knew that it was usually only summoned when the Emperor wanted money. This situation led to appeals to the Emperor to take back lost rights and revenues and Maximilian's father Frederick III had tried this but without success.

When an imperial reform movement emerged in the 1480s Maximilian supported it in the hope that it would enable him more easily to exploit German resources in pursuit of non-German aims. He inherited from his father a package of dynastic claims and ambitions. Frederick III had a long but undistinguished reign, which lasted from 1440–93, though he handed power to his son Maximilian in 1486. His hold on the Austrian lands was never secure, he was forced to neglect German affairs and his reign was a period of instability. Traditional historiography has not been kind to him but he can be seen as the real founder of Habsburg power after the family had raised itself to prominence in Germany from minor origins. From early days the Habsburgs sought to elevate themselves above their fellow princes, for example by awarding themselves exclusively the title of archduke. Duke Rudolph IV of Austria claimed this title in 1358–9 on the basis of forged documents and it was confirmed by Frederick III. Thereafter the Habsburgs saw themselves as special, the arch-house, and their possessions as a special entity among the states of the Empire. Frederick III's adoption of the mystical device *AEIOU*, which in various translations is said to have promised Austria domination of the globe, was another sign of this, though the significance of the motto perhaps owes more to hindsight than reality.

Frederick did not want to be king/Emperor and it is not clear why the electors chose him — perhaps there was no other obvious candidate— but his election began a continuous Habsburg possession of the imperial title which lasted with one brief interruption (1742–5) until 1806. He was the last Emperor to be crowned by the pope in Rome; Maximilian proclaimed himself Emperor at Trent in February 1508, though he stated his intention of obtaining papal coronation in future. Charles V proclaimed himself Emperor and was subsequently crowned by the pope. After him German monarchs simply adopted the imperial title on their election. Frederick founded the first institutions of a distinct Austrian state and built up the power of his lands. This process was continued by Maximilian I, who benefited from good fortune. His uncle Siegmund, the ruler of the Tyrol, had no heir and handed over his lands, with substantial silver reserves, to Maximilian. Innsbruck became his "capital" and he used the revenues from mining to build up powerful infantry and artillery forces. As a result by 1500 Austria was probably the only German state with large enough dynastic resources (*Hausmacht*) to shoulder the burdens of the imperial title. In this way he helped to create the conditions for a potential revival of the *Reich* but at the same time he launched his family in pursuit of a number of wide-ranging ambitions, which distracted them from German affairs. They carried forward the long-established imperial ambitions in Italy. By marriage they acquired claims to Bohemia and Hungary. After the fall of Constantinople in 1453 they took over the old crusading ideal of liberating Byzantium.

The betrothal of Maximilian and Mary was a deliberate attempt by Frederick to link his house to the rising star of Burgundy. Charles of Burgundy also planned by this means to acquire a share of power over the Empire. When Frederick and the Duke of Burgundy met in Trier in 1473, Frederick had to slip away as the Burgundians were demanding too much. In spite of that and although the Burgundian state collapsed in January 1477 after defeat by the Swiss, the marriage went ahead. Maximilian immediately became involved in prolonged warfare against France, which also claimed the Burgundian inheritance, and the Netherlanders, who resisted his claims. Frederick III, after years of lethargy, showed remarkable energy in his old age and his successful prosecution of the war culminated in the Peace of Senlis in 1493, under which the Habsburgs kept the bulk of the Burgundian inheritance.

Although dead, the Burgundian state left behind a brilliant afterglow and the Habsburgs took over all its claims and sought to take over all its prestige by, for example, the adoption of the trappings of the Burgundian court including the Order of the Golden Fleece. Maximilian imitated Burgundian administrative techniques in his own lands and used Burgundian notions of chivalry in his propaganda to reinforce the message that the rising power of France in the West was a real threat to Germany. The re-creation of a powerful "middle kingdom" between Germany and France stretching from Switzerland to the Netherlands would not only give the Habsburgs a magnificent power base but could also be portrayed as a shield-wall for the *Reich*. Frederick also handed on to his son claims to Brittany. In 1515 Maximilian's grandson Ferdinand was married to the heiress of the Hungarian and Bohemian crowns, which, under agreements negotiated by Frederick III in 1491, fell to the Habsburgs on the death of Louis, King of Hungary at Mohács in 1526. If these claims could be made good against the Turks they would represent a great extension of Habsburg power.

All these ambitions and more were to be inherited by Maximilian's successor Charles V: in 1496 Maximilian married his son Philip to Joanna of Castile, heiress of Ferdinand and Isabella, the unifiers of Spain. A series of deaths made Maximilian's grandson Charles the unplanned universal heir to the possessions of Austria, Spain and Burgundy, adding the claims and ambitions of Castile and Aragon to those already pursued by the Habsburgs. Extensive possessions gave them extensive commitments and ambitions and Germany remained very much a side-show. Just at the time when Germany needed a monarch of her own she had to make do with a small share of someone else's. At the same time the Emperor was more than ever dependent on German resources, which were rarely forthcoming. In 1492 the *Reichstag* voted 94 000 *Gulden* to Maximilian for war against the French but only some 16 000 were actually paid over. Understandably the German princes were unsympathetic to the use of German blood and treasure in the pursuit of foreign ambitions even under Frederick III and realized that, if the Emperor became powerful as a result of foreign successes, any help they provided might simply be making a rod for their own backs. The majority of the princes were also motivated by a lively fear of becoming involved in wars of no direct concern to Germany, especially as there was before the reign of Charles V no formal provision in the German constitution for princes to come to the aid of a fellow prince under external attack.

The imperial reform movement reached its height in the 1480s and 1490s. The significance of the *Reichsreform* has often been distorted in the past in German nationalist historiography. It was not the culmination of a great campaign for change going back decades nor was it a step towards, or away from, the creation of a German nation state. From the outset there were two reform parties, one imperial, led by the Emperor, and the other led and organized by a group of princes. Their aims were broadly the same, to equip Germany with some of the institutions of government which it so obviously lacked, but the motives of the two parties were very different indeed. Maximilian planned to create a system which would guarantee him regular tax payments and military resources from the *Reich* plus a working regency system to run Germany in his absence on foreign campaigns. He also planned to establish a new supreme court which would make the princes more dependent on him.

The princely group saw reform as removing abuses, restoring proper balance to the imperial constitution, and dealing with practical problems, especially internal and external security. It was led and organized ably by a pupil of Nicholas of Kues, Berchtold von Henneberg, Archbishop-Elector of Mainz (1484–1504), a title which brought with it the post of arch-chancellor of Germany. This was the only ceremonial office held by an elector which gave its holder functions of real political weight, in this case control of the procedures and business of the imperial diet. Henneberg's party planned to give Germany an organized federal structure. The main instrument for the achievement of this was the proposed *Reichsregiment*, a standing committee containing representatives of the Emperor and the princes and equipped with considerable powers to act as a permanent executive to administer the *Reich*.

Henneberg drew his strongest support from the ecclesiastical states, the free cities and the small, poor and vulnerable states, especially in the west and south west, that is the weakest political units in Germany, which had most to fear from foreign intervention, a powerful Emperor and powerful princes. Henneberg was strongly opposed by Maximilian and the rulers of the stronger states, who had no deep interest in the Empire as long as there was no restriction on their freedom of action in their own lands. It was at this time that the concept of *teutsche Libertät* (Germanic liberty) was floated as propaganda against both imperial and princely reform plans. This was based on the totally spurious claim that the individual German states and territories had existed at some point in the remote past as sovereign entities and had then voluntarily subjected themselves to imperial control, while retaining their princely liberty. Particularism, the slow gradual devolution of the functions of government from a central authority to the individual states, was legitimized by this and resistance to attempts to restore centralized government could therefore be portrayed as the defence of the traditional freedom of the German rulers against a usurping power. Ironically, the claims of "Germanic liberty" were strengthened by Maximilian's own actions. As well as resisting the reform party, Maximilian employed an alternative policy of negotiating directly with the greater princes in order to sabotage Henneberg's plans. This was a tacit recognition that the Emperor and the greater princes were political and diplomatic equals.

The reform movement started in the Frankfurt *Reichstag* of 1486 and lasted into the 1520s.[5] It achieved some significant successes. In 1486 a general peace was proclaimed throughout the Empire, to last initially for ten years. This extended to the whole Empire the ban on all forms of violent self-help, which had earlier applied to specific places and times. At first only geographically and chronologically limited *Landfrieden* were enacted and the activity of the king's supreme court was intermittent. A peace covering the whole Empire *(Reichslandfrieden)* was first proclaimed at the Mainz *Reichstag* in 1235 and a temporary one-year *Landfrieden* was issued in 1467, involving an absolute ban on *Faustrecht*. In 1489 there was a further regularization of the procedures of the *Reichstag* (previously called the *Hoftag*), which was being summoned more frequently as the Emperor's need for money to finance his wars increased. The membership of the diet was fixed and lists were drawn up of those entitled to send delegates. It met in three houses or *curiae* and debated in secret. The towns had permanent representation in the *Reichstag* after 1489 but no vote until 1648. After the 1512 diet it was accepted that a vote of those present in the diet was binding on those who absented themselves. The principle of majority voting was already accepted in imperial elections.

Further major reforms came at the Worms `Reichstag` in 1495. Maximilian was very vulnerable, being simultaneously involved in several wars, and was forced to make concessions to the reformers. The peace of the Empire was declared perpetual. The Emperor and the German rulers signed a formal agreement to maintain peace and justice, a significant sign of how they were growing apart: *Kaiser* and *Reich* were becoming distinct and opposing concepts. Proposals were also put forward for the creation of a standing imperial army, to be financed by a general tax on all subjects under the control of the *Reichstag*. Nothing came of this. To deal with disputes, an imperial supreme court, the *Reichskammergericht* (imperial chamber court), an institution long needed in Germany, was re-established, equipped with a new ordinance and given a permanent seat in Frankfurt-am-Main. Maximilian was forced to concede a large measure of control over the new tribunal to the princes, who appointed some of its judges and, in theory, financed it. Initially it was regarded with great hostility by the towns and imperial knights, who had no say in its running, though very soon the latter group was able to win an important role in staffing the court. It was the first German central institution independent of the crown. It played a major part in the standardization and proper organization of justice in the Empire and the states in line with advanced judicial thinking at the time. In 1498 Maximilian set up a separate supreme tribunal under his total control, the imperial aulic council *(Reichshofrat)*. The two courts were to remain in existence and rivals until the end of the Empire in 1806.

The Worms diet also instituted a regular imperial tax, the Common Penny, a universal progressive property and poll tax, to finance the *Reichskammergericht*. The funds, collected by the clergy, were to be administered by an imperial treasurer in Augsburg under the control of the *Reichstag*. A population survey was carried out to assess liability to the tax. As it turned out, this system could not be made permanent because of the opposition of powerful princes and in 1505 the *Reichsmatrikel*. the old system of matricular contributions, was restored. Under this each state's obligations to the *Reich* were laid down in proportion to its size. The tax was levied as Roman Months (*Römermonate*), so called because it was originally a tax raised to finance the Emperor's journey to Rome for his coronation by the pope. Under the *Matrikel* the collection and apportionment of imperial taxes were left to the state governments. This allowed traditional exemptions, for example of the nobility, to remain, unlike under the Common Penny. The diets of 1507 and 1510 also accepted the principle that subjects could be called upon to pay imperial taxes, an important constitutional point.

The 1497 diet issued the first imperial recess (*Reichsabschied*), a collection of the laws passed during the session, a recognition of the shared legislative authority of the Emperor and the *Reichstag*. The reform party pressed for the establishment of a *Reichsregiment*. Maximilian was able to block this but had to accept annual meetings of the diet, which was to become the supreme legislative authority in the *Reich*, making it a constitutional monarchy. By the meeting of the diet of Augsburg in 1500 Maximilian could no longer resist pressures in favour of the *Reichsregiment* and had to agree to its establishment. It was to consist of twenty members under the presidency of the Emperor or his nominee and was to include the seven electors and other members appointed by the German rulers. Plans were again floated for a standing army of 300 000 under the control of the *Reichsregiment*. In fact the *Regiment* only lasted until 1502 and in its brief life it was unable to achieve anything. The German rulers refused to provide funds for it, it had no bureaucracy to service it and no means of executing its decisions. Maximilian refused to accept any decisions affecting his own territories. He also refused to pay the yield of the Common Penny from his lands into the central treasury but appropriated it for his own use. He was as guilty of particularism as any of the German princes.

The final major achievement of the reform movement came in 1500 with the creation of the system of imperial Circles (*Reichskreise*) based on the constituencies electing members to the proposed *Reichsregiment*, regional unions of state designed to maintain internal order and external defence. By 1512 there were ten Circles in all. They covered the whole Empire except the Habsburgs' possessions in the east, Bohemia, Silesia and Lusatia, the lands of the imperial knights and a few other small territories. The Habsburgs' other lands dominated the Austrian Circle. The rulers in the Circles were supposed to hold regular meetings to concert arrangements to fulfil the functions of the organization. The majority never operated in the way intended.

Although it came after Maximilian's death, a list of major constitutional changes during the reform period should include the first capitulation of election (*Wahlkapitulation*), a list of promises and undertakings imposed by the electors on Charles V on his election in 1519. This document included, among other things, a formal guarantee by the Emperor to the German rulers of undisturbed possession of their lands and rights, even if these had originally been acquired as temporary grants from earlier monarchs. That was an open recognition of the federal nature of the Holy Roman Empire. Similar capitulations of election were given by all subsequent Emperors and became part of the law of the Empire.

In the light of the wide-ranging ambitions and lavish plans he pursued, Maximilian's reign must be judged unsuccessful. This was recognized by the Emperor in the instructions given while he was dying that his corpse was to be disfigured and was not to be embalmed before burial. Although his marriage policy was eventually to add Bohemia and Hungary to the possessions of his house, he failed in France and Italy. He introduced reforms in the government of his lands on which his successors could begin to build the institutions of an Austrian state but his assertion of monarchical power, involving infringement of the special rights of the various provinces and on the political power of the nobility and towns, aroused opposition. His death was followed by a period of disorder in various parts of his lands. In the Empire he failed to persuade the electors to elect his grandson Charles as king of the Romans, an office which enabled its holder to succeed to the imperial title without an election. This involved the Habsburgs in massive expenditure in bribes. The reform movement failed as neither the princely nor the imperial party gained its objectives; some argue that Germany was anyway too far advanced along the road of particularism for the trend to be reversed.

Arguably Germany was potentially far more united at the beginning of the sixteenth century than for centuries. The missing ingredient was a German religion and Luther seemed to provide this: he was an anti-foreign German nationalist who deliberately used the German language. A sign of the times came in August 1518 when Maximilian asked the *Reichstag* for money for a crusade. Instead the German states presented a list of their grievances against the papacy. The Worms diet of 1521 debated lavish plans to build on the foundations laid down in the *Reichsreform* but it was too late as the Lutheran Reformation was already sweeping the country.

[handwritten notes]

- Hapsburg dynastic gains imperial reform

nationalism / rise of the state / vs. nobility
economic changes / (silver, ↑ prices) / econ individ
population pressure / cities
    rural → urb
    migration
turks
nominalism
Roman law / (Italy) / Univ.

- tradition of reform church
(not mentioned here) →

3 The Reformation in Germany

The history of the German Reformation and its effects is readily available in a number of excellent works. Its analysis in this chapter will therefore be restricted to a few aspects. The role of Luther and theological elements in the Reformation will be examined only briefly. An excessively Luther-centric view is anyway dangerous as there were other movements at work at the same time which could have overtaken and swamped Lutheranism. More attention will be given to the mass movements associated with the Reformation and, in particular, to the effects of the events of the period 1517 to 1555 on German political and constitutional life.

These effects were momentous. Martin Luther certainly considered the Reformation a substantial break with the past: in a letter written in March 1542 to Jakob Probst he stated that Germany was finished and would never again be what it had been. Although it was deeply rooted in essentially medieval attitudes, the Reformation acted as a modernizing force in social, political and intellectual life. It was not, however, part of an early bourgeois revolution in the marxist sense, arising from the crisis of the feudal production system. There was nothing resembling the bourgeoisie in the modern sense in sixteenth-century Germany and the old medieval orders of society were not replaced by modern classes during the Reformation. [1]

The Reformation was a complex multi-level phenomenon, affecting Germany from top to bottom, the imperial and princely courts, the diets of the Empire and of individual states, universities, towns and villages. Within it a large number of different religious, political and social movements were at work, all seeking different ends but all united by the common theme of discontent with the prevailing situation and all reaching a decisive point at the same time. People at

30

all levels of society had grievances. There was social tension between lords and peasants, rich and poor peasants, nobles and middle-class people, guild masters and apprentices, urban patricians and guild members. Many princes were dissatisfied with the state of the imperial constitution, many educated laymen and clerics as well as ordinary people were profoundly unhappy about the Church and its theology and ordinary Germans had much to object to in the social and economic situation. All these different discontents were mingled together inextricably and it is impossible to attribute the troubles of the Reformation period to any single cause, economic, political or religious.

The Church had a political importance in Germany only equalled in the papal states. Its landholdings were huge and many of its prelates, archbishops, bishops, abbots, abbesses, deans and the heads of the Teutonic Order and the Order of St John, were political rulers of states as well as senior clergymen. Three archbishops were electors. Many prince-prelates employed subsidiary bishops to carry out religious functions while they devoted themselves to government. At a lower level clergymen drawing incomes from Church livings carried out educational, charitable, administrative and academic functions. Religious changes, when they happened, had a huge impact on the lives of ordinary Germans, not just the elites.

The period of flux which preceded and accompanied the Reformation, could have had several results, including the destruction of the Roman Catholic Church throughout Germany, a social revolution, a united Germany or a totally disunited Germany. In fact a combination of particular circumstances produced a very strange outcome. In the early years of the sixteenth century a national Germany was emerging throwing off earlier universalist pretensions and becoming more self-consciously German, though still, apparently, hovering between potential unity and a formal federal system. As it turned out, the Reformation was to produce a new factor of disunity. It ruined Charles V's plans to revive a strong Empire as the core of a revived Latin Christendom rescued from the ills of national and dynastic selfishness, which threatened its inner cohesion just when the Ottoman Empire was organizing itself for expansion under Suleiman the Magnificent. Charles' efforts could have succeeded as there was a yearning for *renovatio imperii* and disappointment over the unfulfilled potential of Maximilian's reign. But Charles refused to place himself at the head of the Lutheran movement while at the same time he tried to force the papacy to reform the Church. As a result he fell between two stools. Charles had too many obligations and was able to devote very little of his time to German affairs. At the height of his power after the victory over the Protestant rulers at Mühlberg in 1547, he was unable to make his will felt. Increasingly he left conduct of German and Austrian affairs to his brother Ferdinand, who preferred the policy of winning over the princes by concession rather than confrontation.

The Reformation also strengthened individual German rulers, both Protestant and Catholic, and further weakened the Emperor, whose efforts to increase his power in Germany were interpreted as part of the militant Counter-Reformation. The German princes were provided with ideological justification for their particularism. It is interesting that other European monarchs were also frightened by the potential of Charles' empire and some began to create a cult of imperial monarchy for themselves as a counter-measure, including Henry VIII of England and Francis I of France. Even Charles' brother, Ferdinand, effective ruler of the Austrian parts of the Empire, undermined imperial power out of fear that the imperial title would pass to Charles' son Philip of Spain and that "Spanish tyranny" would become a reality in Germany.

The Reformation produced a period of religious chaos and Luther eventually turned to the German rulers to restore order and take over the organization of the churches. As a result, state churches emerged, each with a prince or urban magistracy at its head, and the Protestant rulers acquired a substantial field of government in which they had no superior but God and were not even nominally subordinate to the Emperor. In many cases this was not immediately obvious as the period saw many great battles between princes and their subjects and parliamentary Estates, often involving the question of control of the resources of the newly reformed churches. The Reformation revived the idea of the restoration of power, ecclesiastical and political, to the local community; the idea that the German Protestant princes were able to seize the wealth of the Church and use it at will is wrong. The political power of many Catholic rulers was also increased as a result of the Reformation. The papacy was often glad to give them wide powers over the revenues and personnel of their churches in order to further the battle against heresy. Bavaria was a striking example of the successful use of the opportunities offered. By the second half of the century it was established as a major local power in southern Germany.

The social discontent which played a major role in the Reformation also helped the cause of particularism as it demonstrated the need for strong government which only the German princes could provide. The revolt of the imperial knights in 1522–3, although easily put down, seriously frightened the authorities. Chronic rural unrest, leading to the great peasants' revolt of 1524–5, major disturbances in many cities, serious economic and social problems and the perceived menace of the revolutionary Anabaptists, culminating in their seizure of Münster in 1535, were regarded as the outcome of a spiral of disorder and signs of the imminent dissolution of society which only the concentration of power in the hands of an authoritarian government could prevent.

The Reformation period also increased foreign influence in Germany as Catholic and Protestant rulers called on the help of their foreign co-religionists, setting a very dangerous precedent. German national pride suffered a number of severe blows with territorial losses to the Turks and to the French during the wars of religion, especially the bishoprics of Metz, Toul and Verdun, which opened up western Germany to French penetration, a constant feature of German political life until 1814.

Martin Luther, an Augustinian monk and from 1512 professor of theology at the Saxon university of Wittenberg, founded in 1502, is seen as the originator of the German Reformation. [2] The theatrical events of October 1517 in Wittenberg, Luther's attack on the sale of indulgences and his publication of the ninety-five theses, have been frequently described. Their significance is traditionally exaggerated. Perhaps a more decisive turning point came on 10 December 1520 when Luther, in response to an order to burn his works, burned books of Canon Law and the papal bull of excommunication at Wittenberg. The movement for change in the Church was already established before 1517 and Luther had published theological works anonymously in German before 1517, a sign of his German patriotism and wish to appeal beyond a purely academic audience.

Under different circumstances Luther might have been completely forgotten. Criticism of abuses in the Church was long-standing and was another aspect of the deep piety and enthusiastic popular religious observance in the fifteenth century. Orthodoxy was the rule. Heretical movements such as the Waldensians, Hussites and pre-Christian nature religions existed in Germany but they had few supporters. Spontaneous reform within the Church commenced well before 1517, for example in the restoration of the spirituality of the Benedictine Order which began in the early fifteenth century and proceeded with the support of many state and city governments.

Other leaders like Melanchthon, Bucer, Oecolampadius and Osiander, who did not give their names to Churches, were as important as Luther in consolidating the Reformation. Luther's historic reputation is based on a double distortion. In Catholic myth he was demonized as the man who, single-handed, smashed the unity of Christendom while in later German nationalist historiography he became a German hero, fighting alien forces undermining the father- land. Luther contributed to the latter as he was certainly virulently xenophobic. He wrote of the Reformation as leading to the partition- ing of Germany into Roman and free Empires and he consciously looked back to Arminius as a forerunner in resisting Roman tyranny over Germany.

His importance lay in his popularization of a clear theological alternative to Catholic doctrine and in the fact that he came to lead the first established Protestant Church. Luther, an idealistic, zealous and learned man, went through a deep personal religious crisis which led him to produce a new statement on Christianity. He was not modern. His attitudes had little to do with the Renaissance or humanism but were very characteristic of the late Middle Ages. Like most people living at the time, he had a deep fear of the tortures of hell, which the propaganda of the Church had made very real to them, and terrifying doubts about the possibility of salvation. [3] Much ink has been spilt on the question of whether Luther derived his ideas from earlier writers or in seeking psychological causes for his actions. Certainly there was nothing new about his basic ideas, which had been present as a kind of puritan element within Catholic theology for centuries. What made Luther important was the moment and circum- stances in which he chose to publicize his views and the immoderate language which he used.

Although he made use of anti-clericalism to win support for his ideas and painted a very unflattering portrait of the pre-Reformation Church in his writings, he did not seek the regeneration of the Catholic Church by removing its abuses. He attacked what had become one of the fundamentals of the Catholic faith, the very essence of Catholicism, on which the entire structure of the Church was based, good works, and offered an alternative faith, by means of which a thorough rejuvenation of Christian society might be achieved. Scripture should take precedence over tradition in the Church. His basic position was that, since the Fall, man had been so utterly sinful that even to worship God was an act of gross presumption. The sacrifice on Calvary had assembled a reservoir of grace which enabled God arbitrarily to ignore the sinfulness of some men. This grace gave its recipients faith that they were saved, producing the key Lutheran doctrine of solafideism, salvation or justification by faith alone. Luther came to this conclusion at some point between 1515 and 1518. He later described how this realization, after a period of deep despair, made him feel reborn. The gates of paradise had opened for him and he had gone in.

For people unsure of salvation the new certainty offered by Luther was very appealing. All this was a perfectly tenable theological presupposition which, if taken to its logical conclusion, had the implication that man can do absolutely nothing to secure his own salvation and that therefore the Mass, the sacraments, the clergy and the whole visible Church could be dispensed with, except as a community of Christians. Luther also wished to admit the layman to what he saw as his rightful place in Christian life, which led to his doctrine of the priesthood of all believers. Certainly Luther was no believer in religious individualism; he sought freedom to interpret the faith for himself but not for everyone, although he was strongly influenced by the movement towards a more individual faith, with its emphasis on private worship and study, seen within the Church in the fifteenth century. Luther did not share the belief of, for example, the humanists, that political and social reforms would produce better men. For him man remained irretrievably sinful.

This system of ideas was complete in Luther's mind by 1512 though its implications were not worked out until the 1520s. When he was later forced to consider the organization of an external Church, the essential medievalism of his thinking became clear. He thought in terms of a collective act of praise in the vernacular with hymns and sermons, the election of clergy by congregations and the provision of local funds to maintain the clergy, charities and schools. On economic and social questions, which he considered trivial in the light of the imminent end of the world, he was very reactionary and was in no sense a father of capitalism. He believed that the disappearance of moral restraints in economic activity before 1517 was one of the causes of rising discontent and part of a general decay of old standards of behaviour. He held that many of the individual good works promoted by the Catholic Church were a waste of time and preferred organized communal good works. In his view, the resources of both state and Church, including monastic wealth, could be put to better use, particularly for welfare, charitable and educational ends. Here again, his well-documented links with late medieval humanism and the *Devotio Moderna* movement are clear.

When Luther chose to act in 1517 he was caught up in a great wave of undifferentiated enthusiasm at all levels of society. The process was initially gradual. The first impact was felt in very limited circles, in the universities and among urban intellectuals. The Church authorities at first ignored Luther's protests against the sale of indulgences, part of a massive financial transaction involving the Hohenzollern Archbishop of Mainz, the Fuggers and the Holy See. The ninety-five theses were published without Luther's knowledge in Nuremberg, Basle and Leipzig. The whole Reformation then exploded on the indulgence issue. The fact that there was such a huge popular demand for indulgences demonstrates the spiritual needs felt by the people; Luther provided an alternative answer to such needs. His ideas spread with remarkable speed and he became a German hero. This cannot be explained by the printing press alone. Personal links within clerical and intellectual networks were also very important. His appeal fell on very receptive soil, long fertilized by frustration at the mechanistic practices of the Church, virulent anti-clericalism, growing since the fifteenth century, a desire to return to a simple faith and a lovable Church and caring clergy, thought to have existed in the past. Luther represented a political as well as a religious challenge. There was also yearning for a German leader to solve Germany's problems. The Elector Frederick of Saxony (1486–1525) was being spoken of as a candidate for the imperial title at the next election and this idea was encouraged by the papacy nervous of the excessive power concentrated in the hands of Charles of Habsburg. This fact was to protect Luther for a long time. A German religion was perhaps the missing ingredient needed to cement the long-growing revival of German national sentiment.

Dissatisfaction with the state of the Church was widespread and long-standing. Criticism of the low standards of the Church in Germany came from the top to the bottom of society. There were calls for spiritual reform after the Great Schism of 1378, seen in growing calls for a Church Council, the Lollard and Hussite movements, pressure for monastic reform and groups such as *Devotio Moderna* and the Brethren of the Common Life, which tried to involve the laity more closely in the life of the Church. There were symptoms of growing religious individualism and the pursuit of personal piety rather than the mechanical worship of the organized Church, such as the rise of travelling evangelists and mass preaching and an increasing use of sermons. At its most extreme it gave rise to violent millenarianism and social revolutionary religious movements such as the

Taborites in Bohemia. The climate of opinion was changing with the Renaissance and the rise of humanism. The humanist movement was based on a dense and active network of groups and individuals all over Central Europe maintaining contacts with one another. They placed emphasis on the power of education to enable men to understand the world in which they lived. A greater proportion of the laity, especially in towns, were receiving an education and had access to new ideas.

At the Augsburg diet of 1518 a comprehensive list of the grievances (*Gravamina*) of the German nation was handed to the papal legate. This had been a frequent event in the fifteenth century. The Council of Constance (1418) tried to draft a Concordat regulating the relationship between the German Church and the papacy, including restrictions on Church taxation and indulgences and higher standards for the clergy but it did not come into effect. The *Reichstag* of 1439, 1445 and 1446 spelled out the grievances of the German nation against the papacy, proposed measures to limit papal interference in the German Church and called for a German Church council to deal with abuses. The 1521 diet of Worms, which condemned Luther for heresy, again listed over one hundred complaints against the papacy. Throughout the complaints changed little. Too many cases in Church courts were summoned to Rome in order to extract fees. Too many German benefices were given to foreigners. Church taxes were too high. Indulgences were scandalously abused. Charities and church buildings were neglected. These claims were, in reality, grossly exaggerated.

When Luther was declared an outlaw at the *Reichstag* at Worms in May 1521 he was taken under the protection of the Elector of Saxony, whose subject he was. Saxony was specifically excluded from the operation of the edict because of the political power of the elector. He was then effectively away from the public scene for two years, during which time his ideas spread rapidly from the students of the university of Wittenberg to the Augustinian Order, which adopted them as a weapon against their great rivals, the Dominicans, and beyond to the whole country. The reputation of Wittenberg as a university was made and it rapidly became the biggest in Germany. Monasteries emptied, clergy married and the Mass was abolished in many towns and on the estates of many nobles. The uniformity of Catholic worship was replaced by a bewildering variety of "reformed" Churches. Hundreds of independent centres of reformed doctrine, such as that of Martin Bucer in Mainz, later moved to Strasburg, appeared inside and outside Germany. Between 1517 and 1521 only four cities in the Empire banned Luther's writings and two of those were in the Netherlands.

The new ideas spread quickly among Germans in the Baltic and Scandinavia, Bohemia, Transylvania and the Low Countries. Had it not been for disputes over details of scriptural interpretation between Luther and Zwingli, which the Marburg debate of 1529 was unable to settle, Switzerland would also have gone Lutheran. This explosive spread was fuelled by Luther's enormous writing energy and power of communication, a charisma of the written word or "inspired journalism". The Lutheran press campaign, the circulation of Luther's sermons and pamphlets and the writings of a host of other reformers in hundreds of thousands of copies, was in itself a remarkable phenomenon and a sign of the fevered nature of the times. As important were the thousands of woodcuts, which spread the message of the Reformation, and later the Counter-Reformation, to the ninety per cent of the population who were illiterate. In spite of efforts by various authorities to stop their spread, because of fear of putting the scriptures in the hands of ordinary people and of religious disputes igniting unrest, pamphlets by and about Luther became a very profitable commodity, for which demand was high. They were cheap and easily concealed and distributed. In the absence of copyright laws and the effective collapse of censorship until the late 1530s, they continued to spread.

Luther's translation of the Bible, not the first in German but the first to achieve a mass readership, and a host of tracts and cheap news sheets appeared in numerous editions. Very soon Catholic counterblasts began to appear. In the ten years after 1510 the number of books alone printed in Germany quadrupled, with dozens of presses catering for a market which seemed insatiable, in spite of high prices. Germany was not again to experience a similar publications explosion until the late eighteenth century. In addition to the religious impact, this, along with the use of German in church services, was an important step in the final emergence of a literary High German (*Hochdeutsch*) based on the language spoken across central Germany from Mainz to Saxony, accelerating a process of linguistic standardization which had begun in the later Middle Ages. Without this, the political fragmentation of Germany might have led to the development of two or more mutually incomprehensible languages in north and south, as was to happen in the case of Dutch and German.

To most of his early supporters Luther was to prove a profound disappointment. He failed to fulfil their hopes and over the next eight years he was to lose the support of the peasants, the lower nobility, humanist intellectuals, who disliked his pessimistic view of mankind — in 1524 Erasmus published an attack on Luther's doctrines — and most of his fellow theologians. At the same time he won over a substantial section of the German princes and governments, which ensured the survival of his movement. By 1523 Luther was saying something rather different from what he had been saying in 1517. The notions of a personal interior religion, a Church free of state control and wide toleration of different religious views had gone and Luther had come to realize the need for a Church with a distinct clergy, external organization and state protection, if only to bring some order to the religious anarchy and threatened social revolution which his early actions had unleashed in Germany. Between 1525 and 1526 he accepted the Elector of Saxony's right to inspect and organize a state Lutheran Church, which began in 1527. The prince thereby became head of the Church and acquired control of a vital sphere of government, with a major role in education and the administration of charities, potentially substantial revenues and an important organ of propaganda, in which for the first time he was truly sovereign as he was supreme bishop by the grace of God and not acting as an agent of the Emperor.

The Church claimed total authority over major aspects of peoples' daily lives. Saxony was followed in installing a new state Church structure by other states, including Mansfeld, Brunswick-Lüneburg, Ansbach, Hesse, Mecklenburg, Anhalt, ducal Prussia and Brandenburg. State Churches on the Lutheran model were, however, initially the exception in the towns. Apart from a few like Nuremberg and Magdeburg, most German free cities, when they decided on their own form of Church, opted at first for the Zwinglian Zürich reformation and entered the Lutheran community only in the 1530s. [4] Some commentators have argued that Lutheranism, in contrast to the second-wave Reformation movement Calvinism, bred apolitical attitudes in its followers. This is oversimple and exaggerates the differences. Calvinism was to teach the duty of Christians to strive for the improvement of state and society in an effort to create a Godly community. Lutheranism urged an abstention from political involvement, preferring a cultivation of the inner spiritual life. It did not teach mindless obedience of authority, as those who sought to portray Luther as a proto-Nazi were later to claim. To Lutherans the spiritual was all-important and the secular incidental. Legitimate authority was to be respected as long as it did not infringe religious rights. It is significant that Luther later had to be pressurized into endorsing the Lutheran political alliance, the League of Schmalkalden.

Monocausal explanations of the early success of the Lutheran movement are unacceptable. Recent work has revealed clearly the importance of social, economic and political factors, alongside spiritual concerns, in producing an audience receptive to Luther's ideas. It is often impossible to disentangle one from the other. After 1517 movements for political and religious change came together. Detailed local studies have shown the enormous variation from case to case, particularly in the cities. [5] Anti-clericalism was a common factor: the clergy formed a substantial and usually privileged part of the population of many towns. Cathedrals and their surroundings were often special enclaves exempt from town jurisdiction. In some cases the Reformation movement began among the common people and was used by parties in internal political power struggles. In many towns the Reformation became a genuinely popular movement when it was taken up by non-citizen groups keen to topple the prevailing guild oligarchy and resisted by the traditional ruling groups, who clung to the old faith for political or personal reasons. In others, for example Nuremberg, it was adopted by the ruling elite and imposed on the masses, again as a political device. In some free cities Church fraternities and charitable funds were a major political issue where these were controlled by small elites and there was suspicion of corruption. Even before 1517 many cities had exercised some control over the Church and its associated charitable and educational institutions within their walls and the Reformation enabled them to take total powers. In a few, such as Cologne, the Reformation was eventually reversed but this was rare. More commonly towns acted as bases for the spread of the new faith into surrounding rural areas. Outside the towns the lower clergy, the lower nobility of the individual states and the free imperial knights played a major role in spreading Lutheranism, especially where their status was under attack from rulers, for example by assaults on the rights of the parliamentary Estates. Everywhere the clergy played a very important role. External factors were also important. Many of the small states bordering substantial Protestant states like Saxony and Hesse found themselves under strong pressure to adopt the new faith.

The popular movement for religious reform in the towns and cities spanned the whole Reformation period and continued for most of the century after the establishment of state churches. Out of sixty imperial free cities, only five of the smallest did not adopt the

Reformation and hundreds of other towns were involved, often long before their rulers. The movement has been intensively studied in recent years after long neglect by historians of the role of the cities in German history. The German city states embodied a tradition of urban self-government and communal pride also seen in Italy, Switzerland and the Low Countries. Levels of educational provision were usually high in towns and they often employed modern administrative techniques, for example written law codes, before the princely states. Many were suffering increasing demographic, economic and political problems in the early years of the sixteenth century, producing pressure on the established authorities.

The Reformation saw the last flowering of medieval urban republicanism in Germany. The ruling elites in many cities tried to strengthen themselves in imitation of princes and there were campaigns to win for the imperial free cities, equality with the electors and princes in the imperial diet. The larger free cities began to hold joint meetings, the town diets (*Städtetag*) to concert policy and lend weight to their grievances. The first was held in 1522 in Esslingen, which produced a *Recess* listing grievances and expressing opposition to a common imperial external tariff, the *Reichszoll*, an idea which had long been circulating. This attempt to unite the towns to increase their political muscle in Germany came to nothing; divisions were deep, a factor to be made worse by religious disputes, and too many pleaded poverty. The early sixteenth century saw more frequent riots in towns. Some free cities and many towns in princely states were facing growing encroachments on their rights from rulers modernizing and centralizing their governments and some took advantage of the troubled times to try to reverse this process and recover their autonomy.

Many of the princes and city governments which became "Lutheran" did not regard the schism in the Church as permanent but were compelled to step in and try to control a movement which was becoming essentially popular and threatening to become dangerously radical. It was in order to restore control that Luther left Wartburg Castle, to which he had withdrawn for safety after the diet of Worms, and returned to Wittenberg. In the early stages of the Reformation large numbers of autonomous religious communities (*Gemeinden*) sprang up spontaneously and there was a real fear that this movement would become political. It is also far too simple to see the princes' adoption of the new faith as motivated by greed for the Church's wealth or political independence from the Emperor. Some may have used Lutheranism for base ends but others, such as Luther's patrons the electors of Saxony and Margrave George of Ansbach, were sincerely motivated by a desire for religious reform and saw themselves as the divinely appointed instruments of such reform. There had long been disquiet on the part of many German governments over deficiencies in the Church and what was seen as the squandering of its resources. A strong movement towards state and city control of the Church had appeared in Germany long before 1517 and in some cases the Reformation completed the process of giving princes and city governments control over Church property and jurisdiction. German support for the conciliar movement in the early fifteenth century was strong in the hope that it would lead to reforms and a transfer of powers over the Church into the hands of secular authorities. Before 1500 the rulers of Jülich-Cleves, Austria, Saxony and Brandenburg, for example, had entered agreements with the papacy giving them considerable control over the Church in their states. The Emperor Frederick III gained the right to appoint to a number of important bishoprics within his lands. Secular rulers' ability to interfere in the running of the Church was enhanced by the fact that many high positions in it were held by members of the ruling families or their clients. The 1446 *Reichstag* gave the German rulers substantial rights over their Churches and by the 1448 Concordat of Vienna the papacy confirmed these rights. The pope was left with only vague powers of supervision. It did not, for example, have the right to fill German benefices with Italians.

There was no great rush to seize the wealth of the Church in the early stages of the Reformation. The majority of rulers remained concerned to preserve imperial law and some were very reluctant to act. For example the Elector of Brandenburg Joachim II began to take control of the Church in 1539–40 but initially only as an interim measure until a German Church council was convened. In the 1520s the majority of the "Lutheran" rulers were waiting for the calling of a German national synod to make final dispositions regarding the organization of the Church, including decisions on its property. Plans were circulating to use its revenues to maintain an imperial standing army, as well as for educational, charitable and religious purposes. The heavy additional costs facing governments caused by inflation and mounting military, administrative and diplomatic expenditure made the wealth of the Church very tempting but, unlike in England, the German Reformation did not lead to a wholesale looting of Church property. In some cases, when a ruler became lukewarm in his support of the new faith, defence of the Holy Evangelium passed to the Estates, who were sometimes able to prevent a squandering of Church funds and were prepared to pay their rulers substantial taxes to induce them to act as defenders of the faith. Eventually the position of most rulers was strengthened, even if it took time. [6] Church property was secularized and often taken into the prince's domain, providing extra income. It was frequently sold to the nobility. The elimination of the clergy from the parliamentary Estates and the state's enhanced access to the manpower, buildings and facilities of the Church were additional factors strengthening the state.

It was Charles V's inability to provide a national German solution for the problem, as he was urged to do by, for example, Johann Sleidan (known as Sleidanus) in his *Oratio* of 1544, which called on the Emperor to put himself at the head of the Protestant faith, which forced rulers to take the initiative into their own hands, especially when the Reformation threatened to become anarchic. Charles was absent from Germany during the decisive years, 1521 to 1530. When he returned after nine years in Spain he was at the height of his power and was horrified at the spread of heresy and the social unrest which had grown up in his absence. Recent studies have thrown a great deal of light on the so-called Radical Reformation, an inchoate movement of religious sects. [7] These, condemned by Luther as "false brethren" and "mad saints", sprang into existence independently of Luther's protest but were unwittingly encouraged by him. Luther was horrified by them and they had a substantial impact on the development of his ideas and attitudes.

They appeared very quickly in the first weeks of the Reformation in many parts of Germany and most had utopian social revolutionary programmes. Luther had no direct social teaching as such but what he said was easy to misunderstand, by those who had no privilege, as a general attack on privilege. He also helped to put the Bible in the hands of the semi-educated. The Radical Reformation attracted a mass following and by 1530 in terms of numbers of followers it was bigger than all other movements put together. The Radical Reformation was a Protean development but a number of generalizations can be made. The various movements on the radical wing of the Reformation were very similar. They usually appeared spontaneously. They covered a wide spectrum from the Spiritual and Mennonite movements, pacifist, contemplative and humane, to violent revolutionary sects seeking to initiate God's kingdom on earth by the extermination of the godless. The movement was not new but had existed as an undercurrent for centuries in the form of relics of pre-Christian religions, for example in witchcraft, or as heretical movements driven underground but not eradicated.

Groups known as the Peasant Biblicists or the *Illuminati* also predated Luther. These involved the sudden appearance of a charismatic leader, who claimed to have experienced visions and to have acquired special knowledge of some imminent huge catastrophe, which he or she had to pass on to the world. In the century before the Reformation several such leaders had quickly attracted a substantial following of disciples and taken on a very threatening character until put down. They were often lower class and violent and preached dangerous egalitarian and democratic ideas. The best known leaders of the Radical Reformation were Andreas Karlstadt, who had great influence in Switzerland, Gabriel Zwilling in Wittenberg and Thomas Müntzer. One of the most prominent groups to appear before Luther were the Zwickau Brethren in Saxony, led by the weavers Niklas Storch and Thomas Drechsel. This was influenced by the earlier Taborite movement in neighbouring Bohemia.

The best known of these sects was the Anabaptist movement, a very diverse and fissiparous collection of groups united only by the belief in regeneration by adult rebaptism. It had developed in the Netherlands and spread into the Rhineland before Luther appeared on the scene, a product of the deep economic crisis which was striking the Dutch urban poor and middle classes. During the Lutheran Reformation it experienced a final upsurge, attracting about ten thousand people concentrated in Switzerland and south and central Germany, again fuelled by a sharp recession from 1528 to 1534, which caused another wave of religious extremism. In 1529 the *Reichstag* banned Anabaptism. It culminated in 1535 in the seizure of the city of Münster by a group of revolutionary Anabaptists under "King" Jan of Leyden. For years before thousands of religious extremists had moved into the city from the Netherlands and neighbouring German states, producing a mounting political confrontation with the authorities. In 1532 Münster became officially Lutheran and in 1534 Anabaptism won hundreds of converts in a wave of millenarian hysteria. For some reason, it was believed the end of the world would begin in the city. The Anabaptist New Jerusalem held out against a siege for months during which terrible atrocities were committed. The *Reichstag* voted funds for its capture which happened in June 1535. This brief experience of the fiery breath of anarchy sent a shudder of horror through Europe and unleashed another wave of terrible persecution against the sects. The last serious outbreak of revolutionary Anabaptism occurred on the Lower Rhine in the late 1560s.

Although the majority of the Radical Reformation movements were docile, tolerant and egalitarian, they were viciously persecuted, being seen as a threat to all order, religious, social and economic. The development is well illustrated in the recently-studied career of Melchior Hoffmann, a fur dealer from south western Germany, who became a convinced follower of Luther and acted as a missionary of the new faith among the German-speaking communities in Scandinavia and the Baltic. In 1529 he broke with Lutheranism because it had become the faith of rich urban patricians in northern Germany. He went to Strasburg, which until 1534 was ready to tolerate a wide variety of different faiths within its walls. He gravitated into a spiritualist Anabaptist movement but quickly moved on to lead a group within the revolutionary wing, known as the Melchiorites, which had a substantial following among the lower classes facing severe economic and social problems. He was imprisoned from 1535, when the city turned against extremists, until his death in 1543.

The sects were deeply involved in the most important event of the Reformation period, the great peasant revolt in southern and central Germany in 1525–6, called the Peasants' War. It was the long-predicted culmination of long-developing movements in Germany and other parts of Europe, which had produced a series of major risings at the turn of the century, the most serious in Germany and Hungary. The best known outbreaks were associated with the *Bundschuh* in south west Germany before 1500 and the *Arme Konrad* in Württemberg in 1514. Both were wide-spread conspiratorial movements with known ringleaders. In the areas where the rising of 1525–6 was most intense, stability had already been undermined by a local war between the towns of the Swabian League and some of the aristocracy and the rebellion of a number of imperial knights (1522–3).

The Peasants' War took the form of risings all over southern and central Germany and was perhaps the greatest mass movement in German history. From the outset the rising adopted a defensive attitude. It began with meetings, petitions and calls for mediation and only later did it become violent. [8] It began in the summer of 1524 near Lake Constance and spread rapidly up the Rhine, into the Moselle valley, east into Austria and north into Saxony and Brunswick. A second wave of risings came later in 1525 and 1526 in the Rhine valley, Alsace, the Tyrol, Salzburg, Franconia and Thuringia.

Detailed research into the rising has modified older views which saw it as a uniform movement of the dispossessed. It was in no sense a national movement and remained provincial and localized, though certain common features were visible. The rising was most intensive in those areas where the rural economy was most advanced and where a man's land was always divided among all his children on his death, leading to overpopulation and serious land hunger. Significantly, Bavaria and most of northern Germany were spared. These were areas with stronger state governments, with fewer ecclesiastical states and free knights and where land-hunger was less acute than in the south and west. A variety of factors, including the proximity of towns, closeness to main roads and population densities, influenced village prosperity. Only peasants able to sell products directly on the market could take advantage of the price rise. Jurisdiction over villages in these areas was often shared between several lords, the Habsburgs, the Church and the nobility. The competition between them to impose a single lordship often added to the peasants' problems. The composition of the peasant "armies" varied from region to region. It was more than a large-scale riot but highly organized and led by men with military experience. It was joined by the poor and not-so-poor and leadership of the movement was taken over in some areas by townsmen, richer peasants who wanted to rise more quickly and enjoy higher status, and even officials and minor noblemen, who were casualties of the political and economic changes taking place and who used the grievances of the peasants to win over a following. Well-known examples of the last were Götz von Berlichingen, Florian Geyer and Tilman Riemenschneider, Mayor of Würzburg. Though it was an overwhelmingly rural phenomenon, many towns, especially those in decline or experiencing serious internal problems, played a prominent role, for example Mühlhausen in Thuringia. A series of urban risings in Speyer, Worms, Frankfurt, Mainz, Cologne, with echoes in the Netherlands and Poland, was sparked off by the rising.

In some of the towns of the south west there was a movement to secede from the Empire and join the Swiss confederation and they were accused of wishing to spread Swiss-style republicanism throughout Germany. The example of "free" Switzerland, where the peasants believed there were autonomous self-governing peasant communes, was important, especially in Swabia. In the Tyrol and Salzburg the movement took on a constitutional tone, with plans for the parliamentary Estates, the *Landschaft*, which contained peasant representatives, to retake political power. Some more extreme groups put forward radical utopian plans for a new German state of burghers and peasants under a paternal Emperor with the nobility reduced to the status of paid officials. It is on these aspects of the rising that East German historians have concentrated, who portray it as a failed bourgeois national revolution. From the outset a prominent role was played by Thomas Münzer, a charismatic leader who had emerged in the Zwickau Brethren in 1520, had quickly broken with Luther and who then went around among the peasants and workers in the Saxon mining areas preaching that the apocalypse was imminent and advocating a simple social Christianity based on the freedom and equality of all men. The peasants, he said, were to purge the world of the ungodly, especially the nobility, in preparation for the second coming. In Thuringia under Münzer and in the Tyrol under Michael Gaismair (or Geismair) a kind of primitive Christian communism also emerged within the movement but it was not typical.

The peasant revolt involved a complex mixture of economic, political, religious and social motives but it was at basis reactionary and restorative, growing out of a general yearning for a return to the "good old days". The peasants resented the growth of the intrusive and standardizing state, assaults on village self-government and the price rise. They sought to put the clock back to what was seen as a fairer world before their position had started to deteriorate. They opposed the village ordinances (*Dorfordnungen*), imposed by the state and supervised by its officials, which replaced the self-government of village communes based on traditional unwritten laws. Their support of a "moral economy" was part of a wider anti-monopoly movement arising from a conviction that the sufferings of the poor were due to the activities of wicked men, monopolists, usurers and engrossers. They called for "Godly law" (*göttliches Recht*) and return of the "old law"; the Reformation provided a link between the two. Godly law was to become a new universally applicable criterion of right and wrong, overriding the variety of local laws and conventions. The peasants were prepared to have their grievances judged by learned and pious men of the new faith, who would decide on the basis of Godly law.

The peasants also looked for the return of a powerful mystical Emperor who would step in to humble their oppressive landlords, the nobility and higher clergy, who, under pressure from falling grain prices and rental incomes since the late fifteenth century, sought to cushion themselves against economic change by exploiting their tenants more harshly. The measures adopted by lords seeking to increase their take from the peasants varied from place to place and included restricting their access to forests and pastures and employing jurisdiction as a source of revenue, major causes of grievance. No one seemed able to protect the peasants against restrictions on their freedom, increasing since the late fifteenth century, and the loss of their traditional rights. The main targets of peasant anger were not the higher lords but their agents in the localities, especially if they were based in the towns. Rural resentment of the towns was an important factor, made worse by a movement of urban capital into the countryside in the later medieval period, which ruptured long-standing personal ties. Divisions within the peasant community were also a factor, with landless labourers seeking to acquire a share of common land and the richer peasants seeking to stop them.

The most important statement of the peasants' "programme" was the Twelve Articles of Memmingen of February/March 1525. This was issued after three peasant "unions", those of the Danube valley, Lake Constance and the Allgaü, came together there. Subsequently many copies were printed in several widely spaced centres. It was a document full of biblical quotations, combining social, economic, political and religious demands. The notion of community (*Gemeinde*) was central to everything. The peasants called for community owner-ship of woods, waters and meadows, the abolition of rents, tithes and serfdom. They wanted a restoration of their traditional rights of access to common lands, forests and fisheries. They were horrified at the steady encroachment of the state on their lives, a state which claimed to own everything, the fish in the river, the birds in the air, the wind which turned the mill and the current in the river. They opposed the expansion of the state at the cost of village self-government and the spread of Roman Law, although they sometimes benefited from it.

Hostility to the legal profession was a powerful unifying element among the different strands of the peasant revolt. The damage caused to their lands by the lords' exercise of their hunting rights and increased taxes and tithes had long figured in lists of peasant grievances. Christian love and justice were to determine relations between lords and tenants: the lords should protect their subjects and they should in return pay him just dues. They condemned the failure of the clergy to give them the comfort they needed in hard times and demanded the free preaching of the gospel by clergy elected by the community and paid from the yield of tithes. Any surplus was to be used for purposes useful to the community. They stated that they had looked in the Holy Evangelium and could find there no justification for the things they objected to.

The peasant leaders' call for the creation of a great tribunal of princes and reforming clergy to judge their cause, of course, came to nothing and violence spread. It was very easy for the authorities to split the peasants and defeat them piecemeal. The risings were put down with great harshness from April 1525 into the summer of 1526 by German mercenary troops returning after Charles V's great victory at Pavia. The Swabian League and rulers of both faiths co-operated to crush it. In mid-May a great peasant "parliament" was held at Heilbronn, which put forward a number of draft proposals, some including plans for reform of the Empire, the significance of which has sometimes been exaggerated, but it only lasted a short time because of the approach of the Swabian League army, which on 14 and 15 May crushed the main peasant army at Frankenhausen. Other defeats followed. It is estimated that about 75 000 peasants were killed. For areas which were overpopulated this was not a catastrophe. In the subsequent judicial procedures many ringleaders were killed but the majority were given corporal punishments or fines. Collective fines were also levied against whole villages.

The defeat of the peasantry had significant long-term effects. Probably, except at a local level, there was no immediate sharp deterioration in their position, which was poor anyway. An attempt was made to avoid further trouble. In 1526 the imperial diet at Speyer considered the grievances of the peasantry, including the Twelve Articles, and a special committee was established to deal with this matter. This eventually put forward a number of proposals for reform, at the same time, significantly, taking the opportunity to attack abuses in the Church. It recommended that no more taxes should be paid from the German Church to Rome, restrictions on the operations of Church courts and steps to improve the quality of the clergy, including higher pay for them. For the peasants it suggested steps to remove their most obvious grievances, such as lighter labour services and improvements in the administration of justice. The report was rejected by the full *Reichstag*, which recommended firmer measures to deal with any future risings rather than steps to remove their causes. A few empty exhortations to lords to behave with more humanity to their peasants were widely ignored, except by the Swabian League, which tried to enforce them on its members.

The picture remained very varied. In some parts of Germany, for example the Tyrol, the peasantry was able to resist attacks on its position through its representation in the local Estates. Elsewhere governments, where they were strong enough to do so, took steps to remove grievances and to negotiate compromise settlements between peasants and lords. In most parts of Germany the bulk of the peasantry was effectively excluded from political, economic and social power before the rising and this was to remain the position until the nineteenth century. Their position deteriorated because of the growing burden of payments to the state, the lord and the tithe-owner but it would be very wrong to regard them as leaderless and voiceless after 1525. They could and did defend their rights in the imperial courts or, ultimately, by violence. It was widely accepted that the Emperor had a duty to protect subjects against the tyranny of their lords. Peasant communities, especially in the south west, funded appeals to the *Reichskammergericht* and often showed remarkable sophistication. If in sixteenth-century Japan villagers went in search of seven samurai, in Germany they went to find lawyers. Unrest was endemic in the German countryside until the French Revolution. The Church and the lower nobility were also badly hit by the rising and the main beneficiaries were the greater nobles and the larger secular rulers. The need to restore order gave the German rulers an excuse to increase their power while a growing determination to bring an end to religious chaos speeded up the movement towards state control of the Protestant churches.

There has been great debate about the links between the revolt and the Reformation. No doubt the general effervescence which accompanied Luther's protest encouraged the movement and aroused an expectation of change. At first Luther's attitude towards the rising was ambiguous. He had no sympathy with the peasants' social and economic aspirations, arguing that they had a duty to obey their lords. Their rebellion was a sin. Equally the lords had an obligation to protect their peasants. He considered that some of the peasants' grievances were justified and condemned lords whose maltreatment of their peasants had helped to cause the rising. He believed the peasants had been led astray by false prophets. He firmly denied that the peasants had any right to find their own religion on the basis of individual interpretations of the Bible or to use religious arguments to justify attacks on the social order. He is condemned for his famous strongly worded and bloodthirsty pamphlet of May 1525 against the peasants, urging the lords to put them down with brutality, which led to a hardening of attitudes. The first edition of this contained an earlier pamphlet calling for a mediated settlement but this disappeared from later printings and was forgotten.

This was probably not, as has been suggested, a sign of his political dependence on the ruling class but originated in his theological views.

Luther accepted a hierarchical society and the need for authority. In this he differed from Zwingli, who taught that subjects had a right, or a duty, to overthrow an authority which did not maintain a proper Christian order in the world. He put forward his famous doctrine of the two kingdoms (*Zwei-Reich-Lehre*), which drew a clear distinction between religious and secular spheres. Rebellion was wrong as no man could be judge in his own cause. Because of his innate sinfulness, man deserved a harsh life on earth but could console himself with the hope of bliss in heaven. Neither lords nor peasants were behaving in a manner suitable to prepare them for the imminent end of the world. It is anyway doubtful if Luther's whole-hearted support for the peasantry would have done them much good as the trends against which they were revolting were already too well-established. After the failure of the revolt the revolutionary sects were persecuted and driven underground and conservative state-run Churches came to dominate Protestant Germany.

The impact of the Reformation on German political life was profound. The religious and social tensions cut across political developments and contributed to the accelerating decline in imperial power and an even more decisive movement towards federalism in Germany during the reign of Charles V. [9] In the past attempts have been made to assign Charles' motives to neat categories, imperial, Habsburg/dynastic and Catholic. Men of his generation did not think in terms of such water-tight compartments. For example, Charles and his brother Ferdinand continued Maximilian I's policy of using imperial feudal rights and jurisdiction to try to extend Austrian political control among the little territories north of Lake Constance. Up to 1530 he was strongly influenced by his grand chancellor Mercurio Gattinara, a northern Italian in Burgundian service, then by Nicolas and Anthony Granvelle, father and son, also Burgundians, as first secretaries and later by his Spanish advisers. As his reign progressed he became increasingly Spanish in outlook, though he continued to regard the imperial title as providing a spiritual basis for the great empire he possessed and for his claims to universal monarchy. Charles inherited a whole complex of policies along with each of his various possessions and the balance between them shifted constantly during his reign. From Burgundy he took the policy of building a powerful "middle kingdom" between France and Germany, from Spain the crusading zeal of the *reconquista* and the expansionist ambitions of Castile and Aragon and from the Austrian lands a desire to make a reality of the German imperial title and ambitions in Italy and the Balkans. Common to all was a desire to stop the eastwards expansion of France and the westwards expansion of the Ottoman Turks. Charles made no attempt to create a super-state, to co-ordinate all his separate territories into a single structure of imperial power. It was probably impossible anyway. All his possessions suffered from having to share their ruler with other territories. This was particularly true of Germany.

Charles V was elected as Emperor by the unanimous vote of the electors on 28 June 1519 after spending 852 000 *Gulden* (*Fl.*) in bribes. The French king, a rival candidate, mounted a vigorous campaign to stop Charles' election, which included making large payments to German rulers. The election of the "German candidate" was popular and produced a wave of national enthusiasm. Charles was expected to act as a strong leader and defender of German national interests. Such hopes were soon disappointed. His reign in Germany must be regarded as a total failure, though there is a danger of judging it entirely from the perspective of 1556, when he abdicated. On more than one occasion he seemed close to asserting his authority in the Empire, though the problems facing him were formidable.

From the outset relations between the Emperor and the German princes were strained as the princes were afraid of Charles, not only because of his huge *Hausmacht* but because of the risk of Germany being dragged into foreign wars for him. This fear was seen in the imposition on the new Emperor of a restrictive capitulation of election (*Wahlkapitulation*) in 1519. Although this was modelled on the similar promises given on their accession by many German rulers, it went further than the usual undertaking to observe existing rights and agreements. Charles had to promise, among other things, to respect the rights and privileges of the German rulers, to appoint no foreigners to office within the *Reich*, to bring no foreign troops into the *Reich* and not to declare war without the consent of the electors. This last provision created the concept of the imperial war (*Reichskrieg*), a war declared and fought by the whole Empire. German and Latin were to be the only official languages of the Empire. The Emperor was obliged to consult the *Reichstag* or the electors on all imperial matters. All subsequent emperors and kings of the Romans had to issue a capitulation of election, which gradually extended these restrictions and became part of the law of the Empire alongside the Golden Bull, the perpetual peace of 1495, the religious peace of 1555 and the treaties of Westphalia of 1648.

The election of Charles marked a break in the imperial reform process which had begun under his grandfather but it revived soon after. Eighteen imperial diets were convened between 1521 and 1555, a large number compared with earlier and later periods, and at these the work of the imperial reform movement was completed, almost entirely in the manner desired by the princely party. A committee structure was established within the imperial diet, the *Ausschüsse*, to deal with specific items of business. This grew out of the earlier *ad hoc* committees set up to deal with petitions to the diet, the *Supplikationsausschüsse*. Provision was made for the calling by the arch-chancellor of Germany, the Elector of Mainz, of a delegate diet (*Deputationsreichstag*) of representatives of the Circles in an emergency, extended in 1555 into a standing committee with power to deal with any business left over at the end of a meeting of the full diet. This was to be abolished in 1603, when the electors vetoed its further operation and insisted that they alone should exercise decision-making functions between diets.

The functions of the Circles, increased to ten in number, were extended to include nominating judges to the imperial chamber court (*Reichskammergericht*), the maintenance of defence and internal peace, economic and coinage regulation, discussion of common concerns and the collection of taxes and recruiting of troops under the *Matrikel*. This was significant because it gave the states a pretext to extend their tax-levying powers. Imperial taxes were privileged as they overrode all constitutional conventions in force in any state. The later sixteenth century saw a sharp increase in the volume and frequency of imperial taxation to fund warfare against the Turks. Rulers habitually levied more than they were entitled to and used the surplus for their own purposes. Where financial control was exercised by Estates, either exclusively or jointly with the government, there was an incentive for rulers to switch the bulk of taxation from traditional land taxes to excises and taxes on consumption, which were easier to collect. All this led to increasing constitutional conflict in some states.

The leading rulers in each Circle were designated as convening princes (*kreisausschreibende Fürsten*), with the tasks of supervising the work of the Circle and calling assemblies of its members. This amounted to an active and viable federative political structure which could work, as was shown in 1544 when an imperial army was brought together to fight the Turks, but its operation always varied from area to area. It functioned best in the south west, especially in Swabia, where the Swabian League had created habits of co-operation between the states and the Circle became a real working union.

In 1532 the Regensburg diet accepted a common criminal code, the *Carolina*, which was to become the basis of the penal procedures of the states just as the ordinance of the imperial chamber court (*Reichskammergericht*) was supposed to be the basis for civil procedures. The last act of the reform movement came in 1559 with the issue of a coinage ordinance attempting to establish a common standard for the various coinages circulating in the Empire.

In 1521 a *Reichsregiment* was established, not, as Maximilian and Charles intended, a docile regency council to run the Empire in his absence but a body controlled by the German princes. It sat in Nuremberg until 1530 and put forward sensible schemes to give the Empire a professional civil service and military, economic and financial unity while preserving its federative nature. These plans were to remain on paper as the *Reichsregiment* was crippled by religious disputes and the rivalries of the greater princes. In 1526 it was responsible for the interim decision that questions of choice of religion were to be left to the individual rulers until a national Church council, vetoed by Charles in 1524, could be called together. This was to have major consequences; when Charles returned to Germany in 1530 Protestantism was already established.

Relations between the Emperor and the German princes did not improve as time passed. As Spain became increasingly the centre of gravity of Charles' *imperium*, the main source of money and troops, the prospect of a Spanish Emperor loomed larger. The phrase "Spanish tyranny" entered the German political vocabulary as a major threat to *teutsche Freiheit*. In his proposition to the 1521 *Reichstag* Charles stated that, in future, Germany should not have many masters but one. This was a silly statement as Charles had no means of enforcing his rule and it served only to antagonize those whose co-operation he needed to run the Empire. From 1521 to 1530 he was absent and left his brother Ferdinand as regent. The Nuremberg diet of 1522–3 called for a Church council and ordered Luther's supporters to remain quiet until it met. Action against the Lutherans was avoided out of fear of provoking a violent reaction, especially from the population of the towns. Religious polarization began early. In 1524 the Regensburg Union and in 1525 the Dessau Alliance were formed, unions of Catholic rulers, the main aim of which was to prevent disorder. In October 1525 Saxony and Hesse formed the Torgau Union, later joined by other Lutheran states in the north. In July 1524 Charles issued another mandate against Luther repeating the Edict of Worms and calling for its enforcement. Some members of the Swabian League began to burn Luther's works, which had only happened so far in the Austrian lands. This caused riots in a number of cities and was ignored in north Germany and most towns.

The 1526 diet in Speyer effectively gave the governments of the German states interim powers to make decisions on religious matters until a Church council was convened. This was tacit acceptance that individual states had to find a temporary religious settlement appropriate to local conditions in order to avoid spiralling disorder. In 1529 Ferdinand tried to reverse this, which led to the issue of a formal protestation by a small body of Lutheran rulers, princes and free cities, the Protestants, claiming a right to make decisions on religious questions and not to be bound by the decisions of the *Reichstag*.

Charles returned to Germany in 1530 after making peace with the pope. From 1530 to 1532 he was at the height of his power. Charles underestimated the religious conviction of the Protestants and believed that the whole thing was just a squabble over details. His main aim was to unite the Empire in the far more urgent task of fighting against the Turkish threat. In fact, the need to deal with the Turks constantly distracted Charles and played a major part in allowing Protestantism to survive and grow. He made energetic but vain attempts to preserve the unity of the Church. He saw the schism as easily curable and was ready to agree to the Mass in both kinds as an interim measure and put pressure on the papacy to carry out reforms in the Church and to call a joint council of the Church including the Protestants.

Several attempts were made to find a settlement. In the 1530 diet at Augsburg there was a serious attempt to find a compromise after the pope refused to call a council of the Church. The Protestants issued a statement of their faith, the Augsburg Confession, drawn up by Melanchthon in close consultation with Luther. This was very conciliatory, too conciliatory in the eyes of some Protestants. It left open the possibility of reconciliation with the Roman Catholic Church and made clear the differences between Lutheranism and the other sects. It was answered at once with a Catholic counter-statement which made clear the deep theological differences between Catholicism and Lutheranism. Papal and French agents helped further to sabotage the negotiations and the Lutherans refused absolutely to accept papal supremacy. There was also growing unrest among the Catholic princes because of the secularization of Church land and the gradual erosion of Catholic power in the Empire but Charles was able to find few allies among them. The prospect of an imperial victory so frightened even the Catholic rulers that they turned to foreign friends, especially France, for protection against their own sovereign.

In February 1531 the leading Protestant princes and Bavaria set up the League of Schmalkalden to defend the reformed religion *and* the rights of princes. It was eventually joined by seven princes and sixteen cities. Luther, after serious reservations about an act of defiance against the Emperor, accepted it. This was significant: earlier leagues, like the Swabian, had operated nominally as agents of the Emperor to preserve peace but the Schmalkaldic League was openly partisan and opposed the Emperor. Its formation provoked a lively debate among the Protestants, which highlighted divisions between the Lutherans and Zwinglians, about a right of resistance. The League was eventually justified by an assumed general right, shared by nobles and towns as well as princes, to resist a superior who behaved as a tyrant. This was an important step in the emergence of the states' claim to sovereignty. The League became an important political factor, an organized centre for the spread of Protestantism before the rise of Calvinism, especially important after the alternative Swiss centre faded away following the death of Zwingli. In 1534 the League restored the Lutheran Duke of Württemberg after he had been deposed in 1519 and his country occupied by Swabian League troops in the name of the Emperor. After his restoration the Lutheran Reformation was introduced. In 1542 the duchy of Brunswick-Wolfenbüttel was forcibly converted to Lutheranism and the duke imprisoned by the Schmalkaldic League.

The Turkish threat forced Charles to compromise again. The Emperor was absent from 1532 to 1545, when Ferdinand was again in charge. Ferdinand was elected king of the Romans, automatic heir to his brother, in 1531. He was the last German king or Emperor to be crowned in Aachen. One reason for this was his desire to remove Ferdinand from Spain, where he had been brought up and where he was more popular than Charles. His Interim of 1532 postponed action against the Lutherans and again provisionally accepted the existence of Protestantism. The Catholics were persuaded to accept that questions concerning the disposition of Church property were also, *ad interim*, to be decided by the state governments. Between 1538 and 1541 several colloquies were held in an attempt to find a compromise but all failed. At the same time Charles was working hard to exploit divisions within the Protestant camp, using for the purpose the Elector of Saxony's expansionist plans to absorb bishoprics on his borders and the landgrave of Hesse's bigamous marriage.

Friction between the Emperor and the Protestants was increased by other than religious factors. By 1541 Charles was resolved on war against the Protestants and their defeat seems to have become his prime aim, especially as the movement was again spreading and threatening Cologne, Münster, the Palatinate and the Netherlands, areas vital to Spanish communications in Europe. In 1538 relations between the Netherlands and the neighbouring Protestant German territory of Cleves-Jülich deteriorated sharply. Since 1521 the duke possessed a strategically and economically important area on the Lower Rhine and it was the ambition of his house to expand and convert his lands into a major state. In 1538, when the native ruling house in neighbouring Guelders died out, he tried to take the territory, which Charles also claimed. In 1541 the Netherlands government sent in troops to seize Guelders and to attack Cleves and Jülich. The duke was forced in 1543 to accept the Treaty of Venlo, agreeing to restore the Catholic faith in his lands and to an imperial occupation of his fortresses. The Peace of Crépy with France (1544) gave Charles a free hand. Under its terms Francis I of France had to agree to a joint attack on the German Protestants, the Turks and Geneva. Hungary was also pacified by 1547, freeing Charles' hands further. Since the death of King Louis of Hungary and Bohemia at Mohács in 1526 Charles' brother Ferdinand had been nominally king of both states but his possession was challenged by the Turks and the Transylvanians. Warfare, which threatened to spill over into Germany, continued until 1538 and again from 1540 to 1547, when it was ended by the Treaty of Adrianople.

The Council of Trent opened in March 1545, raising the possibility of redress of the Protestants' grievances. Subsidies and military aid were obtained from the papacy. Dukes Maurice of Saxony and William of Bavaria were prepared to ally with the Emperor in return for a promised elevation to the rank of elector. Maurice, head of the ducal or Albertine line of the Saxon ruling house, [10] initially remained Catholic when the electoral or Ernestine line adopted the reformed faith. The Emperor wooed him with promises of territorial gain. Here dynastic rivalry was an important factor in a religious decision, as it was in the case of the House of Brunswick. There were also deep divisions among the Protestant rulers. In 1546 Charles went to war against the Schmalkaldic League to execute an imperial ban against the Elector of Saxony and the landgrave of Hesse as punishment for their attack on Brunswick-Wolfenbüttel. On 24 April 1547 he inflicted a decisive defeat on the Saxons at Mühlberg, after which the elector and the landgrave were imprisoned. Charles again seemed to be in a position of unassailable power.

On the pretext that he had gone to war in order to suppress a rebellion and therefore had the right to tear up all existing agreements, he proposed a harsh settlement including a strongly Catholic religious settlement and a thorough-going reform of the government of the Empire. An imperial commission took over the government of free cities which had turned Protestant, the guilds, blamed for the rush of their cities into heresy, were deprived of their power and oligarchic city governments were installed, as had happened to Ghent after it revolted against Charles in 1540. An attempt was made to revive the Swabian League as an instrument of imperial power at a meeting of representatives of selected German rulers at Ulm in 1547, at which Charles announced that the new League would have himself and Austria as members and a common law court, army and treasury.

At the Augsburg *Reichstag*, which opened on 1 September 1547 and lasted ten months, there was a strong imperial military presence to make clear who was master now. This produced the religious Interim of 1548, a provisional settlement until the Council of Trent completed its work. Charles' plans to restore unity to the Church by compromise were ruined when he again fell out with the pope, who, worried at Charles' growing power, encouraged his opponents and moved the Council, which very few German prelates attended because of conditions in Germany, to Bologna. The Interim, while allowing communion in both kinds and married clergy, made no theological concessions to the Protestants and did nothing to remove abuses from the Church. It was therefore acceptable to neither side. It soon became clear, in the form of disturbances in a number of states and cities, that there was considerable popular support for the Lutheran faith. As a political system for Germany Charles proposed the creation of a perpetual *Bund* or confederation of states under imperial control, with regular taxes, a standing army and a permanent administration and law courts, all under the direct control of the Emperor. An additional Circle, the Burgundian, was created out of Charles' possessions in the Netherlands and Franche Comté as a means of extending his personal power into the Empire. This was to be in perpetual alliance with the Empire but largely outside its jurisdiction. Charles had no intention of subjecting his dynastic possessions to a structure of imperial government which might slip out of Habsburg hands. Had all this come into effect, it would have started Germany down a constitutional road very different from the one along which it had been proceeding for centuries.

There were other changes. Maurice of Saxony, labelled by the Lutherans the Meissen Judas, was awarded the lands and title of the deposed Elector of Saxony, whose sons were given small duchies carved out of Maurice's former possessions. There was a strange after-shock of all this in 1563–7, when the son of the deposed Elector John Frederick II allied with the last of the robber knights, Wilhelm von Grunbach, in a combined attack on Maurice to recover the electoral lands and title. It came to nothing. All this was seen by the German rulers as a breach of the Emperor's capitulation of election and an attack on the German constitution. Eventually Charles abandoned his far-reaching constitutional plans in the face of growing opposition.

In 1550 Maurice of Saxony deserted Charles and reconstituted an alliance of Protestant rulers against him. This entered the Treaty of Chambord with France in January 1552, under which Henry II, as defender of German liberty (*Vindex libertatis Germaniae*) provided military aid in return for Cambrai, Metz, Toul and Verdun, which considerably strengthened the French position in Alsace and Lorraine. The Schmalkaldic princes resumed war against the Emperor in the spring of 1552. A nominal imperial war against France was declared but a very limited effort was put into it. Some seized the opportunity of the disorder to pursue their own interests. For example, the Hohenzollern margrave of Kulmbach, Albert Alcibiades, in a pioneering exercise of the predatory habits which were later to characterize his house, tried in 1553 to seize Nuremberg, Bamberg and Würzburg. Maurice of Saxony was killed during the suppression of this. The Catholics remained neutral, including Ferdinand, installed by Charles as ruler of the Austrian lands in the partition of his empire in 1551, who signed a separate peace with Saxony in 1552. In 1551 Charles made public his intention to have his son Philip succeed Ferdinand as Emperor, which caused considerable concern among the German princes. This was an early sign of growing divisions between the Spanish and German branches of the Habsburg House, which were to become significant later. Charles was defeated and had to flee from the *Reich*. He abdicated from all his thrones in 1556, the first Emperor to do so.

In 1555 Ferdinand, given a free hand by Charles, who was in Brussels, very much a bystander, mediated the Augsburg Settlement, which brought the religious war in the Empire to an end and annulled the 1521 Edict of Worms. The diet which agreed to the settlement met after several postponements in February 1555. It made ritual noises about an eventual reconciliation of the two faiths but eventually accepted an agreement which recognized that its efforts were too late. The settlement recognized the primacy of the states but at the same time confirmed the imperial constitution, restoring the balance which

Charles V after 1547 had threatened to destroy. It also confirmed the *Reichsfrieden*: in future disputes between Catholics and Protestants could be settled only according to the law. One of the motives behind this was continuing nervousness about popular unrest caused by religious issues.

The basic principle behind the religious settlement was *cuius regio, eius religio*, the ruler had the right to determine the faith of his subjects, with some restrictions on the rights of the governments of free cities. The rights of dissenters to leave states with their possessions were guaranteed. Although Augsburg gave the Lutheran faith legal recognition in the Empire it also helped the Catholic cause. Calvinism and Zwinglianism were banned, a blow to many free cities in the south west, which had adopted these faiths, and further secularizations of Church lands were forbidden. The settlement embodied two incompatible principles, the preservation of the status quo and the right of the two legal religions to grow. Initially this did not produce problems.

By 1555 some of the fire had gone out of the Reformation, which was represented by less extreme figures like Melanchthon and Bucer. The creation of established Lutheran churches with a married well-educated clergy represented a substantial social change as this group, with its interest in status and property and therefore in stability, reinforced the middle classes.[11] In most of the free cities there was a return of stability by the middle of the century with the restoration to power of small patrician groups and tighter control of established churches. A new less dogmatic generation of German rulers was emerging, more attached to the ways of compromise in religion, concerned with the internal problems of their own states and anxious to avoid war. Typical was the pragmatic Ferdinand I, eager to meet the Turkish threat to his own possessions and preferring a quiet life in Germany.

4 Peace and Polarization: Germany 1555–1618

Traditionally the early part of this period of German history has not received much attention. It is seen as rather uneventful, a time of settlement after the troubles of the Reformation, and only becomes interesting again with the revival of tension caused by the advance of the Counter-Reformation, culminating in the outbreak of the Thirty Years' War. For Germany it was a period of peace and comparative stability at a time when other parts of Europe were engaged in warfare. The French wars of religion, the Spanish-Dutch war and the Turkish wars in Eastern Europe all touched the periphery of the Empire but Germany remained immune from serious trouble. During these years a number of well-established trends were consolidated. The federalization of the Holy Roman Empire continued, with measures enacted at a series of major *Reichstag* meetings. The Empire was a functioning political entity, which existed in its institutions and ceremonials. Descriptions of the situation after 1555 as "the glass peace", for example, are perhaps too influenced by hindsight. The settlement of 1555 created a remarkably successful *modus vivendi* between the Emperor and the princes and among the German states.

At the same time tensions seethed below the surface. All three major religions in Germany went in for proselytizing of varying intensity. This, and the readiness of all parties to look outside Germany to foreign friends, was a dangerous development. Within individual German states the extension of an absolutist system of government continued, culminating in some cases in serious constitutional struggles between rulers and Estates. Economic decline and stagnation deepened, marked particularly by the ossification of many German towns and cities partly as a result of the rise of the territorial states. A few states remained economically buoyant, for example Brunswick-Wolfenbüttel with its ample mineral resources in the Harz Mountains, but the majority accumulated mounting debts. As before, the urban picture was very mixed. The emergence and consolidation of a distinct Austrian state proceeded. All these trends came to a head in the Thirty Years' War, which accelerated and, in some cases, completed the processes.

The Habsburg successors of Charles V were very different from him. Ferdinand I, who was Emperor from 1556 until 1564 (although the electors accepted Charles' abdication and Ferdinand's automatic succession only in 1558) was more open and less inclined to heaviness and melancholy than Charles. He was also more German and more *politique* than his brother. At the Regensburg diet 1556–7 he tried to bring the two religious parties to conversations — a meeting was actually convened in Worms in 1557 — and he put pressure on the pope to permit clerical marriage and communion in both kinds in an effort to build bridges. At the same time he sought an internal revival of the Catholic Church. To this end he promoted the Jesuits in Germany in an effort to win people back to the Catholic faith by persuasion instead of force. Peter Canisius was especially successful in this work.

Ferdinand, strongly influenced by Spanish absolutist ideas, also continued the building of the Austrian state. In particular he saw the need to create strong central institutions to give some unity to a collection of disparate provinces. He had begun this process in 1527, while acting as regent for his brother, with the creation of the first all-Austrian organs of government. It should be noted that no clear distinction was drawn between Austrian and imperial institutions until 1620. The Austrian state grew gradually as an extra layer of administration spread on top of existing well-established provincial organs and, in that respect, could be regarded as unnecessary. He also moved the centre of gravity of the Austrian state eastwards from the Alpine core to Vienna, the more easily to control the newly acquired lands in Bohemia and to assert claims to the whole of Hungary, of which he held only a small strip.

Ferdinand was a careful ruler. In Bohemia he slowly extended his power by exploiting class and religious differences and building up a pro-Habsburg Catholic group among the nobles. Throughout he was conciliatory, a wise move as ninety per cent of the population were Protestant. His hold in the small territory of Royal Hungary, the only part of the kingdom not held by the Turks, was very weak. The powerful nobility was able to play off the Habsburgs against the Turks and keep their autonomy, as expressed in the diet. In some ways Ferdinand was oddly old-fashioned. On his death in 1564 his lands were partitioned among his three sons, creating three separate states. The senior line ruled the Austrian archduchies, Hungary and Bohemia. Inner Austria, Styria, Carinthia and Carniola formed a second unit and the Tyrol a third. This showed a conflict in his mind between state-building and the essentially medieval practice of creating appanages, though it has been argued that this device was seen as a means of preventing inheritance disputes before the principle of primogeniture was clearly accepted.

His successor as Emperor, Maximilian II (1564–76), has traditionally been seen as secretly inclined to Protestantism. He was, in reality, in matters of religion a *politique* like his father. He saw toleration as the only means of avoiding the destruction of the *Reich.* He challenged Spain's oppressive religious policies in the Netherlands, nominally still part of the Empire, although the 1555 settlement did not extend to the Burgundian Circle, of which they were part. He faced a growing problem within his own possessions from the parliamentary Estates, dominated by Protestant nobles, which were able to exploit the crown's problems with the Turks and financial weakness to demand political and religious concessions.

An influx of American silver was undercutting the production of Austria and Bohemia which, in any case, was facing growing technical problems. A decline in production was marked from the middle of the century. There were temporary recoveries but the trend was quite obviously downwards. The same was true of the Saxon and Thuringian mines. Lutheranism and Calvinism were spreading among the politically dominant Austrian aristocracy, which faced little challenge from the weak towns. The Estates in the Austrian lands, increasingly powerful from the 1530s, were able to extort major concessions in the late 1560s and early 1570s, which gave them control of taxation and considerable religious freedom. Austria came close to becoming Protestant. At the same time Maximilian undertook a major reform of the standards of the Catholic Church in his lands. In 1552 he brought in the Jesuits and set up universities for them in Vienna and Graz. In this he was strongly influenced by the example of Bavaria, where the Jesuits had their first German centre at Ingolstadt. Maximilian's policy seemed to stem from a desire to build bridges between the two faiths and end the schism between them. His reign was peaceful.

During this period the *Reich* was also remarkably tranquil. A serious effort was made to solve by compromise points of religious friction left over after the 1555 settlement. Speeches in the *Reichstag*, in a spirit of German patriotism, called for measures to preserve the Empire and the *Reichstag* voted taxes for the Turkish wars with little dissent. Apart from the Turkish threat, serious after 1576, other aspects of the international situation reinforced this. French influence and the French alliance with the Protestants were nullified by the wars of religion and only began to revive after the accession of Henry IV. Two elections of kings of the Romans, in 1562 and 1575, confirmed the Habsburgs' possession of the imperial title. The second such election, that of Archduke Rudolph, later Emperor Rudolph II, did lead to expressions of suspicion because he had been brought up in Spain, but only the Elector Palatine actually voted against him. Maximilian and Rudolph organized an active imperialist propaganda campaign, particularly through the clergy, calling for internal unity in the face of external threats and emphasizing the identity of the Empire and the House of Habsburg. Imperial propositions to the *Reichstag* were a useful vehicle for such appeals and were clearly intended for wide publication. As a result of cautious policies Ferdinand and Maximilian were able to build up considerable influence in the Empire. This was facilitated by the fact that the princes were no longer as afraid of the Emperor as under Charles V but were now more frightened of their neighbours, foreign powers and of being dragged into wars. Many rulers also faced internal constitutional problems with their subjects. In the second half of the sixteenth century many of the German Estates were reaching the pinnacle of their power and serious clashes between them and the nascent bureaucratic states took place.[1] At the same time the German princes were unwilling to support positive steps to strengthen the institutions of the *Reich*. At the diet of 1570 an imperial plan was floated for a new military system to give the Empire effective armed forces but this came to nothing.

There was no hard opposition to imperial authority as no single German ruler seemed willing or able to place himself at the head of such a movement. Moderation and pragmatism seemed the keynotes of the age. Dukes John III and John V of Jülich-Cleves sought to find a compromise or middle way between Catholicism and Protestantism, avoiding persecution and tolerating unorthodox practices. Their capital, Düsseldorf, became a centre of humanist ideas in the north west of the Empire.

With the legal acceptance of Lutheranism, Saxony's role as stand-ard-bearer of opposition waned and it was not to be taken up by the elector palatine until the emergence of militant Calvinism later in the century. Elector Augustus I of Saxony (1553–86) was a frugal ambitious ruler, who gave his state modest prosperity and educational reforms, including a new university at Leipzig. Another leading Lutheran state, Brandenburg-Prussia, also became passive. In 1525 Albert of Hohenzollern had begun the construction of a substantial state by secularizing the lands of the decaying Teutonic Order, of which he was master, and converting them into the duchy of Prussia, a fief of the Polish crown. The ban of the Empire was decreed against Albert but, because of circumstances, it was not put into operation. This policy was continued by his successor Elector Joachim I. Joachim II (1535–71) was, however, a puppet of the noble-dominated Estates. The *Junkers* were able to achieve political and social domi-nance, enserfing the peasantry, and destroyed the prosperity of the towns. The crown could do little to stop this due to financial weakness and other factors.[2] Other potential leaders of a princely opposition party, such as Hesse, lacked the means: on the death of Philip of Hesse, his possessions were divided into three separate states.

Matters began to change in the 1570s and 1580s after the accession to the imperial throne of a man unsuited to the tasks facing him, Rudolph II (1576–1612).[3] He was an extremely odd character, perhaps insane at times. He was deeply interested in art, including a large collection of erotica, and science, the latter covering the whole spectrum from the new astronomy to alchemy. He made his chosen capital Prague a major cultural centre for Europe. Resisting the mixing of religion and politics, he sought to draw the best from Catholicism and Protestantism to produce an amalgam acceptable to everyone. He spent long periods during the later years of his reign in self-imposed isolation in his palace in Prague, from where he con-ducted relations with the world through low-born favourites. This produced a serious vacuum in leadership in the Austrian lands and the Empire at a time of growing political and religious tensions in both.

Germany entered a period of confessionalism. Permanent religious/political networks, educational, personal, diplomatic and military, developed above the states as German life became increasingly confessionalized, a reflection of development taking place throughout the whole of Europe. Two Germanies began to emerge, with clear differences in culture and ideology. A new generation of young self-confident princes appeared, which had not experienced the earlier religious troubles. Most German states were essentially confessional, in that one religion was regarded as the basis of the entire political structure and toleration of other faiths was seen as inherently dangerous, an open door to treason and social disorder. In addition many aspects of government previously controlled by the Church, education, poor relief and marital law, were now in state hands.

The sixteenth century saw the foundation of a number of new universities, which, like the states, were confessional. The Lutheran and Calvinist universities were state-controlled while in the Catholic states the Jesuits and Benedictines remained important in their running. The administrative personnel in states were usually of one faith. There is evidence that some Catholic leaders, for example Philip II of Spain, believed in a kind of domino theory, to the effect that, if religious diversity was allowed to infect one province, it would spread like a disease and threaten all authority. On the Protestant side there was fear of a Catholic plot to exterminate them: memories of the St Bartholomew's Day massacre of 1572 lingered for a long time. A feeling of insecurity quickly spread fuelled by pamphlet warfare, in which vicious attacks by one faith on another were common although such material was illegal under imperial law. Typical of the atmosphere of suspicion caused by all this was the Protestant reaction to Pope Gregory XIII's reform of the calendar in 1582 to replace the outdated Julian calendar. It involved the disappearance of the days between 5 and 14 October and the year was to begin on 1 January instead of 1 March as previously. This was seen in Protestant areas as a plot to rob men of ten days of their lives and attempts by the Emperor to impose the new system throughout the *Reich* as imperial despotism. Protestant Germany refused to accept the new calendar until 1700 and the issue produced serious violence in some places. After riots in 1584 the city of Augsburg postponed the introduction of the new calendar until 1586 and many Protestants there clung to the old system.

Large areas of the *Reich* were affected by religious warfare in neighbouring countries, France and the Netherlands. In 1567 the Spaniards occupied Cleves-Jülich as part of their campaign against the rebellious Dutch provinces. Religious confrontation again became a serious problem in Germany. Each faith began a creeping encroachment on the territories of the other and extremists on both sides began to adopt deliberately aggressive policies. The Catholic Church, aware of divisions in the Protestant camp and the quietude and divisions of

Lutheranism, made a determined attempt to win back lost lands. In 1566 Austria and Catholic states in the Empire adopted the decrees of the Council of Trent, which had ended in 1563 and had confirmed traditional doctrine and practices, finally closing the door on compromise with the Protestants. Under Pope Gregory XIII a major Catholic renewal movement was launched in Germany with the establishment of the German Congregation in Rome and the despatch of a number of energetic nuncios, based in Munich, Cologne and Graz, who often operated without the Emperor's approval. A new harder line in religion became visible. The activities of the Jesuits in Austria, Salzburg, Bavaria, Mainz, Trier, Würzburg, Münster, Augsburg and Fulda increased, resulting, for example, in the expulsion of Protestants. The bishopric of Eichsfeld in Thuringia and the Lutheran state of Baden-Baden returned to Catholicism.

This was answered by a Protestant revival. In 1577 a conference of Lutheran theologians at Bergen Abbey near Magdeburg produced a clear statement of Lutheran doctrine, which breathed new life into the Church. In 1580 a declaration of agreement based on this was published, signed by fifty rulers, thirty-eight imperial cities and eight thousand clergymen. The state of Württemberg emerged as the powerhouse of revitalized Lutheranism, with the university of Tübingen as a centre. At the same time a militant Calvinist movement, inheriting the Zwinglian legacy, was spreading rapidly and became especially strong in the same areas as the earlier radical Reformation movements. At first it spread spontaneously from Switzerland, the Netherlands and France into the western areas of the Empire and from there to all parts. Under the 1555 settlement it was an illegal faith and was persecuted by many rulers, Catholic and Lutheran.

Solidarity between the two Protestant faiths was very limited, though initially in 1566, to avoid making a concession to the Catholics, the Lutheran establishment went along with the fiction that Calvinism was only a variant of the Augsburg Confession. It was tolerated or actively promoted by a number of princely and urban governments, beginning with the palatinate. Elector Frederick III converted to Calvinism in 1562, after a long search for religious truth, against very powerful resistance from his Lutheran subjects. The Palatinate was followed by Nassau, Hesse-Cassel, Saxe-Anhalt, Lippe, Cleves and, briefly, electoral Saxony. Unusually for something regarded as "the religion of rebels" the initiative for this often came from governments and met opposition from subjects. In the case of

Germany there was no necessary link between a particular religion and a particular class or political programme, though political troubles in some free cities in the early seventeenth century were attributed to the dangerous "democratic" spirit of Calvinism. The organization of the Calvinist Church in Germany was more authoritarian than elsewhere and the power of the ruler was more firmly entrenched. Some princes adopted Calvinism as a means of defeating Estates dominated by Lutheran establishments. This produced some odd results. In Lippe[4] the Calvinist Reformation was introduced by the ruling count between 1590 and 1610. It was resisted by the main city of the state, Lemgo, which obtained a verdict in its favour from the imperial aulic council. The city's Lutheran Church was retained under its own control. The opposite process took place in East Frisia, where the city of Emden went Calvinist under the influence of the neighbouring Netherlands, with which it had close ties, while the ruling prince remained Lutheran. In Brandenburg in 1613 the elector became a Calvinist while the state remained officially Lutheran. The co-existence of different faiths in a single state did not inevitably lead to conflict. Economic and political considerations often led to *de facto* toleration of minorities and the avoidance of extreme positions. There were cities in the south west where all three faiths established a pragmatic *modus vivendi*, though this was rare and such arrangements were usually fragile and susceptible to periodic friction. In many of the south German cities forcibly recatholicized after Mühlberg a system of *Parität*, the legal existence of two or more faiths in the same polity, was introduced in 1555. These arrangements were individually negotiated city by city and many were very complicated indeed and full of potential for trouble. In some a *Simultaneum*, an arrangement for shared use of a single church building, funds or other facilities by two faiths, was introduced, for example in Ravensburg and Augsburg.

Under the 1555 settlement it was unclear whether the religious status quo of that year was permanently established as far as the free cities were concerned or whether their governments had the right to change the established faith. This became important as circumstances changed, if religious issues became political, as they often did, or if waves of proselytizing zeal affected one side or the other, as was becoming more frequent in the last decades of the century. Demographic and economic changes could also alter the whole picture. Friction grew in Aachen, a Catholic city, when large numbers of Calvinists, many of them refugees from the Netherlands, began to move in, forming a majority of the city's population by the end of the century. Religion was not the decisive factor in determining the social and political structures in the towns; other factors were more important in this. The tradition of popular participation in government did not die away and even in the towns in princely states, called in German *Landstädte* to distinguish them from the free cities (*Reichsstädte*), some self-government remained. Many of the free cities were to experience chronic political instability from the Reformation until the eighteenth century.[3]

The causes of religious tension, apart from encroachment by one faith on the territory and rights of another, were breaches of the 1555 settlement, the continued secularization of Church lands in Protestant states and the advance of Protestantism among the free cities. The Augsburg Settlement had established parity in some cities but some Protestant magistracies had subsequently abandoned this unilaterally. The Ecclesiastical Reservation clause, which prevented Catholic prelates who became Protestants from converting their sees into secular states, was regarded by the Protestants as a barrier to their expansion. Catholic ruling houses, on the other hand, were able to expand by placing members in ecclesiastical posts. In a secret unpublished declaration at the time of the Augsburg Settlement, which did not become imperial law, Ferdinand I had guaranteed the religious liberties of Protestant nobles and towns in the ecclesiastical states, a breach of the principle of *cuius regio, eius religio* and a cause of great irritation to many bishops and archbishops.

Many of the twenty-six cathedral chapters, which elected bishops, contained, contrary to the Tridentine decrees, Protestant nobles, as the prebends and benefices available were a useful way of providing for younger sons. Where a chapter had a Protestant majority, it often wished to elect a Protestant prelate. If the see was then secularized, the prebends could be turned into fiefs. Some were elected and accepted as bishops by pope and Emperor if they gave guarantees that they would accept the decrees of Trent. For example, two sons of the Duke of Brunswick became bishops of Halberstadt and Osnabrück and this was a clear sign of the ambitions of the House of Brunswick to possess these territories. Even more spectacular, Albert of Hohenzollern secularized the east Prussian territories of the Teutonic Order. Saxony absorbed Merseburg, Meissen and Naumburg. It was obvious that Saxony, Brandenburg, Mecklenburg and Pomerania were casting covetous eyes on ecclesiastical territories within or near their borders, Magdeburg, Bremen, Verden, Schwerin, Minden, Halberstadt and Lübeck, and used the same procedure, having members of the ruling family elected to the sees in preparation for later annexation. This was another weapon in the ongoing campaign by the larger princes to extend their power over their smaller neighbours. Some of the sees did not have representation in the imperial diet but problems arose when other Catholic states refused to accept the right of Protestant prelates to control Catholic seats and votes in the imperial diet. There was a chronic dispute over the admission of Magdeburg from the 1570s until the outbreak of the Thirty Years' War.

Many Catholics realistically accepted that north Germany was lost to them but real trouble appeared when Protestants threatened to take over sees on the "border" between the two faiths, such as Cologne and Strasburg. Cologne was very sensitive indeed. It was an established ambition of the Bavarian Wittelsbachs to turn Cologne into a *de facto* permanent secundogeniture of their house, a device employed by other houses. In 1582 the Archbishop Elector of Cologne, Gebhard Truchsess von Waldburg stated his intention of becoming a Lutheran in order to marry. This would have seriously upset the balance of power in Germany, involving the loss of a Catholic electoral vote and of a substantial and strategically important Catholic outpost in the north west. The Estates of the archbishopric were strongly Catholic. Waldburg was deprived of his see in 1583 and Ernest of Wittelsbach, brother of the reigning Duke of Bavaria and already the holder of a number of important sees, was elected in his stead. War seemed likely as Spain and Bavaria were ready to support the new elector while the Palatinate supported the deposed Waldburg. The Dutch refused to become involved and eventually, after some localized violence in the electorate, Waldburg was bought off. Thereafter, members of the Bavarian house were to hold Cologne until 1761. Problems appeared in Strasburg between 1583 and 1604 because the cathedral chapter was divided between Catholic and Protestant parties. This eventually led to a double election of two bishops with useful international connections, a French Guise and a relative of the Elector of Brandenburg. Again war was avoided but the affair increased tension.

Rudolph II, like his immediate predecessors, was anxious to avoid trouble with the Protestant princes and feared the accusations that he was bringing Spanish influence into the Empire and threatening to drag Germany into Spain's wars. In 1579 Rudolph was betrothed to the Infanta Isabella, the daughter of Philip II, which revived hopes of an eventual revival of Charles V's empire, enlarged with Portugal and its possessions. This aroused great hostility in Germany and the marriage came to nothing. Rudolph was also unable to prevent direct papal contacts with German Catholic princes behind his back. In 1582 he apologized to the Protestant electors when the nuncio published a papal bull in Germany without his permission. Rudolph was increasingly out of step with his times. Within both religious camps aggressive "activist" parties were gaining strength and elbowing aside the moderates. By the later years of Rudolph's reign, especially after 1606, it was impossible to achieve anything concrete in the *Reichstag*, as it had become paralysed by religious squabbles. The Protestants complained, inaccurately, that the Catholic ecclesiastical states represented a solid bloc vote for the Emperor and demanded extra votes for themselves to balance it. They began meeting separately as a group before the opening of diets to concert policies. In 1598 a long and significant debate took place in which some Protestant states argued, contrary to the prevailing convention, that majority votes of the diet were not binding on all Estates of the Empire on non-religious as well as religious questions.

The imperial diet met only five times during the reign. The imperial deputation (*Reichsdeputation*), a small committee of the full diet, which became active in the 1570s, met more frequently. Other imperial organs like the imperial defence organization and the two supreme courts were also crippled by religious differences. In 1588 a long overdue inspection of the imperial cameral court was torpedoed when the Catholics refused to allow a Protestant to represent the Archbishop of Magdeburg on the inspecting commission. The Protestants complained in the *Reichstag* when the imperial courts found in favour of Catholic litigants appealing against a loss of rights and property to Protestant rulers and in 1600 they refused to participate any more in hearing appeals against cameral court verdicts, normally dealt with in the imperial deputation.

Rudolph became involved in a major war against the Turks between 1592 and 1606 but could obtain only limited help from the princes of the Empire or from the Estates of his own lands. A prominent figure at Rudolph's court, Andreas Haniwald, secretary of the imperial aulic council, was a strong Catholic imperialist and absolutist, who planned to rebuild his master's power in the Austrian lands by an alliance with the towns and peasantry against the nobles, who dominated the Estates, but this came to nothing. The only policy available to the Emperor's representatives in the Empire was co-operation with the Catholic party but this made the position of the majority of moderate Protestant princes around Saxony increasingly difficult and gave ammunition to the militant party growing up around the Wittelsbach elector palatine.

The Palatinate was emerging as the leading anti-imperial state, using Calvinism as a political weapon. It organized opposition to the Turkish taxes and mounted campaigns of obstructionism in the imperial diet. The Elector Palatine John Casimir (1583–92) opened his territory to Calvinist refugees. Unlike many of his fellow rulers he had no constitutional problems in his main territory as there were no Estates in the Lower Palatinate. A kind of Calvinist International was developing led by Prince Christian of Anhalt, a close adviser of the elector palatine. Its headquarters were in The Hague but it had major centres in the Empire, including the universities of Heidelberg and Altdorf and military academies established in 1606 at Sedan in the Calvinist duchy of Bouillon, ruled in the early seventeenth century by Turenne, a prominent Huguenot leader and uncle of the elector palatine, and in 1617 at Siegen in Nassau. It derived intellectual legitimacy from the work of a group of Dutch, French and German anti-absolutist writers, labelled by their opponents the *Monarchomachs* (king-killers). This "organization" maintained a network of contacts with sympathisers in many parts of the Empire, including members of the Austrian and Bohemian nobility, and other states.

The Emperor's position in Germany was further weakened by the clear ambition of another branch of the Wittelsbach family, the Duke of Bavaria, to become leader of the Catholic party not for religious reasons but as the basis for Bavaria's role as a regional power in southern Germany. The Duke of Bavaria, Maximilian I (1598–1651) issued propaganda offering the prospect of a Catholic Wittelsbach Emperor as an alternative to the Habsburgs. The emergence of a powerful Bavaria represented a serious threat to Habsburg influence. Since subjecting the nobility to their rule in 1495 and achieving primogeniture in the early sixteenth century a series of talented rulers had built Bavaria into a well-organized state. Albert V (1550–79) broke the power of his Lutheran nobility, who dominated the Estates, and created a powerful central administration in Munich in close alliance with the Catholic Church, over which the duke had substantial control. In 1570 a Spiritual Council (*Geistlicher Rat*) was set up, a joint body of laymen and clergy, which ran the Catholic Church. William V continued along the same lines. By a concordat signed in 1583 the papacy accepted ducal control of the resources and personnel of the Church. The relationship between Church and state was not always harmonious, as the bishops chafed under secular control, but in general it functioned well. The work was completed by Maximilian I, the most able of the three, whose long reign saw the creation of an advanced administration and the consolidation of absolutism.

A new office, that of *Rentmeister*, was created. Its holders took charge of financial administration in the four *Aemter* into which the duchy was divided. Later they also took over judicial powers, leaving the noble governor or *Viztum* with little more than ceremonial functions. In 1591 all Bavarian officials were required to take an oath to the Tridentine decrees and to live as observant Catholics. This was later extended to all Bavarian subjects: the obligation to produce regular certificates of confession and attendance at the Mass was an effective instrument of social and political control. The court, which took part in a regular programme of Catholic ritual and observance, widely reported among the population, became a model of baroque piety, which added to its authority and standing in Catholic Germany. What had begun as an imposition quickly, thanks mainly to the skill of the Jesuits, became popular and Bavarians came to identify closely with their Church and dynasty. Good relations between the crown and the nobility were restored by the issue of new law codes in 1616 and 1618, which considerably weakened the rights of the peasantry. This helped to console the landowners for the loss of their political power in the Estates. Prussian absolutism was later to be founded on a similar bargain between the crown and the nobility of Brandenburg in 1653.

The Bavarian example was imitated by others, including the later Emperor Ferdinand II and the Archbishop of Salzburg. Archbishop Wolf Dietrich von Raitenau (1587–1612), was a strong ruler who eliminated the political power of the Estates and the cathedral chapter, ironically in order to strengthen his state against Bavarian and Austrian encroachments. In 1606 he forced the cathedral chapter to accept an agreement never to elect a Habsburg or Wittelsbach prince to the see. In 1612 a Bavarian army invaded Salzburg and arrested and deposed von Raitenau after border clashes.

Growing religious tension was accompanied by a revival of social problems, which added further to the atmosphere of instability in Germany in the last decades of the sixteenth and early years of the seventeenth century. There was a widespread belief that Germany had suffered a general moral decline, manifested in conspicuous consumption, excessive eating and drinking, profanity, libidinage, dishonesty and greed. The Turks were again seen as God's agents for the punishment of wicked Germans.

The Reformation period had seen important social changes, which added to a growing feeling of unease. Any disturbance of the social order was regarded as dangerous because of the built-in limits of the economy: one group could only acquire more by taking it from others, threatening the whole structure. The effects of the changes were extremely complex and difficult to reduce to simple formulas. Old concepts, such as the patriarchal household, including family and servants, as the basic unit of society and a society divided into traditional Estates, survived but there was an increasingly fluid situation within each Estate. There was certainly greater social mobility, especially in the towns, where the opportunities were greater. It was made possible by the expansion of education, the emergence of professional administrators and, probably the least important factor, changing economic opportunities. Attitudes were also changing. Although the supposed link between Protestantism, especially Calvinism, and capitalism has been exaggerated in the past, there was certainly a new attitude to work and accumulation after the Reformation. The Catholic clergy, as before, could not own or inherit property but Protestant clergymen could do both and marry, leaving heirs. The old view, that the lowest in society did physical work while the highest did no work, was changing. Work was no longer seen as something to be done only in order to acquire enough capital to make further work unnecessary but as valuable in its own right. Criticism of a nobility which did nothing to justify its status was becoming more common. Protestant nobles began to engage in trade and manufacturing, though usually only in the products of their own lands, without derogation, loss of status. New groups were increasing in wealth and social and political power, while older elites clung on to what they could of their former position, with varied success.

Changes in Church/state relations disrupted old systems, bringing about significant changes in the distribution of power, wealth and status in both Catholic and Protestant states. Political power and social power were not always in the same hands: in many free cities the old patricians, although forced to admit wider circles of citizens to a share of political power, clung on to their old social status. A visible raising of social barriers among the nobility and urban patricians in the last decades of the century was a reaction against a perceived excess of social mobility earlier. Some successful townsmen moved sideways to become land-owning nobles. Perhaps the most striking example of this was the Fuggers, who became counts of the Empire and princes of Babenhausen. Although there are dangers in exaggerating the extent of the change, economic classes in a modern sense were just beginning to emerge alongside the surviving traditional medieval orders. Yet it remained an oddly ambivalent world, with the same men practising proto-capitalist methods in order to enrich themselves while continuing to give lavishly to charity in the medieval style.

The economic situation was also becoming more difficult. It would be inaccurate to talk of a general economic decline in Germany in the later sixteenth century though changes were occurring which caused decline in some areas and growth in others. The general commercial situation in Europe continued to change to Germany's disadvantage and the German economies could not be isolated from developments elsewhere. There were marked signs of economic change and decline, especially in the cities. Stettin and its hinterland were badly hurt by the collapse of its biggest trading company in 1572. Many of the formerly prosperous free cities of the south were declining and experiencing pastoralization of their economies, adding new fuel to internal political divisions and sharpening religious divisions. There was a marked withdrawal of capital from enterprise and investment in land as many urban patricians became nobles. The position of the guilds was often a potent source of trouble. As cities began to experience decline, the guilds, where they were traditionally important, often tried to increase their power in order to defend the livelihood of their members. This bred conservatism and resistance to change, which could in turn make the economic position worse. It is significant that many of the few manufacturing bright-spots in late sixteenth-century Germany were in cities like Frankfurt, which had a textile industry free of guild control and open to new methods, or in small towns and rural areas outside the walls and beyond the control of guild-dominated centres like Cologne and Aachen. The first stages of mercantilism, state direction of the economy, caused further disruptions.

Economic stagnation was made worse by a number of years of poor weather, labelled the Little Ice Age, which lasted into the mid-eighteenth century. The inevitable crisis caused by population growth combined with the built-in limits of agricultural productivity had arrived.[6] Governments did not begin to regard overpopulation as dangerous until the eighteenth century; earlier the prevailing view was that population was the prime source of a state's strength. Germany, especially the western parts, began to experience the problems of overpopulation and food shortages. Large numbers of people lived an extremely marginal existence and a natural or family disaster could throw whole families into total destitution. Pauperism and vagabondage were increasing before 1618, adding to public insecurity. The years 1560 to 1600 saw a sharp increase in criminality, mainly as a result of the growth of robber bands. Epidemics of plague, malaria and other diseases hit Europe in the years before 1618. Malnutrition, and the sterility it produces, were chronic. All this, combined with the appearance of comets, created genuine fears about the future. As before the Lutheran Reformation, there was a mounting feeling of imminent catastrophe and growing millenarian hysteria.

The late sixteenth century was marked by serious peasant revolts and political and social conflicts, often violent, in towns and cities, *Reichsstädte* and *Landstädte*. Between the 1580s and the 1620s there was a wave of serious peasant risings, especially in the south west. The peasants were under growing pressure from land hunger and increasing demands from states and landlords desperate to increase their incomes. In some cases princes revived their campaigns to take over free cities, including the most important ones such as Hamburg, Bremen, Cologne and Frankfurt, in alliance with parties inside them. All this was a sign of deep social and political tensions. In some cities these expressed themselves in the form of violent anti-Semitism, which was never far below the surface, with the reappearance of old myths about Jewish ritual murders of Christian children.[7] Typical of all this was the so-called Fettmilch Rising in Frankfurt-am-Main between 1612 and 1614. This was named after a gingerbread baker Vincenz Fettmilch, who led a popular movement among the citizens which culminated in August 1614 in a vicious pogrom against the largest Jewish community in Germany leading to its expulsion. Other "outsiders" such as gypsies also suffered an upsurge of persecution and there was a large-scale witch craze between 1580 and 1600, followed by further waves during and after the Thirty Years' War, all part of the same phenomenon.

There are clear indications that these movements were sometimes deliberately exploited for political purposes by one faction against another and that the authorities in some places encouraged these outbreaks as a safety valve; it was easy to blame visible groups like Jews and witches for economic and climatic phenomena which were otherwise inexplicable. Superstition and survivals from pre-Christian times were not far below the surface, especially in rural areas. In 1631 Friedrich Spee wrote *Cautio Criminalis*, an essay on witch trials showing how ridiculous the whole procedure was, but its impact was only gradual.[8]

Added to all this were symptoms of the further development of the concept of the state in the modern sense, the beginnings of which had contributed to the pre-Reformation crisis. In the later sixteenth century theory and practical developments were proceeding rapidly hand-in-hand. Bodin's *Six Books of the Republic* (1576) put forward the concepts of the sovereign state: indivisible and unlimited sovereignty, the exercise of which could be restrained by divine and natural law, prevailing constitutional agreements or the fundamental laws of the state.[9] The impact of this in the *Reich* was limited, where the long-standing debate on the nature and origins of territorial sovereignty (*Landeshoheit*), the powers of the German princes, was more important. Most German rulers were very far from possessing sovereign power, though many aspired to it. Corporate and individual liberties and privileges remained powerful, though they were often customary and not written down. The growth of the state was, inevitably, at the cost of these rights and the constitutional disputes of the time showed a growing tendency on the part of princes to command rather than to negotiate. The state, it was argued, always knew best.

New administrative methods continued to exist side by side with more traditional systems but the trend was clear; experts were taking over and the old self-governing institutions saw their functions and status being eroded. As governments tried to deal with the effects of structural changes by means of legislation, the size and scope of government had to increase. The most common device chosen for this purpose was the *Polizeiordnung*, an untranslatable term perhaps best rendered as "administrative ordinance".[10] The notion of *Polizei* or *Policey*, which the ordinance was designed to further, can perhaps be best rendered as "good government", with emphasis on the duty of the Christian ruler to protect the good and punish evildoers. These regulations, designed to promote good order and morality, were issued in increasing numbers in the sixteenth century by most governments, from the free cities to the Empire, and covered ever wider aspects of the daily lives of the people. Poor relief, charities, education, public health, medical matters, fire regulations, the guilds, wage and price regulations and control of servants were all covered. Of growing importance in the later sixteenth century were sumptuary laws designed to prevent what was seen as a dangerous blurring of the lines between the different social orders. It was considered important to preserve visibly the status of each order by distinctions of dress. Without this, it was feared, the respect given by one order to another, the glue which held society together, would be eroded. The first imperial *Polizeiordnung*, including sumptuary regulations, was issued in 1530, laying down what clothes and furs each order could wear and how much each could spend on events like weddings and funerals. They were repeated in 1548 and 1577.

Political tensions in individual states were mirrored in Germany as a whole, as was illustrated in 1608 with the Donauwörth affair. This free city, which had a Protestant majority and a Catholic minority with certain defined rights, was in an area of the Empire of great religious sensitivity, where Protestant and Catholic states and cities were very close to one another, including Bavaria and the Calvinist Upper Palatinate. There was a long history of friction between the two groups in the city, in which the Catholic Bishop of Augsburg had played a provocative role. In 1608 it was annexed by Bavaria under the pretext of executing a verdict of the imperial aulic council (*Reichshofrat*) against the city government after a religious riot in 1607. The aulic council was seen as an instrument of Catholic policy, especially when its business increased because its rival, the imperial chamber court, was paralysed by religious disputes. This was not, as the Protestants claimed to believe, the beginning of the long-expected Catholic offensive but an attempt to uphold the constitution of the Empire and, at the same time, to win back something seen as legitimately Catholic. If there was a great Catholic offensive in Germany it came after 1618 not before but the affair caused great alarm.

The Donauwörth affair accelerated the formation of religious leagues in Germany, traditionally seen as an important step in the process leading to the Thirty Years' War. On 27 April 1608 the Calvinists walked out of the *Reichstag*, which stopped its work and prevented the grant of a tax for war against the Turks. At the same time the institutions of the religious conciliation system, in operation since 1555, ceased to function. On 14 May the Evangelical Union was set up, consisting of the Palatinate, Anhalt, Württemberg and a number of free cities, in other words very much the activist minority of the German Protestants and clients of the Palatinate. The membership was later extended in 1612–13 when Hesse-Cassel and Brandenburg joined and it also entered formal agreements with England and the United Provinces.

Frederick V became elector palatine in 1610. He was a very weak character, strongly under the influence of Christian of Anhalt. In July 1609 the Catholic League was established, led and financed by Maximilian of Bavaria. It grew out of the earlier Landsberg League

(1556–98), which had begun life as a non-confessional peace-keeping alliance similar to the Swabian League, taken over by Bavaria. Initially this was also very much a minority movement among German Catholic rulers, but it too expanded as tension grew. A number of ecclesiastical states joined it, including Mainz and Cologne, and Spain became its protector. The League was always much better organized than the Union, thanks to Bavarian control of it, and it quickly built up an effective army under the Walloon general Count Tilly. In 1616 Austria and Saxony, the leading Lutheran state, joined it, at which point Maximilian of Bavaria left it and founded another Catholic League with a few ecclesiastical states. He clearly wanted no rivals to his control. Neither the Union nor the League was ever designed to include all the Catholics or Protestants in the Empire. In reality both were vehicles for Bavarian and Palatinate influence and instruments of their ambitions to become regional powers in the south and west of the Empire. Religion was a useful means of disguising power politics and of attracting powerful foreign friends. Neither the League nor the Union was the spearhead of a crusade to rid Germany of Protestantism or to capture it entirely for one or other of the reformed faiths.

The formation of the German religious leagues has in the past often been quoted as evidence of the inevitability of a religious war in the Empire. This "tinder-box" theory, that Germany and Europe had divided into two armed camps and that only a spark was needed to set off the explosion, owes more to the analogy with Europe in 1914 than to a realistic assessment of the actual situation in Germany in 1618. It is interesting to note that Europe experienced a general pacification in the years before 1618, a peace of exhaustion. The end of the Anglo-Spanish War came in 1604 and the French civil wars, in which Spain was involved, ended in 1598. Spain and the Dutch signed a twelve-year truce in 1609 after the peace party under Oldenbarnevelt came to power in the Netherlands, though the Orangist war party remained influential in north western Germany, maintaining garrisons in Emden and other strong points. Peace came in the Baltic region between 1613 and 1617. Turkish attacks on Austria, regular since 1593, stopped in 1615. Although the position in Germany was becoming more tense before 1618, the majority of German rulers were far more afraid of war than desired it. It was imperial policy to try to play down religious problems. The German religious leagues did not divide Germany into two religious armed camps but they were ominous in that they became vehicles for growing foreign influence in

Germany. This was a clear sign of development of a power vacuum in the Empire, which states like Bavaria and the Palatinate rushed to fill and into which foreign influence was drawn. The Protestant Union was linked to England and to the House of Orange in the Netherlands and the League to Spain.

This was shown very clearly in the Jülich-Berg crisis of 1609–10. The male line of the native dynasty of this substantial and strategically very important territory on the Lower Rhine died out. In order to forestall an imperial take-over, the territory was occupied jointly by the two rival candidates for the vacant throne, the Elector of Brandenburg, who became a personal convert to Calvinism — his state remained legally Lutheran — to win a marriage into the House of Orange and Dutch support, and the Count of Palatinate-Neuburg, a member of a junior branch of the House of Wittelsbach. He became a convert to Catholicism to win Habsburg and Bavarian support for his claims. Such opportunism points to a certain shallowness of religious convictions, at least among the main power-exercisers of the Empire.

The Jülich-Berg affair was important because it impinged on the vital interests of other European powers. The government of Spain was frightened that the territory so close to the Netherlands would fall into hostile hands and encouraged the Emperor to intervene judicially, as he had a right to do when a fief of the Empire fell vacant. The French likewise felt threatened if Jülich-Berg should come into the possession of a pro-Habsburg ruler and were prepared to march in to prevent this. A French intervention had the backing of England, the Dutch and the Protestant Union. There was a real possibility in 1610 of the Franco-Spanish War reviving and spilling over on to German soil. Although this did not happen due to the assassination of Henry IV in May 1610, which prevented an internationalization of the problem, and although eventually the affair was settled by the Treaty of Xanten in 1614, which partitioned the territories between the two claimants and guaranteed existing religious rights there, this event did illustrate very well the basic cause of the Thirty Years' War, mutual fear and misunderstanding, not religious polarization. It added to the growing fear on both sides, the Habsburgs and their enemies, that the other was about to launch a great attack which, according to growing war parties in several states, but most importantly in Spain and the Netherlands, had to be met with a defensive pre-emptive strike. In the final crisis which precipitated the war each side believed it was acting defensively.

The leaders of the Spanish war party were Oñate, Spanish ambassador in Vienna from 1616 to 1617, Baltasar de Zuñiga, Philip IV's
first minister, in Madrid, Archduke Albert, governor of the Spanish
Netherlands and his commander Spinola. They were on the Habsburg
side the equivalents of the Elector Palatine and Christian of Anhalt.[11]
When the Bohemian crisis broke there was a very deep difference of
opinion, especially in the Spanish government, as to whether Spain
should intervene. The war party argued that Spain could not afford
not to intervene. A long debate followed on the costs and political
repercussions of intervention in Germany and of not intervening.
Among the horrors which might follow if Spain did not become
involved were a Protestant Emperor, the loss of Bohemia to the
Calvinists, a severe threat to Catholic Poland, and the loss of Alsace,
which was vital to Spanish communications in Europe, the Spanish
Road.[12] Opponents of war argued that Spain could not afford war
until she had recovered her strength.

To the Austrian branch of the House of Habsburg the prospect of
war was even more frightening. Like Spain it was in a weak state in
the years before the outbreak of war, having been through a period of
severe internal troubles. Between 1600 and 1612 Rudolf II played
virtually no part in the government of his possessions. The noble-
dominated Estates of his possessions took advantage of this to extend
their powers. Calvinism spread rapidly, acquiring an institutional
base in the Estates, towns, villages and schools, and their leader
Georg von Tschernembl had close links to the Calvinist International
described earlier. In 1608 the Estates of Upper and Lower Austria
formed the Union of Horn and expressly reserved the right to use
force to defend their rights, including religious liberties. They also
entered a military alliance with the governor of the neighbouring
Upper Palatinate, Christian of Anhalt. There was growing social
tension as some of the nobles took advantage of their new power to
extend their rights over the peasantry. The Austrian lands were
afflicted with growing religious, social and political tensions and the
monarchy seemed powerless to intervene. There was a major peasant
revolt between 1594 and 1597, part of a wave of peasant risings in the
south of the Empire at this time, and serious disorders in Habsburg
Hungary. There were more serious risings in Upper Austria in 1632
and 1636.

Rudolph's brothers also took advantage of his weakness to build
states for themselves within his possessions. In 1608 Archduke
Matthias allowed himself to become the figurehead of a revolt of the

Hungarians and Austrians. As a result he became nominal ruler of Hungary, Moravia and Austria. Rudolph was only able to keep Bohemia by making massive political and religious concessions to the Estates in 1609, the famous Letter of Majesty. The Bohemian Protestants had sunk their doctrinal differences to form a bloc in 1575 and were powerful in the Estates. The Letter of Majesty allowed them to create a defence system to protect their rights. After Rudolph's death Matthias was briefly Emperor between 1612 and 1619. He was an ambitious mediocrity willing to use any device to gain power but in fact he gained only the trappings of power, not the reality. Though his main adviser, Cardinal Klesl, was a *politique*, he embarked on a more aggressive policy towards the Estates and Protestantism in the Austrian lands, leading to a marked sharpening of internal tensions. In 1614 he called representatives of the Estates of his lands together at Linz and asked for financial help. This was refused.

In the Empire he was even more powerless. Rudolph's inertia had encouraged the princes, including Bavaria and the Palatinate, to carve out little informal empires for themselves. In 1610 the electors met and claimed a right to govern the Empire in the absence, for whatever reason, of the Emperor. This casts serious doubt on the view of the Thirty Years' War as the culmination of a contest between imperial despotism and princely particularism. The opposite seems to have been the case. Rudolph and Matthias were incapable of acting as despots and it was the almost complete absence of imperial authority in the Empire, not rampant particularism, which gave the German rulers the motive and opportunity to look to their own state interests.

Another legend has in the past been considered a major cause of the war, the so-called Madrid-Vienna axis, a supposed close alliance between the two branches of the House of Habsburg to restore their power in Germany and Europe by means of a Catholic crusade. They are said to have had grandiose plans: Spain was to recover the Netherlands and humiliate France and Austria was to restore Habsburg authority in Germany. Together they would recatholicize Scandinavia, turn the Baltic into a Habsburg lake, revive Poland, creating a Vienna-Madrid-Warsaw axis, and launch an attack on the Turks to liberate Hungary and the Balkans and recover Constantinople.

In fact such an alliance between Madrid and Vienna was created by the war and was not a cause of it. Both states were very weak at the outset of war and needed peace. Though the Habsburgs' enemies habitually interpreted the relationship between Spain and Austria as very close, in fact there was, in spite of the family link, no real identity of interest between them. An alliance with France would have benefited each more than the alliance with one another. More than that, before 1618 there was very real mistrust and divergence of opinion between the two over policy in Germany, Bohemia, Italy and the Netherlands, especially as the last two were claimed as fiefs of the Empire, that is under ultimate imperial authority, though they were possessed by the Spanish branch of the family. The Austrian branch was very bitter when, at the partition of Charles V's empire, Spain emerged as the senior line, with the advantages of American silver, a stronger monarchy and an absence of Protestants. This was also a sign of the devaluation of the imperial title, though Philip II would have liked to have been Holy Roman Emperor.

As we have seen, the Austrian branch tended to follow a more *politique* line on religion and the Dutch revolt. Matthias had briefly flirted with the idea of taking over the role of figurehead of the Dutch rebels. The Austrians were greatly irritated when Spain assumed that German territory near the Spanish Road was a legitimate sphere of Spanish influence and acted in accordance with this assumption. This, plus Spanish interference in German affairs, added fuel to the "Spanish tyranny" argument of the German princes and made life difficult for emperors like Rudolph II, who needed German aid against the Turks. The Emperors' position was further damaged by the growing religious squabbles, in which Spain was seen as playing a role. Spain also took advantage of troubles in Rudolph's later years to increase her influence in Austria.[13] Philip II was always ready to give advice to his Austrian cousins, whether they wanted it or not. He was constantly annoyed at the Austrians' obsession with their Balkan ambitions and refused to give any help for their campaign in Hungary unless Spain was given overall charge of it.

The Emperor Ferdinand II, who succeeded Matthias, is traditionally portrayed as the Spanish candidate for the imperial crown but in fact his choice as heir to the Austrian lands after the sons of Maximilian II died out without direct heirs was a defeat for Spain, which also had a claim to the Austrian inheritance. Ferdinand was a member of the Inner Austrian or Styrian branch of the Austrian Habsburgs. He had ruled Inner Austria from 1595. He was an absolutist who, like Maximilian of Bavaria, used the Counter-Reformation for political ends, in particular to smash the noble-dominated Estates. The traditional Protestant view of Ferdinand as a bigot and tyrant is over-simple. While his personal zeal as an observant Catholic was undeniable, he was a rather lazy and easy-going man under the influence of his advisers. His main aim was to turn Austria into a powerful state with central institutions, religiously uniform for political reasons. As Matthias had no children he was recognized as the Habsburg candidate for the imperial title in preference to Philip IV and as heir to the Austrian senior line in 1617 by the Treaty of Graz, also known as the Oñate Treaty, which was kept secret for a long time. He had to buy off Spanish claims by promising to cede to them Austrian possessions in Alsace and imperial fiefs like Mantua in northern Italy, which seemed likely to become vacant soon. He succeeded to an Austria in ruins thanks to his cousins and the last thing he needed at his accession was a large-scale war.

His ambitions lay in Austria, not in Germany. Certainly he needed allies among the German rulers but had great difficulties in winning them. The Catholic League was not immediately available to him, as it was a Bavarian alliance and its leader, Maximilian of Bavaria, was very cautious in the early stages of the war, 1619–20, and only committed himself to Ferdinand when he had strong guarantees. What pushed Austria and Spain together was fear of the Calvinist activism already noted. This was not a factor in areas which were solidly Catholic or Protestant like Bavaria, Saxony, Scandinavia and Brandenburg but in areas where religious confrontation was or had recently been acute, including the Netherlands, England, Austria, France, Hungary, parts of Germany and Bohemia. It was in Bohemia that the Thirty Years' War began.

5   The Thirty Years' War and its Consequences

There was a time when it was fashionable to deny that there was any such thing as the Thirty Years' War: the whole thing was an invention of German nationalist historians in the nineteenth century. The fighting between 1618 and 1648 was a series of separate conflicts, often fought over issues which had little to do with Germany but which happened to spill over on to German soil and to involve German rulers. The war never involved the whole of the Empire. Many of those who fought in "German" armies were not Germans but Walloons, Scots, Spaniards, Dutchmen and Italians. There was a Bohemian phase, a Danish phase, a Swedish phase and a French phase, the first arising from a revolt in the Austrian Habsburgs' territories, the second and third a spilling over into Germany of the Northern War for domination of the Baltic and the last a part of the much longer struggle, fought on many fronts between the Habsburgs and their enemies, for hegemony in Europe. Although the fighting in Germany ended in 1648, it continued elsewhere until 1659–60.

It is easy with hindsight to challenge long-held assumptions about the war but, in doing so, one runs the risk of ignoring the way in which contemporaries viewed it. The war was seen by them as a continuous conflict which lasted for thirty years. Some contemporaries called it "the German war". Important German political and religious questions were at issue in it, not just in the propaganda of the belligerents. It therefore had some characteristics of a German civil war. The treaties of Westphalia which brought it to an end had important long-term consequences for Germany.

The war had its origins in the internal political problems of the Austrian state and, initially at least, there was no sign that it would turn into a German or European conflict. It was the European implications of the Bohemian question which led eventually to the internationalization of the war. Bohemia was seen as one of the areas in Europe on the front line of religious confrontation. It was regarded as vital to the Habsburgs in maintaining their influence in German politics, particularly because of its vote in imperial elections, and in their struggles against the Turks. By extension it was crucial to the religious future of Poland and therefore to the Baltic. If it could be won for the reformed faith, Protestantism would gain a great accession of power in Europe.

In 1617 a majority of the Bohemian nobility, which dominated the Estates, elected Ferdinand of Styria, as the adopted son of Matthias, King of Bohemia in return for a confirmation of the privileges of the kingdom and an affirmation that its throne was elective. Relations between the new king and his subjects quickly deteriorated. Trouble had been foreshadowed during Matthias' reign, when the government attempted to stop the building of Protestant churches in certain areas and committed other infringements of the Letter of Majesty. There was growing polarization, as the majority of moderates in the Bohemian ruling class lost ground to extremist minorities of Catholics and Protestants, and a real danger of civil war. The resistance to Ferdinand was not exclusively Protestant but had the characteristics of a Bohemian nationalist movement, involving both Czech and German nobles of both faiths. The whole movement was portrayed as legitimate resistance to prevent the imposition of a tyranny. A coup attempt was launched from March 1618 by a minority of the nobility planning to depose the Habsburgs and install a Protestant dynasty. The Calvinist "International" became involved after an armed rising in May 1618 following the famous defenestration of Prague. After a mock trial of three crown officials held to be responsible for breaches of Bohemian liberties by a "court" of Protestant nobles, they were thrown out of a high window. Their survival was seen on the Catholic side as a sign of divine favour; a contemporary print showed angels, under the personal direction of the Virgin Mary, wafting them gently to the ground with heavenly parachutes. The Bohemian revolt was followed closely by another in the archduchy of Upper Austria.

In January 1619 a defensive alliance was signed between the Bohemian rebels and the Upper Austrian Estates, after which they began to raise an army. The leading element in this movement was the lesser nobility. The towns and the peasantry played little part and there was an undercurrent of class bitterness accompanying the whole thing. The nobility refused to arm the peasants as they were afraid of them. These divisions weakened the rebel cause from the outset and it was their constant aim to secure foreign help for their cause. Their initial appeals, including to the Turks, had no success but the insurrection gradually spread. In March 1619 Matthias died. The Estates of Upper and Lower Austria refused to accept Ferdinand as their ruler and they were quickly joined by the provinces of Silesia, Lusatia and Moravia. In June 1619 a rebel army came close to Vienna. On 26 August the Bohemian diet elected Frederick V, elector palatine, king. He accepted against the advice of the members of the Protestant Union and his fellow Protestant rulers, including his father-in-law, James I of England, who was trying to establish a reputation as the arbiter of Protestant Europe. It quickly became clear that Frederick was no more than a puppet of a party within the nobility. Ferdinand, in the meantime elected Emperor unopposed, did not immediately move to deal with the rebellions by force, though in reality he had little choice as he possessed no military resources to speak of. The recruiting and financing of troops had fallen largely under the control of the Estates of the Austrian lands, the most important of which were in open rebellion against him.

In spite of this, the Bohemian rebels were vulnerable and had to continue their efforts to internationalize the war. Frederick's coronation in Prague in November raised calls for a Protestant Emperor but only the Transylvanian prince Bethlen Gabor and the Duke of Savoy, who had ambitions on the Bohemian and even the imperial crown, were prepared to go beyond encouraging words to help Frederick. The Catholic League also did nothing to help Ferdinand until Spain entered the war in October 1619. This was after a long debate in the government, which the war party eventually won. They argued that, though Spain was in a financial mess, she had to intervene. Otherwise she ran the risk of lots of dominoes falling, including the total loss of the Netherlands, and ultimately the loss of the South American and East Indian colonies to the Dutch. In August 1618 the Orangists had come back into power in the United Provinces and Dutch interlopers were already making serious inroads in Brazil and the Far East.

Spanish armies from the southern Netherlands and Italy moved into Germany from November 1619 to early 1620, occupying the parts of the Palatinate to the west of the Rhine and giving rise to rumours that Spain planned to annex the whole of the Lower Palatinate. In July the League and the Union signed the Treaty of Ulm, which neutralized the west of the Empire, a sign of a desire to avoid war rather than launch crusades against one another. These events gave Maximilian of Bavaria the security he needed and he was ready to enter an alliance with Ferdinand in return for a promise of territory. In 1621 Bavarian troops occupied Upper Austria. The harshness of the occupation was to provoke a peasant revolt in 1626. It was not clear whether this cession of land would be as security for the costs of Maximilian's military aid or permanent. Maximilian was also given a verbal promise of a share of the Palatinate and an electoral title. In December 1619 Saxony also allied with the Emperor in return for the cession of Lusatia and a guarantee of the existing rights of Lutherans in the Empire. The allied forces won a speedy and overwhelming victory on the White Mountain outside Prague on 8 November 1620. There was a certain irony in the fact that at this battle the Bohemian army consisted mainly of Germans and Hungarians and the imperial army, apart from some Saxons, of Italian and Walloon mercenaries hired by the Catholic League. This was one of the only two occasions during the war when the Habsburg forces were able to combine. The other occasion was in 1634 at Nördlingen, another great victory, which prolonged the war and led to French intervention. The victory on the White Mountain ended the Bohemian revolt but began the real Thirty Years' War.

Detailed accounts of the course of the war are readily available in many places,[1] to which the reader is referred. There were two main theatres of conflict once the Bohemian phase ended, in the Rhineland, where Spain fought against France or her agents, and in other parts of Germany, where the Austrian Habsburgs fought against first the Danes and then the Swedes and their German allies.

Attention here will be focused on imperial policy in the war and the impact of the war on Germany. One issue is the question of imperial absolutism, the supposed ambition of Ferdinand II to deprive the German princes of their autonomy and to restore full centralized monarchical control over the whole Empire. There can be little doubt that Ferdinand did see an opportunity during the war to increase imperial influence in Germany not so much by force as by persuasion and conciliation. Ferdinand was certainly tough in restoring monarchical power in his own hereditary lands, where it was threatened by the nobility, but not in Germany. Three points are traditionally quoted in connexion with the imperial absolutism debate, the Edict of Restitution of 1629, the role of the imperial commander Wallenstein and the Peace of Prague of 1635.

The Edict of Restitution of March 1629, issued after the defeat of Danish intervention in the war, was as much political as religious in motivation. It proposed substantial changes, a great redistribution of religious and temporal power, which would have considerably strengthened Habsburg power in Germany. Under the edict all land secularized illegally since 1552 was to return to the Church including sees in north Germany. Tilly's army was used to enforce the decisions of special imperial commissioners administering the edict and members of the imperial family were appointed to vacant sees, which were occupied by imperial troops. Calvinism was outlawed and German rulers were reminded that, under imperial law, they were not allowed to make alliances with foreign states. All these decisions were issued as imperial decrees without reference to the *Reichstag*, which was profoundly worrying to all the German princes, Catholic and Protestant. The edict was an assertion of existing law but its enforcement by the imperial courts caused outrage among the German princes. It was an exercise of the imperial office not seen since after Charles V's victory in 1547 and was attacked as absolutism and Spanish tyranny. Significantly Maximilian of Bavaria refused to allow his troops to be used to enforce the edict. He also took the lead at a meeting of the electors in Regensburg in 1630, in which French influence was very visible, which demanded the abolition of the edict and refused to elect Ferdinand's son as king of the Romans. In 1631 Bavaria entered an alliance with France, showing the readiness of the German princes to turn to foreign friends when the Emperor threatened to become too powerful. At the insistence of the electors the Emperor was forced to suspend the edict in May 1635. In spite of this, the electors still refused to elect his son king and to give him military aid.

There is dispute about the significance of Albrecht von Wallenstein (1583–1634).[2] He rose rapidly to prominence after the White Mountain, which enabled him to buy up confiscated rebel lands at low prices. 1625 saw his emergence as the leading imperial general. In the spring of that year he offered to raise an army of 40 000 for the Emperor, financed with his own resources and equipped from his own enterprises, to meet the Danish intervention. This was an opportunity for Ferdinand to end his reliance on Maximilian of Bavaria and he appointed Wallenstein commander of all imperial troops in the Empire. Wallenstein's successes were immediate and spectacular and he was made commander in chief of all the imperial forces. Following a series of victories in 1626, northern Germany came under Wallenstein's control. In May 1629 Christian IV of Denmark came to terms in the Peace of Lübeck. The Emperor, not wishing to spread the war, was very generous to Denmark. In July 1629 the two duchies of

Mecklenburg were given to Wallenstein as a state of his own, as an alternative to paying him the huge sums the Emperor owed him. Against the advice of many of his counsellors Ferdinand deposed and dispossessed the two Mecklenburg dukes on the grounds that they had been allies of Denmark. This exercise of the imperial will again caused very unfavourable comment among the German princes, as did the appointment of Wallenstein as general of the Oceanic (Atlantic) and Baltic seas, with plans to establish an imperial navy.

All in all, Wallenstein provided the answer to Ferdinand's prayers, an army which won victories and which could support itself at someone else's cost. Ironically, his great success was his undoing. His great power worried everybody, including his nominal employer, the Emperor. The 1630 electoral diet, which forced Ferdinand to suspend the Edict of Restitution, also made him dismiss Wallenstein and after this the imperial armies were reduced. Unfortunately, Wallenstein's successes in the north precipitated the Swedish intervention in Germany, a revival of the northern wars which had racked the Baltic in the second half of the sixteenth century. Wallenstein's victories revived fears of a Vienna/Warsaw axis. Sigismund III, the Vasa King of Poland responsible for the virtual elimination of Protestantism in that country, was brother-in-law of the Emperor. He had been King of Sweden until 1598, when his attempts to recatholicize the country provoked a coup which deposed him. The Swedish invasion of Germany in 1630 was designed to meet the threat of an attempt to restore the Catholic Vasas by force. A series of imperial defeats, culminating in April 1632 in a Swedish occupation of Munich, led to the recall of Wallenstein as a commander with unlimited powers. Bavaria returned to the imperial alliance. Wallenstein again became too powerful and threatened to undermine the Emperor's carefully constructed system of influence in Germany. There were rumours that he was in secret negotiation with the Emperor's enemies with a view to changing sides and in February 1634 he was killed on imperial orders. His "state", including his substantial financial and manufac- turing empire, collapsed. Command of the imperial forces passed to the Emperor's son, King Ferdinand of Hungary and Bohemia.

Some credit Wallenstein with a desire to restore a powerful Habsburg monarchy in Germany while others argue that he was motivated solely by great personal ambition, in particular to create a state for himself. Some dismiss him as old-style *condottiere*, a type of man Europe had already outgrown, a half-way stage between the private contractors who raised mercenary armies and the commanders of the state-controlled standing armies of the eighteenth century. Others do not regard him as a German but see him as a Bohemian patriot with political and economic ideas way ahead of his time. On balance the policies of Wallenstein seem to have stemmed from personal ambition rather than a desire to promote imperial absolutism.

The Peace of Prague was signed between the Emperor and the Elector of Saxony in 1635 after the massive defeat of the Swedes and their Saxon allies at Nördlingen on 6 September 1634. It took the form of a permanent alliance designed to keep foreigners out of Germany, not an instrument of imperial dictatorship, and other German rulers were subsequently invited to join it. Under the terms of the treaty all the princes were forbidden to enter foreign alliances. It also contained a plan for an imperial standing army to be financed by the princes but controlled by the Emperor. There was to be a general *restitutio in integrum*, a return to pre-1618 conditions, from which only Bohemia and the Palatinate were excluded. The Edict of Restitution was suspended and a new normal date for the division of Germany between the faiths was fixed at 1627. Calvinism was still not recognized as an official faith. The Catholic League was abolished, though Bavaria later reestablished it. The deposed dukes of Mecklenburg were restored. Bohemia was recognized as an hereditary possession of the House of Habsburg. The *Reichstag* and the *Reichskammergericht* were to be restored to regular activity.

The treaty was in reality a manifestation of German national feeling (*Reichspatriotismus*) against the foreigners who were ravaging the country. It was not an instrument of imperial absolutism: Ferdinand was in any case too old for such ambitions. Its main aim was to prevent Germany being dragged into war between Spain and France. In December 1636 Ferdinand's son was elected king of the Romans and succeeded his father as Emperor Ferdinand III in 1637.

By then foreign interference was too deeply established to be easily eliminated. As a result Germany did not have any chance to solve her constitutional and other problems by herself. In May 1635 France declared war on Spain and the final and most destructive phase of the conflict began, which lasted until 1648. The alliance system established in the Treaty of Prague did not have time to establish itself and little could be done to prevent the armies of France and Sweden, and their German clients, ravaging the country. Saxony, Brandenburg, Bavaria, the south west, Mecklenburg and Bohemia all became theatres of war. Many German states tried to save themselves by returning to neutrality but this could be as damaging as belligerency. Saxony and Brandenburg were both plundered by the armies of their nominal protector, Sweden. Bavaria abandoned neutrality in the last months of the war as the elector believed that the settlement being proposed by the French was not beneficial to Bavarian interests and was afraid of a French domination of Germany. His country was again devastated in the last campaign.

It soon became clear that the French and the Swedes were anxious to dictate a settlement to the Emperor and his allies. Sweden demanded money and territory for itself and an amnesty for all its allies among the German princes. French ambitions were more wide-ranging: Germany was a vital component in the French security system which Richelieu was seeking to create and they were already thinking of creating a permanent alliance system among the states of the Empire. The French also wanted substantial territorial concessions to strengthen their eastern borders. Their basic aim was a settlement which would for all time deprive the Emperor of the resources of Germany. In fact, during the long negotiations which preceded the Peace of Westphalia the Emperor was able to defeat such aims. Ferdinand III had some success in building up support among the German rulers and had some very able diplomats at the negotiations, which took place in two centres, made neutral for the purpose, Münster and Osnabrück, for some seven years from 1641. Actual intensive negotiations began in 1645 after the Emperor in August abandoned his claim to negotiate exclusively on behalf of all the states of the Empire.

Eventually the German states divided into Catholic and Protestant *corpora* which prevented individual states holding up the business because of trivia and made the negotiations much easier. The Emperor was able to play on fears of Swedish ambitions in north Germany and the Baltic on the part of Brandenburg, Denmark, the Dutch and the Hanseatic cities. The negotiations revealed a surprisingly large reservoir of imperial sentiment in Germany, especially among the weaker Catholic states, who were afraid of aggressive Protestantism backed by powerful foreign states, and among the electors disquieted by a campaign by some princes, backed by Sweden, to lessen their predominant position in the politics of the Empire. This was one reason why Sweden's favourite client state and the leader of a group of princes seeking radical constitutional changes, Hesse-Cassel, did not achieve what it sought, including the substantial territorial gains it had hoped for. It had to be content with little bits and pieces which did nothing to strengthen it. Catholic predominance in the south was restored by the abolition of the duchy of Franconia, created for the mercenary commander Bernhard of Saxe-Weimar out of the sees of Bamberg and Würzburg.

In particular Ferdinand was able to frustrate plans to include detailed changes in the imperial constitution in the peace settlement, including a permanent capitulation of election agreed by all the German rulers not just the electors, changes in the system of electing a king of the Romans and reform of the *Reichshofrat* to end the Emperor's exclusive control of it. An imperial diet was supposed to meet within six months of the peace settlement to deal with these matters but in fact it did not convene until 1653. These points were never settled and were to remain a source of friction in German politics until the end of the Empire. The only minor concessions made were that after 1648 the princes and towns would be able to comment officially on the contents of the *Wahlkapitulation* and that in future a king of the Romans could be elected only by a unanimous vote of the electors. As before, the election of an Emperor would require only a majority.

The fixing of the situation in 1624 as the basis for the religious settlement was also a minor victory for the imperialists, as was the renewal of the 1555 Ecclesiastical Reservation clause to prevent further erosion of the Catholic position in the Empire. Although a numerical minority, Catholics continued after 1648 to dominate the college of electors and to set the public tone of the Empire. It was accepted that there would always be a Catholic majority in the college of electors. The Bohemian vote, long in abeyance, was revived in 1708 to balance the newly created Hanoverian electorate and it was laid down that if, as happened in 1777, the Bavarian and Palatinate lines were amalgamated, an extra Catholic vote would be created. The Catholic Church remained an important element in the imperial structure. About a third of the Empire consisted of ecclesiastical territories and imperial counts and knights were able to find a useful niche in cathedral chapters. Abbeys and convents were a source of useful employment for younger sons and convenient stowing places for the unmarriageable daughters of the imperial nobility.

The treaties of Westphalia were signed simultaneously in Osnabrück between the Emperor and Sweden and in Münster between the Emperor and France and their allies on 24 October 1648. A Spanish-Dutch peace had been signed earlier in January. The treaties were important at two levels. They were international treaties in which France, Sweden, the Emperor and the electors, princes and towns of the Empire came to terms as equals. It was an attempt at a general and comprehensive settlement of all outstanding European problems, to be rounded off by the treaties of the Pyrenees in 1659 and Oliva in 1660. As such it lasted in its essentials until the French Revolution. It was also an agreement between the head and members of the Holy Roman Empire and among the members of the Empire themselves. The two treaties became a major element in the imperial constitution alongside the Golden Bull, capitulations of election and the religious peace of 1555. The constitution of the *Reich* was rebuilt in its final form; there was, in reality, no alternative to the structure established in 1648.

The treaties are enormous documents, most of them taken up with minor points of detail, mainly concerned with religion. There was an attempt at a comprehensive clarification of the constitutional situation: all existing customs and usages contrary to their provisions were specifically annulled. Perhaps the most important part was paragraphs 1 and 2 of Article VIII of the Treaty of Osnabrück, by which the Emperor recognized "German liberty". This confirmed the German rulers' free exercise of territorial sovereignty, *Landeshoheit*, a term used only from the middle of the seventeenth century. They were not given this by the treaties of Westphalia but their absolute possession of it was confirmed. From now on they exercised this right of government in their own name, not as supposed agents of the Emperor. Now only certain powers were specifically reserved by the Emperor, the *Reservatrechte*. These included the right to charter universities and grant titles of nobility and the Emperor's rights as feudal overlord. All Jews in the Empire were the Emperor's subjects. The princes also now had the right to make alliances among themselves and with foreign powers as long as such alliances were not aimed against the Emperor, the Empire or the peace of the Empire. This completed the process by which the princes secured a monopoly of diplomatic power for themselves. Not only was the Emperor no longer able to speak for them but their subjects, organized in Estates or in towns, could no longer enter agreements with "foreigners" without the prince's consent, as they had sometimes done earlier.

The composition of the *Reichstag* was laid down; it was to consist of three voting houses (*curia*) of electors, princes and, it was now accepted after long dispute, towns. This last provision was of more symbolic than real importance because most of the imperial cities were in advanced decline and the majority never bothered to send representatives to the diet. The subordinate role of the house of towns was shown in the fact that they could not initiate legislation and in joint meetings their representatives stood while those of the electors and princes sat. The legislative power of the diet was confirmed; its consent was required for everything which touched the Estates of the Empire, war and peace, taxes, duties, treaties which placed obligations on the Empire, the imperial fortresses, the movement of imperial troops and the imposition of the ban of the Empire, the ultimate punishment of a ruler, depriving him of land and titles and making him an outlaw.

There were important religious clauses. Calvinism was confirmed as the third official religion of the *Reich*. The princes were given the total *jus reformandi* over their churches. The amendment of the imperial constitution to accept the equality of the two faiths, long discussed before the war, was now accepted. The *Reichstag* was divided officially into two religious *corpora*, Catholic and Protestant, led by Mainz and Saxony, with an "alarm bell" procedure: any matter concerning religion could not be settled by majority vote but only by compromise. This was known as the *jus itio in partes* and would be described in the jargon of modern sociology as a consociational solution. This settled the important constitutional issue of majority voting raised at the 1598 diet. The rights of religious minorities were guaranteed not in a spirit of toleration but out of a desire to end religious confrontation and the use of religion as a political weapon. Article 5, Paragraph 35 laid down that 1624 was to be the key year in the religious settlement: members of any of the three legal faiths established in a state in 1624 could stay there. Those not covered by this provision were to be allowed to leave with all their property or, if they stayed, were not to be persecuted. Members of minority religions were to be allowed private worship in their own homes. Individual princes could, if they wished, extend toleration beyond this minimum level. Catholic rulers usually interpreted the settlement in a narrow sense, Protestants often more generously. All disputes between the faiths were to be settled by the imperial courts and the Emperor was declared protector of all three faiths. There was to be religious equality in the staffing of the two imperial high courts.

A less extreme view of religion was evident during the negotiations leading to the treaties. In both Catholicism and Protestantism there was a movement away from religious persecution and towards a more contemplative inward Christianity, which abstained from involvement in politics. In spite of this desire to see an end of the politicization of religion, which was held to be responsible for the horrors of the war, there remained a constant undercurrent of religious mistrust. Religion was still being used as a political weapon in the later eighteenth century, when Prussia and Austria posed as leaders of German Protestantism and Catholicism respectively. Clearly, after 1648 religious considerations were far from paramount in decision-making, if they ever had been. This was seen, for example, in the refusal of Catholic rulers to take any notice of the pope's objections to the settlement, but it would be misleading to talk of a comprehensive "secularization of politics" in post-1648 Germany. Many governments might have preferred such a development but it was hard to eradicate a confessionalism which had become so deeply rooted earlier. In fact many potential points of religious friction were left unsettled: most German states remained mixed in religion and some, for example the Palatinate, were very mixed.

The situation became more complex still if princes changed their faith or the ruling line changed, though it was very rare after 1648 for such rulers to try to convert all their subjects forcibly. When the Elector of Saxony became a convert to Catholicism in the late seventeenth century this was a purely personal change. Saxony remained a Lutheran state; the elector remained an official Lutheran and head of the Protestant *corpus* in the *Reichstag*, though actual leadership was increasingly provided by the deputy director, Brandenburg-Prussia. The settlement also contained all kinds of compromises, including the *Simultaneum*, the sharing of churches between two or more religions, and *Parität*, the fixed apportionment of public offices between two faiths, in a number of free cities. The town of Siegen in Nassau became the common capital of two states, one ruled by a Catholic line and one by a Protestant line of the House of Nassau. The two faiths could hold processions in the town only on certain days and using certain roads. One church in Protestant Frankfurt-am-Main remained Catholic as the Mass associated with imperial coronations was held there. The Catholic bishopric of Osnabrück, which had a predominantly Lutheran population, passed alternately between a Catholic bishop, elected by a cathedral chapter dominated by Protestant nobles, and a Protestant prince of the House of Hanover, who acted as head of state but did not exercise clerical functions.

There were major territorial changes with long-term implications for Germany. Brandenburg-Prussia, cheated of its legitimate claims to the whole of Pomerania, the more valuable western part of which containing the port of Stettin went to Sweden, gained the sees of Minden, Kammin and Halberstadt and the reversion to Magdeburg, which was taken up in 1680. Although substantial, these were not seen as enough and the Hohenzollerns remained determined to recover what they had lost. Some of these acquisitions added to the central block of Brandenburg territory around Berlin but left the two outlying blocks in the west based on Cleves and Mark, gained in 1614, and in the east, ducal or east Prussia, a fief of the Polish crown inherited in 1618. Saxony retained Lusatia, her reward for helping Ferdinand II put down the Bohemian rebels. This added to the prestige of the Saxon dynasty but was of little value in enhancing its potential as a power. Bavaria kept the Upper Palatinate, adding further to her already compact territory, and the Palatine electoral title with all its precendence and attributes. A new eighth electorate was created for the restored elector palatine, who kept the scattered and vulnerable territories of the Lower or Rhenish Palatinate. In a dispute typical of the Empire, Bavaria and the Palatinate both claimed the imperial vicariate, the regency during an imperial interregnum, which under the Golden Bull the elector palatine and the Elector of Saxony exercised and which came into operation in 1657 after the death of Ferdinand III.

All in all, the treaties of Westphalia contained nothing startlingly new. They rounded off trends visible for over four hundred years. They ratified the states' rights. They were not seen by the Germans as something revolutionary or as a conscious turning point but as a restatement of old rights. The political form of Germany until 1806 was dictated by it. After 1648 the Empire was a federative state. The treaties of Westphalia were not in themselves the cause of Germany's weakness and division but they codified in European public law the factors contributing to weakness and division since the twelfth century. Particularism became firmly established. Disputes as to whether the Empire was a federation or a confederation, that is a state in which a central government devolved some of its functions downwards to lower units or a state made up of a collection of sovereign units devolving some of their power upwards to a central government, is irrelevant as the *Reich* was unique and fitted into no pattern.

A major result of the treaties was to make foreign interference in German affairs a permanent and important factor. From 1648 onwards no major development could take place in Germany without arousing foreign interest. France and Sweden were guarantors of the treaties and on the basis of this assumed a legal right of interference in the affairs of Germany. Sweden became a state of the Empire through its possessions in the north, including Wismar, reputed to be the strongest fortress in the Empire. It also controlled the mouths of the Elbe and Weser rivers. French possession of the three bishoprics of Metz, Toul and Verdun, held since 1552, was confirmed. France also gained Breisach on the east bank of the Rhine, Austrian lands in Alsace, the Sundgau, and a protectorate over ten imperial free cities in Alsace. As was shown in his instructions for his negotiators at Münster of October 1645, the Emperor would have ceded the whole Breisgau, the area around Freiburg, as well in order to preserve the Austrian heartlands intact. As a result of these gains France possessed entry ports, which gave her an open door into Germany. Legally these territories remained part of the Empire but, unlike Sweden, France did not become a member of the Empire as that would have involved a recognition of the Emperor's nominal overlordship. The whole of Alsace and Lorraine was opened to French influence and it was to be easy for Louis XIV to turn protection into possession in the 1680s. France considered it vital to maintain a powerful voice in German affairs and kept diplomatic representatives at the imperial diet, after 1663 in permanent session at Regensburg. These were usually talented professional diplomats not the gilded aristocratic ninnies sent as representatives to less important embassies. It was the ambition of France to build up a system of clients among the rulers of the Empire and in the immediate aftermath of the Thirty Years' War many German princes rushed into Louis XIV's arms, seeking status, subsidies and protection against the Emperor in a French connexion.

After 1648 the majority of the German rulers were very nervous indeed and terrified of a resumption of warfare. France was able to take advantage of this feeling of vulnerability. There were, apparently, two methods of obtaining security available to the German rulers. One, already touched on, was the creation of standing armies. This was an option available only to the larger states; apart from Austria and Brandenburg-Prussia, only Bavaria, Saxony, Brunswick-Lüneburg (Hanover), Hesse-Cassel, Trier, Mainz, Cologne, Salzburg and Münster had respectable forces while many others had small ceremonial armies reinforced with militias and gendarmeries. Other states, for example Mecklenburg-Schwerin and Württemberg, would have liked to have joined the "armed estates" (*armierte Stände*), as they became known, but were unable to do so, mainly because of opposition from their parliamentary Estates. The other method of finding security was an alliance. After 1648 there was a rush into alliances, especially in the south and west, motivated by fear of the over-mighty Emperor and of being dragged into the Franco-Spanish war, which went on until 1659.

The first major shock came in 1651 when it seemed for a time that the north west and west might be engulfed in conflict after the Elector of Brandenburg invaded Jülich-Berg on the Lower Rhine from his neighbouring possession in Cleves, with a view to seizing it. The affair was settled by imperial mediation but sent a shiver through the Empire. From such small beginnings the Thirty Years' War had started. Shortly afterwards two defensive associations were formed, the Protestant Union, known as the Waldeck Union after the memorandum of Count George Frederick of Waldeck, a Brandenburg minister, which led to its establishment in 1654, and the Catholic Cologne Alliance of 1655. These two groupings had the same objectives, the preservation of peace and their members' rights. In 1658 many members of the two alliances came together with France in the League of the Rhine (*Rheinbund*), an alliance formed on the initiative of the Elector of Mainz with the same objectives. It involved arrangements for mutual military support against foreign and internal enemies of the members, including their own subjects. Its most spectacular mobilization under the latter heading occurred in 1664, when a league army, including French troops, helped the Archbishop of Mainz to reduce his previously autonomous city of Erfurt to obedience. This was legitimized by an imperial mandate to restore order in the city. In 1671 the city of Brunswick was seized by force by the Duke of Brunswick-Wolfenbüttel. Brunswick had never been an imperial free city but enjoyed complete autonomy. In the fifteenth century it had been invited to the *Reichstag* and had paid imperial taxes directly. There is some doubt about Erfurt's status but it too had in the past been treated as a free city. The League, which lasted until 1668, was a most useful instrument of French policy; it increased French influence in Germany and it ensured the neutrality of the Empire during the French invasion of the Spanish Netherlands, nominally part of the Empire, in the War of Devolution, 1667–8.

There were other foreign influences in addition to those of France and Sweden. Denmark, although much weaker than Sweden, was a force in the north. North western Germany was subject to Dutch and Spanish influence, the latter from the Spanish Netherlands. The period after 1648 saw mounting friction between the Dutch and the substantial prince bishopric of Münster, a Catholic outpost in a largely Protestant area. The energetic Bishop Christoph Bernhard von Galen (1650–78), who crushed the opposition of the Protestant city of Münster by force, recatholicized it, installed an absolutist system of government and created a sizeable standing army, fought the Dutch and pursued a policy of territorial expansion which threatened the stability of the whole region.

The Thirty Years' War had other major consequences for Germany. Its effects on the German collective consciousness were considerable. The war produced a deep feeling of insecurity as well as severe material deprivation, made worse by the post-war economic depression. It was attacked by Grotius in 1625 as a war without reason, far worse than the wars of barbarous nations. Although it was not, in fact, a pointless war, it was certainly seen by contemporaries as especially terrible in its length, viciousness and in the size of the armies involved. The common man was held to have suffered in it more than was normal. It bred a belief, which gained wide currency in Germany in the Neo-Stoicism of the Dutch phililogist Justus Lipsius, that hard times need hard remedies, a yearning for government. It helped further to legitimize the modern state and accelerated its emergence. It speeded up modernization through absolutism, a process already well-established before 1618. Absolutism as a system of government was both necessary and fashionable. Germany experienced some of the most disturbing manifestations of the so-called general crisis of the seventeenth century, a period of deep and dramatic changes lasting from about 1630 to 1670, which affected all aspects of life. The culmination of the period of instability which had been growing through the sixteenth century, with its implicit threat of civil war, it was a time of flux and chaos, uncertainty and fear. [3] Only strong government could save society from the terrible internal and external dangers which faced it. In particular the dangers of war, brutally illustrated by the Thirty Years' War, justified the taking of extra powers by governments.

A strong state was needed to regulate a society with an inherent tendency to anarchy and to control inevitable conflicts over the distribution of scarce resources. Only the monarch, elevated above the mass of the people thanks to his office, was able to understand the mysteries of government (*arcana imperii*). Subjects were, in contrast, unable to see beyond their narrow class or local interests. This contributed to the revival of the image of the monarch as the stern father of his people, with a duty to promote the common welfare by good *Polizei*. The model of classical Rome, with its supposed virtues of obedience, discipline and respect for authority, was held up before the people as an example to imitate. An important description of a good state in action was given in 1656 in the *Teutsche Fürstenstaat* (*The German Princely State*) of Veit Ludwig von Seckendorff, an experienced administrator.

Fashion also played a major role in the spread of absolutist ideas: the great success of Louis XIV's France was attributed by many contemporaries not to the large population, fertile soil and skilled ministers and generals of France but to its system of government and economic management. This bred a great desire to imitate the absolutism of Louis XIV and the grandeur and pomp of Versailles among many German rulers. From 1648 French culture and fashion were to be predominant among the upper classes in Germany. [4] The vogue of absolutism was also seen in the theatre, opera, literature, elaborate court ceremonial, architecture and garden design, in which order and discipline were given visible expression. Only Vienna, among the larger German courts, resisted the French wave and stuck to the Burgundian/Spanish ceremonial until the reign of Francis I (1745–65). Although none of the German rulers was able to reach the level of Versailles, many fine German palaces and gardens are products of this period, including Mannheim, the new residence of the elector palatine after the French destruction of Heidelberg in 1689, Karlsruhe in Baden, Schleissheim and Nymphenburg outside Munich, Herrenhausen near Hanover, Favorite near Rastatt in Baden, Monrepos near Ludwigsburg in Württemberg and Solitude near Stuttgart. These palaces were the stage for elaborate court rituals, "theatrical" representations of the supremacy of the ruler, which were such an important part of the political system. They also functioned as focal points, "capitals" for the emerging states. One beneficial result of this was the great cultural and architectural richness of Germany: even small capitals could, like eighteenth-century Weimar, become intellectual centres.

The new structure of government which was emerging in the German states showed common features, which is not surprising as it was often copied from foreign states such as France or Sweden — this imitation often went as far as the adoption of foreign titles for officials — or from other German states. Fiscal concerns were central. The war taught states many lessons on the management of their finances. Most emerged from the war heavily indebted. The 1654 *Reichstag* passed a general exemption (*Indult*) allowing them to write off three quarters of the accumulated interest on their debts. There was no prospect of the capital being repaid. Many governments had already issued unilateral *moratoria* on their debts during the war, which had damaged the financial system and contributed to the decline of towns. Now only a state which could cast the tax net as widely as possible and mobilize ample resources could survive and become considerable. A poor state would be a victim state. The emergency situation created by the war gave rulers, especially in the larger states, the excuse to by-pass their Estates.

In 1634 the Elector of Bavaria seized his Estates' funds without ceremony and elsewhere taxes were collected by force without the Estates' approval. Under absolutism this special war situation was to be prolonged into peace-time and to become the basis of government. War councils played an important part in the process of state-building. Initially their competence was limited to military matters but, in many cases, it was quickly extended into other fields. The Vienna aulic war council (*Hofkriegsrat*) was set up in 1556 but it had limited powers. More effective was the war council in Ferdinand II's Styria, which organized defence against the Turks in frontier regions. Although it operated at first in close co-operation with the Estates, it quickly became the heart of the government. In 1620 a war council was established as the key institution in the Bavarian government and this was later copied in Brandenburg, where the General War Commissariat, created in 1655, became the most important department, with competence in military and financial matters covering all the provinces of Brandenburg-Prussia.

The idea of the state as something distinct from the personal property of a ruling dynasty emerged slowly and was still incomplete in the eighteenth century. In practical terms the movement towards absolutism aimed at the greatest possible measure of uniformity and standardization. It also sought to concentrate power at the centre and to eliminate the intermediate corporate bodies, with which the prince had earlier shared power, the nobility, parliamentary Estates and self-governing towns. Middlemen and amateurs were to be eliminated. Absolutism meant simplification and standardization. Civil services and armies, under complete state control, became bigger, better-equipped and more professional, making them more expensive. This in turn made tighter centralized state control more necessary in order to increase revenues to fund them. In the electorate of Hanover there were seven separate Estates bodies representing the provinces from which it had been built up. Territorial sovereignty, recognized in the Westphalian treaties, was seen as a uniform set of prerogatives enjoyed by all German rulers which could override the constitutional agreements in force in any given state.

Even when they survived, the Estates were often much weakened. A favourite device adopted by many rulers was to persuade them to dispense with regular full meetings, supposedly to save money, and to leave the conduct of affairs to small standing committees. These were usually easier to manage or intimidate. Urban self-government was weakened or eliminated by the introduction of a state official, often initially with limited powers, a procedure again supposedly made necessary by the war. Another device frequently adopted by rulers was the creation of a common central court of appeal for all their territories. This symbolized the unity of the state above provinces and was a useful way of by-passing courts controlled by the Estates. Another was the creation of ever-narrower inner cabinets or committees, which made the real decisions under the ruler's personal control while the privy council or *Hofrat*, in which representatives of the nobility often sat as of right, retained purely administrative functions. The Churches, both Catholic and Protestant, exercised wide supervisory powers in moral and family matters and often controlled education and charities. Increasingly they became little more than departments of the government, giving the state an information and propaganda organization with a branch in every village. Education, designed to teach obedience and the duties of good subjects, expanded. In some German states a comprehensive system of schools was created. [5]

In general, new methods and a new professional mentality began to prevail in the localities as well as at the centre, with orderly procedures. The state became more inquisitive, conducting censuses and land surveys and making regular inspections. Written reports and questionnaires replaced the often more haphazard practices of the older semi-amateur administrators. Proper accounting and the collection of accurate statistics, at a time when many noble Estates were floundering because accounting was a total mystery, became standard practice. Ordinances, once a comparatively rare device, began to rain down in ever-increasing numbers on the Germans. Absolutism and mercantilism, [6] its economic counterpart, involved growing state control of and intervention in the daily lives of the subjects. Nothing was regarded as being outside the competence of the state. In the person of the prince and his officials, the state defined the interests of the community as a whole, the common good (*das gemeine Beste*). As a result, it became real and immediate to the Germans to an extent not often seen elsewhere while the Empire became more and more remote and irrelevant to their lives.

Austria was in the lead among German states in the early stages of absolutism. Although the Emperor lost the war in Germany, he won it in his own hereditary lands, where his authority was considerably strengthened. Monarchical power in Austria and Bohemia, which had come close to being undermined in the early seventeenth century, was fully restored. Bohemia lost its nominally elective crown and became an hereditary possession of the Habsburgs. The resistance of the nobility was ended, helped by another major peasant revolt in Upper Austria from 1625 to 1626, which cemented the alliance between the crown and the nobility. In 1621 a new system of government was introduced, followed in 1627 by a new constitution, imposed by the crown, which destroyed the power of the Estates. Urban and village self-government was abolished. Much tighter state control of the Catholic Church was imposed and religious orthodoxy strictly enforced. Protestants were given twelve months to convert to Catholicism or to leave the country. The same was done in other provinces. Well over 100 000 Protestants of all classes are estimated to have emigrated from the Habsburg lands, which had a substantial political and social impact. A new multi-national nobility was imported and rewarded for their service to the crown with the lands and status of the defeated rebels.

In 1621 Ferdinand II declared the unity of his lands, although he immediately gave the Tyrol to his brother as a secundogeniture, and began the creation of Austrian state machinery separate from imperial organs. This gave him a more secure power base. He still had plenty of opportunities to exercise influence in Germany. It is wrong to assume that after 1648 Austria in some way turned its back on Germany in order to concentrate on war against the Turks in Hungary and the Balkans. Any idea that there was after 1648 a dichotomy in Habsburg policy between imperial and Austrian or dynastic interests is as false as it was in the time of Charles V: Austria retained important territories inside Germany, which was her back door when she turned her main attention to south eastern Europe. She could not afford to ignore it and allow it to come totally under the control of foreign powers. In addition, the situation after 1648 made the small states of the Empire even more dependent on the Emperor for protection. The Thirty Years' War left a legacy of fear among them of a general war of all against all and of more foreign intervention in Germany. This helped to create a large reservoir of imperial loyalty especially in the west and south west. The treaties of Westphalia did not reduce the Empire to a crowned Polish republic, as France and Sweden had wished. There were many loopholes in the treaties and vague points open to different interpretations which enabled Emperors to keep their influence in Germany alive.

Although the spread of absolutist methods of government was speeded up by the war, it would be a mistake to exaggerate its success. Most of the German states were too small for anything but an imitation of the externals of the Sun King's France and the old personal links between ruler and subjects in the little states could not easily be eradicated. Even in Bavaria and Brandenburg absolutism remained an aspiration as rulers tried to deal with remarkably flexible and resilient pre-absolutist structures able to adapt to the new system and, by outward conformity, to neutralize some of its effects. Many Estates retained some administrative and judicial functions and a role in recruiting and the collection and administration of taxes even if their political power was taken away. Similarly the nobility in most German states retained important administrative functions as well as social predominance.

Governments faced other problems: many Estates clung to the *Inkolat*, the rule that only natives of a province could hold office there. It was important for rulers to break this and to be able to choose their servants at will. Led by the Habsburgs, they often solved this by employing foreigners.They then had the problem of controlling the new officeholders, especially when they were nobles. New nobles too often adopted the habits and attitudes of the old. Within a century of the White Mountain the Bohemian nobility, descended from Ferdinand II's new ruling class, had acquired a corporate Bohemian identity. There were often divisions within the nobility, with the court nobility usually dominant. Factions at court, fluid alliances and groupings within the nobility and bureaucracy and intermarriage between old and new nobility were other factors which limited total monarchical power. It is not surprising that many states tried to keep the nobility out of the central financial administrations, which were usually the heart of the new administrative structures. New universities were founded and old ones expanded to train more professional administrators, teachers, lawyers and clergymen for state service. The freeing of universities from the straitjacket of clerical control initially benefited the Protestant states and was only much later copied in Catholic states. The Prussian university at Halle in Magdeburg, opened in 1694, quickly became the best university in Germany which helped to make Brandenburg-Prussia the intellectual capital of the Empire. Halle was overtaken only in the 1730s by the new university at Göttingen in Hanover.

Stronger government was needed to deal with the aftermath of the Thirty Years' War. There has been a long debate about the economic and social consequences of the war. It is very complex and the picture is still unclear. The first point which needs to be made is that much of the evidence was falsified in advance: town councils often exaggerated the damage they had suffered in order to obtain tax cuts. The same arguments had been used by several states in the later sixteenth century to try to obtain reductions in the level of imperial taxation. In 1594 the *Matrikel*, which apportioned imperial taxes between the states of the Empire, was revised to shift the burden of contributions on to the free cities.Thereafter they paid about a quarter of the total. The cities were usually better payers than the princely states though, with few exceptions, they all suffered from mounting debts long before 1618. [7]

Many deserted villages were attributed in folklore to the Thirty Years' War, when in fact they had been empty since the fourteenth century, though the war *did* destroy villages. In the course of the Black Death some parts of central Germany, for example Saxony, suffered an estimated population loss of fifty per cent. Rulers also exaggerated the effects of war in order to enhance their achievements in post-war restoration work: a good example is the work of Pufendorf as a historian of the reign of the Great Elector. Some commentators have adopted opposite and extreme views: some minimize the extent of the damage and population losses. [8] Some argue that the south German cities were successfully diversifying their economies before 1618 to meet changing circumstances, by moving, for example, into new textiles or luxury metalwork, and that this hopeful development was cut short by the war. This may be true of some cities but it was not a general development. The traditional German view was that Germany lost two thirds of her population and suffered massive economic damage in the war, which set her back a hundred years, excluded her from the race for colonies and commercial expansion and kept her weak and disunited when other states were carving out places in the world for themselves. It was easy and convenient for the Germans to blame the weakness of their country on the actions of foreigners.

In spite of these disputes there is some consensus on the effects of the war. [9] The general view is that the whole of Western Europe was struck by a period of economic recession, part of a general crisis, in the early seventeenth century. Economic decline in parts of Germany had started before 1618 and the war accelerated and completed it. The war was followed by a long recession in southern and central Europe as a whole, marked by stagnant population growth and stagnant or falling prices, and it took Germany between fifty and a hundred years to recover. Before 1618, among the problems besetting the German economy were a chaotic coinage, a multiplicity of tolls which hindered the movement of goods, disruption of the Rhine trade because of the Spanish-Dutch war, the Jülich-Berg troubles and religious persecutions. It is undeniable that the soldiery was usually brutal and destructive but the effects of the war were patchy. Not surprisingly, the costs of war fell most heavily on those areas directly touched by it. Large areas of the *Reich* suffered little while others were devastated.

The economic effects similarly varied. The war stimulated certain sections of the economy while disrupting others. There were some bright spots. For example, Hamburg did well, drawing trade from eastern Germany and taking advantage of disruption in the Netherlands to capture some Dutch trade with Spain and Portugal. Hamburg was very much the economic and diplomatic "capital" of northern Germany. Frankfurt-am-Main was also buoyant. The Saxon and Silesian linen manufacturies experienced expansion while those of south Germany collapsed. After 1648 capital was diverted into reconstruction and absolutist state-building. Extensive reconstruction work had to be undertaken all over Germany, for example in rebuilding destroyed towns and villages, and it diverted capital from other forms of investment. The contributions taken by the Swedes had a similar effect. These *were* spent in Germany but the contributions diverted resources from investment into consumption. During the war Germany suffered serious inflation, with many coinage debasements. Local booms caused by expansions in weapons production were short-lived. One effect of the war was a general diversion of state funds into military spending from areas seen as dispensable, such as education. After the war the reconstruction of agriculture absorbed a large share of the limited capital available. The loss of animals during the war caused serious long-term damage. Many of the gains of the sixteenth century were temporarily lost.

After 1648 Germany became an economic colony of Western Europe, exporting raw materials and importing manufactured goods which had earlier been made in the country. The mouths of the Rhine were controlled by the Dutch and other rivers by the Swedes, who continued to take illegal tolls on them after the end of the war. Sweden's status as a great power was based on very insubstantial foundations and the Swedes were concerned primarily with security and revenue-raising rather than long-term economic growth. For a long time after 1648 Germany's main Atlantic ports, Hamburg and Bremen, were troubled by internal political problems and constant harassment by Sweden and Denmark. This was part of a common pattern: the last attempt to establish an urban league took place in 1668 when Cologne and Regensburg were being threatened by their princely neighbours. It came to nothing. The last town diet was held in 1671. Towns like Lübeck and Rostock, which had thrived earlier, experienced the pastoralization of their economies seen earlier in the south. Germany was also hit by the silting of rivers, for example the Ems.

The situation was made worse by the rise of economic particularism combined with the economic management techniques later given the collective name of mercantilism. This involved state management and control of the economy, exercised through a variety of different techniques but all aimed at promoting manufacturing, excluding imports and accumulating wealth in the form of bullion. Most German states pursued interventionist economic policies designed to foster what they perceived as their own economic best interests, usually interpreted as the maintenance of a large population, which meant peasants. State attempts to plan the economy were generally unsuccessful, though there were some exceptions. Some of the measures undertaken in Brandenburg-Prussia, for example canal building, had beneficial effects in the long term. The basic problem was that mercantilism was based on a number of false assumptions about the nature of commerce and manufacturing, in particular that the amount of wealth in the world was fixed and that one state could only thrive by taking trade away from another. Mercantilists thought of the economy as an extension of warfare by other means. Also most states did not have the capital to invest in economic growth or were not prepared to divert it from other spending, especially for military purposes which seemed more pressing. Too often states funded huge enterprises like the giant textile factories in Berlin and Linz, which were totally reliant on the state as supplier of capital and as customer and were quite incapable of competing in open markets. All this caused further distortion and fragmentation of the German economy. A special significance has been given by some commentators to

Germany's failure to develop a substantial maritime trade. As a result, it has been said, authoritarian agrarian traditions remained predominant and German states did not develop the cosmopolitan democratic attitudes which business on the high seas supposedly promotes.

There is still dispute about the war's impact on population levels. It is difficult to sort out losses as a result of military action from those caused by disease — Germany was hit by a series of plagues between 1634 and 1639 — by the reduction of fertility resulting from malnutrition, and by malnutrition itself. Some of the population "loss" was in fact accounted for by the movement of people into fortified towns, which hit agriculture. The most commonly accepted view is that Germany's population fell from between fifteen and twenty-one millions to between ten and thirteen millions, a loss of between thirty and forty per cent, that is all the growth of the sixteenth century. The variations in losses between different regions of Germany were marked. Some areas, for example the Austrian lands and the north west, were barely touched and population levels were not affected. Economic and demographic damage as great or even greater was to befall certain areas, such as the south west and the Palatinate, during French invasions later in the century and it was to take even longer to recover from these. Population growth after the war varied from region to region but was rarely sufficient to act as an engine of economic expansion. In general high fertility resulting from earlier marriages and smaller demand for food produced rising birth rates but it took a long time to recover losses. Badly hit areas like Mecklenburg, Pomerania, Brandenburg and Württemberg took a century to reach their former population levels. Governments remained obsessed by the problems of underpopulation well into the eighteenth century. Resettlement began quickly after the war with large-scale population movements within the country. There was a large influx of immigrants from the Netherlands and Switzerland into the west and south after the decline of industries there. Dutch experts in new farming methods were attracted to Brandenburg, where they faced the hostility of the locals and had only a limited impact. There was also movement resulting from religious emigration, for example of Bohemian Protestants to Saxony, Austrian Protestants to Franconia, Waldensians from Savoy and Huguenots after the revocation of the Edict of Nantes in 1685, from which many German territories benefited.

In social terms, perhaps the most significant development was a reversal of the trend towards greater social mobility seen in the sixteenth century. There was a further intensification of the social reaction, which had started to appear in the late sixteenth century with a hardening of visible class barriers. The rise of a substantial independent middle class stopped. The majority of the towns, except the princely capitals which fostered employment and attracted population, stagnated. The fastest growing city after 1648 was Berlin, mainly as a result of the Great Elector's policies designed to attract immigrants. There were a few new towns, for example Erlangen, built in 1686 in Ansbach for Huguenot refugees from France, Mannheim, built on a strictly geometric grid pattern in 1689 as a new residence by the elector palatine, and Ludwigsburg, the residence of the Duke of Württemberg, built in the early eighteenth century. There was no strong economic middle class. The urban oligarchies were usually guild dominated, often corrupt and narrow of horizons. Religious and social exclusiveness was common, especially in the free cities. Ossification and stifling parochialism were characteristic. After 1648 large-scale textile production began at Nördlingen but by 1698 this had been destroyed by a revolt of the guild weavers.

Most states favoured, as far as possible, a simplification of social divisions. Except in the city states and a few princely territories such as Württemberg, the nobility of which were all free imperial nobles, and East Frisia, where the nobility was weak, noble dominance was reasserted. Noblemen moved into government service as administrators, diplomats and officers. It was not difficult to portray this as an extension of the old feudal obligation to aid and advise the ruler, though in some cases, for example Brandenburg-Prussia, this happened only after substantial pressure from the crown. Economic factors were very important; agrarian stagnation after the war hit land values and the yield from land, making nobles more willing to work for the state in order to maintain their status. Some states, such as the Mecklenburgs, had very large nobilities, members of which habitually sought employment in the governments of German and foreign states. Special training schools (*Ritterakademien*) were established for the nobility in many states. Another symptom of this development was an increase in the number of nobles taking degrees in German universities.

The most important element in the German middle class was made up of lawyers, teachers and administrators, dependent for their livelihood on the nobility and the princes. Dynasticism in offices was becoming increasingly common, with sons following fathers in posts. Officials enjoyed special privileges and in some states developed into a self-perpetuating elite like the French *noblesse de robe*. Although most German states did not develop the system of venality of offices seen in France, offices, and the fees and privileges which they produced, were seen as hereditary property. After 1648 the nobility remained socially and economically if not politically dominant and it remained the ambition of successful middle-class men to obtain noble status and land and to give up enterprise or a profession in order to live nobly on their estates. Where this was legally forbidden or was difficult, for example in Brandenburg-Prussia in the eighteenth century, middle-class confidence and esteem were damaged. This again represented the reversal of a trend seen in the sixteenth century.

A significant result of the war was the so-called Second Serfdom, the growth or intensification of serfdom in eastern Germany. The description is misleading as it was in fact not a second serfdom but the first in many parts of the Empire. For example, in 1652 legal serfdom was introduced in Lusatia. It was not a new system but the completion of a process which had begun long before the war and it varied from region to region. It resulted from a shortage of labour and new agricultural market opportunities. Many lords took advantage of the indebtedness of the peasants, made worse by the war, to increase their power over them. Many peasants had left their holdings because of the terrible conditions during the war. In north eastern Germany many landlords had taken advantage of this to take land into their demesnes and create great *latifundia*, an extension of *Gutsherrschaft*.

The hiring of temporary wage labour or giving generous inducements to persuade people to take over devastated farms and work the lord's land were possible answers to the shortage of people. The easiest solution to the labour problem was to tie the peasants to the soil by making them unfree and depriving them of the opportunity, readily available in post-1648 Germany, of moving to better conditions. Much of German agriculture was experiencing serious troubles before the war, with falling prices. The war delayed the fall but the general trend was downwards. The war also caused a disruption of grain exports from the East. The Prussian *Junkers* did well shipping grain through Danzig and Königsberg until about 1660. It was ironical that closer economic links between Eastern and Western Europe caused greater political and social divergence between them. The movement towards serfdom was speeded up by other developments. Some eastern landlords sought to diversify by promoting rural manufactures but this option was available to few and most had to find an economic life-buoy in more intensive cultivation of the soil. A new form of cultivation for the market, the Holstein *Koppelwirtschaft*, spread eastwards. The new methods, which involved dispensing with regular fallows by creating larger fields for mixed arable farming and cattle-rearing, needed more labour. Free peasants survived in parts of eastern Germany, for example the *Köllmer* in east Prussia and Saxony, but they were the exception. In the west serfdom existed but in general it survived there only in the form of relics of unfreedom. There were some areas of peasant prosperity, including the north west, southern Bavaria and parts of the Black Forest, but the general position of the peasantry was depressed. A major factor determining the fate of the peasants was the role played by the state. The peasant was protected when the state intervened to restore the land which peasants had been forced to sell during the war, especially when noble land was exempt from taxation. In such cases the state was afraid of losing tax revenues. Bavaria and Hanover were good examples of this. Elsewhere the state was too weak or was unable for various reasons to intervene, as was the case in Mecklenburg, Brandenburg-Prussia, Pomerania and Bohemia. The lords built up substantial economic, social and political power, including judicial and police powers over their peasants, and the right of presentation to Church benefices. The reduction in the prosperity and autonomy of the towns of north eastern Germany was completed. The nobles had the right to import goods free of toll for their own use. They used this to undercut the economies of the towns. In 1653 a significant *Recess* or agreement was signed between the Elector of Brandenburg and the nobility of the Mark. Under this the nobility granted the elector taxation in order to finance a standing army, in return for which their economic and social privileges were confirmed. This was the beginning of the "historic compromise" between the Prussian crown and the *Junkers*, upon which the whole state was built. The emerging Prussian absolutist state was a life-belt for the Brandenburg nobility, especially welcome as international grain prices collapsed between 1660 and 1670.

Germany after 1648 was further away than ever from economic and political unity. Absolutism and mercantilism had become the typical German forms of government and economic organization. Germany was a cultural and economic colony of her neighbours, a prey to foreign political influence, foreign fashions and even a foreign language, as French became increasingly the preferred language of the upper classes. The greater German states were looking outside Germany for their expansion. By the middle of the seventeenth

century the crisis of the late sixteenth and early seventeenth centuries
was over and Germany entered a period of relative stability even more
of a backwater than before.

6 Absolutism and Particularism: Germany after 1648

German history after 1648 was marked by three characteristics which were to remain dominant until the Empire ended in 1806. The first of these was the paramountcy of foreign influence. The other side of the coin was the growing tendency of the larger German states to seek an extension of their power outside Germany, Austria in Hungary and the Balkans, Saxony, the third largest German state, in Poland and Hanover in Britain. Bavaria dreamed of re-creating the Burgundian state by exchanging German territory for the Netherlands. Of the leading states only Brandenburg-Prussia saw serious opportunities for expansion in Germany by means of its "rounding off" policy (*Arrondierungspolitik*), trying to join together the various blocks of territory of which the state was composed, but in the eighteenth century Prussia also looked to Poland for territorial expansion.

The Empire was also seen as a European necessity, a vital component in the European balance of power, the disappearance of which would lead to an orgy of wars and conquest, as seen in collapse and dismemberment of the Spanish and Swedish empires. To contemporaries the Empire could still behave like a proper state to preserve internal peace and external defence. It was not regarded as simply a power vacuum to be fought over by the first-comers. Germany was part of a European states system which emerged after 1648 and, in a changed form, after 1714.[1] The German states, especially the medium-sized ones, possessed a kind of continent in microcosm in the Empire, in which they could behave like powers. Even pigmy states could engage in diplomatic wheeling and dealing. These factors produced a diplomatic situation of extreme complexity in Germany after 1648. It is often forgotten that the period after 1648, when the princes enjoyed, to all intents and purposes, total sovereignty, was a period of peace and cultural blossoming. This is perhaps not surprising as very few of the German "states" had the resources to act as European or even German powers, whatever the rights guaranteed them in 1648. For many "German liberty" meant the liberty to be unimportant. The majority remained weak and vulnerable and continued to be motivated more by fear than by a desire to throw their weight around. The lessons of the Thirty Years' War, in particular the extreme vulnerability of most German states, were not forgotten.

Germany contained states which were of European significance, possessing the resources in population and wealth plus the organization for power which, in combination, produced great-power status. After 1714 Austria, with a population within the *Reich* of about six millions, was a great power. The controls on her established in the Westphalian treaties were much less effective in the eighteenth century as the guarantors of the settlement, France and Sweden, were weaker after 1714–21. After 1740 Austria was joined as a great power by Prussia, whose population by then was about two and a half millions. In addition there were German "regional powers", strong enough, for various economic, strategic or military reasons, to be desirable allies of European great powers. These included Bavaria, Württemberg, Hesse-Cassel, Cologne, Trier, Mainz, Münster and the Palatinate.

The second dominant feature was what has come to be known as dualism, the emergence by the mid-eighteenth century of two German states powerful enough to dominate the whole country, Austria and Prussia. As early as 1708 the Venetian ambassador in Vienna, Dolfin, reported that the Emperor had made a serious mistake in allowing Prussia to adopt the royal title in 1701. As a result Prussia had taken over the leadership of the Protestant group of German rulers and was a potential rival for the imperial crown. In fact Dolfin was pre-dating a development which came later in the century but it was a perceptive observation.

The third trend visible after 1648 was a hardening of the dichotomy between the Emperor and the Empire. In 1727 the Emperor Charles VI protested in vain against the growing practice of the *Reichstag* of describing the states of the Empire as *das Reich* rather than the earlier formula "electors, princes and Estates". The concept of "German liberty" remained firmly established. Germany in the late medieval period was a complex patchwork of feudal rights and possessions and this continued to be the case in the period after 1648. Power and influence were shared among a host of institutions at all levels from the Emperor through the princes to the lower levels of administration. Within this system a trend established at least since the thirteenth century, the concentration of power at the middle level in the states, continued.

The Holy Roman Empire remained the political framework of the German nation until 1806. The Empire after 1648 has suffered from an almost universally bad press, especially in Germany. It is known in the form of belittling quotations about it, such as that of Samuel von Pufendorf, who in his pseudonymously published *On the State of the German Empire* (*De statu imperii Germanici*, Geneva 1667) described the Empire as irregular and monstrous. This famous quotation is always taken out of context. Pufendorf, professor of public law at Heidelberg and later the official historian of the Elector of Brandenburg, was an opponent of imperial power in Germany but a keen supporter of the Empire, which he wished to see converted into a true confederation of states. As well known are an anonymous Englishman's remark in the 1740s that it mattered as little who was Emperor as who was Lord Mayor of London and Voltaire's jibe that the Empire was neither holy, Roman, nor an empire. "Borussian" propaganda in the nineteenth century consistently portrayed the *Reich* as a barrier to the rise of Prussia, with its mission to unite and lead Germany. Too often forgotten are the verdicts of commentators like Leibniz and Rousseau, who saw great virtues in the Empire and recognized its importance to the stability of Europe. There have been too few serious studies, the Empire has been dismissed too glibly and there has been a tendency to regard the decline of Germany into impotence as complete by 1648: the Empire was already in its coffin then but the funeral was postponed until 1806.

There has also been a tendency to write off the imperial constitution as no more than the codification of weakness, a practice in which modern commentators are only echoing the views of some contemporaries. The Thirty Years' War and the period after it saw a heated debate among academics and polemicists about the exact nature of the German constitution. Speculation about the constitution and its improvement seemed to become particularly intense in periods of instability, war or post-war adjustment. For example, the religious troubles of the 1530s produced a lively debate on the issue of the German states' right of resistance against the Emperor, which expanded into considerations of the nature of the imperial constitution. The periods after the religious peace of 1555 and the Thirty Years' War saw similar peaks.

After 1648 friction between the Emperor and the princes, between princes and their subjects and between factions in the free cities all increased. The relationship between the confessions was still uncertain and the smaller states in particular were aware of their vulnerability. All this contributed to a lively interest in the nature of the *Reich*. Polemicists, often sponsored by the German governments, especially the Protestants, mobilized arguments drawn from history, political theory and law to attack or defend the position of the Emperor, the electors, the princes and the free cities. Opponents of imperial authority usually had as their target not the existence of the Empire but the supposed ambition of the Emperor to subvert the constitution and establish a despotism. Most German universities offered political science courses, including study of the history and constitution of the *Reich*, for future civil servants. A major problem with this debate was that the Empire was a bizarre growth quite unique in European history and impossible to fit into any morphology of state forms. Traditionally states had been categorized, according to the criteria laid down by Aristotle, as monarchies, aristocracies or democracies and their degenerated forms, tyranny, oligarchy and mob rule. The Empire fitted none of these; it was a mystery. The modern world has some analogues in the form of loose unions like the Commonwealth or the EEC. In the eighteenth century one jurist and avid collector and publisher of imperial law, J. J. Moser, came to the conclusion that it was empty hair-splitting to try to define the form of government of the Holy Roman Empire. Germany was ruled in the German manner and could not be subjected to academic analysis or measured against the forms of government of other states.

Many contemporaries believed the imperial constitution was perfect for Germany as it enshrined the virtues of German liberty, about which the Thirty Years' War was thought to have been fought. It combined the diversity which allowed each state to develop in its own way and at the same time gave a necessary measure of unity to the German nation. In the constitution a balance had been found which it would be dangerous to disturb, expressing as it did the true nature of Germany as it had evolved over the centuries. The post-1648 German political system was a mixture of different features, an exotic hybrid, the geological record of successive accretions: the relics of a unitary German monarchy, important survivals of a feudal political structure, the skeletal remains of an aristocratic limited monarchy and distinct traces of federal elements. The Holy Roman Empire had become a German habit. A system of checks and balances had developed over time, in which every interest group could be sure that, though it might never get its own way, it could be confident that its opponents never would either.

Because of its earlier development, Germany had a form of federative system which had evolved and had not been designed. The treaties of Westphalia, by codifying the duality of *Kaiser* and *Reich*, probably gave the Empire a new lease of life by clearly defining the powers of each. The imperial constitution was, apart from minor changes later, finalized in 1648. Under the Westphalian treaties an imperial diet was supposed to be called within six months of ratification to deal with outstanding constitutional issues. No diet had been held since long before the outbreak of the war and between 1613 and 1640 only meetings of the electors had taken place for the conduct of imperial business. The Emperor Ferdinand III was able to delay the next full diet until 1653. By then his position was much stronger and he was able to show, during the ceremonies at the opening of the diet in Regensburg, that the Habsburgs were still very much in the saddle.

In May 1654 this diet passed the last *Reichsabschied*, known later as the *jüngste Reichsabschied*, a collection of laws passed during its sittings, but this largely reaffirmed the constitution as it stood and did not include the permanent capitulation of election and other restrictions on imperial power which France and Sweden had intended in 1648. It did restrict the Emperor's right to create new princes with voting rights in the *Reichstag*. The next diet, which opened in Regensburg in 1663, remained in session for the rest of the life of the Empire until 1806 and did not produce an *Abschied*. It became permanent because the Emperor would not accept the constitutional reform plans of a group of princes, on which they were trying to make a grant of aid against the Turks dependent. It legislated by means of recommendations of the *Reich* (*Reichsgutachten*), of which almost 600 were produced between 1663 and 1717. The diet only left Regensburg in 1713 to avoid the plague and between 1742 and 1745, when it met in Frankfurt during the brief tenure of the imperial throne by the Elector of Bavaria.

One of the great virtues of the imperial constitution was its flexibility and looseness (characteristics which are sometimes seen as particular strengths of the British constitution). Made up as it was of a large number of different agreements and conventions, it was to be a bottomless well from which could be drawn arguments to support a wide range of constitutional positions. It could be adjusted as necessary, as in 1555 and 1648, to accommodate changes in the balance between the two elements, the imperial central authority and the states. The balance between the various power-exercising bodies at work within it provided opportunities for a wide range of possible developments. The system had the virtue that it placed no serious restrictions on the freedom of the individual states. There was no longer any threat of imperial despotism. The relative weight of imperial influence and the power of the individual states changed in a shifting and kaleidoscopic manner depending on the political situation inside and outside Germany.

In the opinion of many contemporary commentators the imperial constitution still contained the potential for development and reform. Emperor and Empire were not necessarily rigidly opposed and incapable of acting together. After 1648 there were brief revivals of imperial patriotism, seen in the Empire's opposition to the aggression of Louis XIV's France and during the last attacks by the Turks against Austria in the 1680s. German national feeling was visible during the imperial war, that is a war declared by the *Reichstag* and involving in theory the whole *Reich*, against France in the War of the Spanish Succession from 1700 to 1714. The Empire aimed to put the Emperor's son on the Spanish throne and to win back lost lands in the west: Strasburg remained a powerful symbol of German irredentism after its loss to France in 1681. Fear of the French later kept alive imperial sentiment in the west and south west.

A measurable decline in imperial loyalty and German national feeling began later in the eighteenth century. In the Treaty of Herrenhausen (1725) Hanover and Prussia made a secret agreement involving the possibility of a joint war against the Emperor in alliance with his foreign enemies. This was treason against the Empire. Prussia's behaviour, especially from the reign of Frederick William I (1713–40), marked as it was by a lack of respect for other states' borders and an increasing use of violence, was incompatible with the imperial constitution. Forced recruiting and plundering expeditions by Prussian troops gave rise to frequent complaints. It was clear that Prussia had taken a decision not to observe the common norms of behaviour in the Reich. In 1740 Prussia invaded Silesia beginning the War of the Austrian Succession, ending nearly a hundred years of internal peace in Germany. Austria was unable to recapture her lost province.

In 1756 Prussia began the Seven Years' War by an invasion of Saxony, a pre-emptive strike to ward off another Austrian attempt to retake Silesia. During the ensuing war most of the states of the Empire went to war against Prussia. Only Prussia's clients and allies, Hanover, Hesse-Cassel, Brunswick-Wolfenbüttel and Saxe-Gotha, refused to participate and the *Reichstag* refused to declare imperial war on Prussia. On 5 November 1757 a combined French and imperial army was defeated at Rossbach, an event exploited by Prussian propaganda to ridicule the Empire. The war ended in 1763 with Prussia still holding Silesia. This established dualism, shared informal control of the Empire between Austria and Prussia, neither strong enough to destroy the other. Dualism perpetuated the existence of the Empire but sustained it like a caliper on a paralysed limb, in a state of rigidity with movement made very difficult indeed.

The Empire had institutions which functioned. The imperial diet was an important political forum for Germany, in spite of the formality of its procedures and the obsession of many of its members with the petty rules of precedence so important to *ancien régime* minds. For example, there was extreme sensitivity to the distinction between the "old" princely houses which had held their seats before 1582 and the more recent "new" houses. The Wittelsbachs claimed to be the oldest house and on this basis took precedence on the bench of lay princes. To avoid troublesome squabbles about the Habsburgs' claim to the same distinction the Austrian representative sat with the ecclesiastical princes.

The diet contained representatives of about 150 "states" which enjoyed *Sitz und Stimme* (a seat and a vote) there. These included nine electors (the Duke of Brunswick-Lüneburg/Hanover was elevated to an electorate in 1697), about 45 free cities out of about 150 and about 60 lay and ecclesiastical princes, representing some one hundred separate territories. The imperial abbeys and free counties had collective votes but the imperial knights were not represented. After 1529 they paid "voluntary" donations to the Emperor in return for confirmation of their direct subjection to him. After the Thirty Years' War the *Reichstag* was an assembly of ambassadors representing virtually sovereign states and often one man represented several principals. In the later eighteenth century only about thirty representatives met regularly and the sessions of the diet were increasingly infrequent. Decision-making was difficult: members could hold business up while waiting for instructions from their principals and there were problems in achieving agreement between the three houses. The diet was inoperative between 1697 and 1701 and 1718 and 1723. As a result there was little imperial legislation especially after 1714, though a few important acts were passed.

In 1681 a new military system (*Kriegsverfassung*) was enacted, which enlarged the imperial army and passed the organization of it and the apportionment of the costs of its maintenance between different states to the Circles. The military role of the Circles was enhanced further in 1703 and 1706. Under this system it was possible for the smaller states to pay their larger neighbours to provide their contingents to the imperial army, thus avoiding the trouble and expense of maintaining their own little armies of a few hundred or even a few dozen men. This led to the *de facto* emergence of two distinct groupings among the German states, the armed, those with standing armies, and the unarmed (*armierte und nicht armierte Stände*). One problem was that the larger states were often unwilling to place their troops under any kind of imperial high command and insisted on keeping control in their own hands. This made imperial armies very unwieldy and inefficient. Only during the Spanish Succession War was an imperial command structure created. Typically, the imperial general field marshal's office had to have a Catholic and a Protestant member. After 1707 the Catholic post was held by Prince Eugene of Savoy. Another problem was that the armed states often found the provision of troops for smaller neighbours a useful means of extending political control over them and turning them into satellites, for example, if they fell into arrears with their payments for military substitution. Emperors from Leopold I were not anxious to see an imperial standing army created as it would certainly not be under their control.

In 1731 the *Reichstag* also passed an ordinance designed to place restrictions on the guilds, powerful institutions with a power base in many free cities and an organizational structure covering the Empire. Many state governments complained bitterly about their conservatism and obstructiveness. This led to a ban on some of the social and racial discrimination earlier practised by the guilds — members of the minority nationalities, the Wends and Sorbs, were excluded, as were the children of people engaged in a whole range of "inferior" occupations — and an increase in the number of apprentices entering crafts, including women in some. Another guild ordinance in 1772 attacked other abuses, including "Holy Monday", the widespread practice of extending the weekend by an extra day. Another law, the 1737 coinage ordinance, was an attempt yet again to bring order to a chaotic system, in which there were over 600 separate minting authorities and over forty German and foreign coinages circulated, and to establish a common standard. These acts depended for their operation on the willingness of the individual states to put them into effect. More significant than its legislative functions was the *Reichstag's* role as a major centre of German and European inter-state politics, as one of the "capitals" of Germany.

The Circles were another imperial institution which worked, at least partly. Each Circle was supposed to have regular meetings of the Circle diet to discuss matters of mutual concern, to appoint judges to the imperial chamber court, to pass legislation and to make provision for defence, internal order and the like. These meetings were supposed to be called by the convening princes (*kreisausschreibende Fürsten*), usually the most important rulers in the area. Those in the north were dominated by the larger states like Brandenburg and Saxony, or foreign powers like Sweden, and were the least effective. The most active were the Swabian and Franconian Circles in the south west. In the late seventeenth century the former, which contained a host of tiny states and free cities, developed a very successful system of co-operation reminiscent of the Swiss confederation. There was also effective defence co-operation between the exposed Circles of the south west, which began with the Frankfurt agreement of five Circles in 1697. This organized an army, which defended the Rhine frontier against the French during the War of the Spanish Succession and lasted into the 1720s. In all there were twelve associations between 1697 and 1748.[2]

At the same time the Emperor retained his reserved powers (*Reservatrechte*), which enabled him to exercise considerable influence. He possessed a range of privileges stemming from his personal feudal overlordship of the whole Empire, including formal enfeoffment of princes with newly acquired territories, a process essential if the holder was to exercise any representation in the *Reichstag* attached to the territory. Within the Empire only the Emperor could ennoble commoners or grant higher grades of nobility. He could grant pardons, exemptions from the jurisdiction of the imperial courts, legitimations of illegitimate children and university charters. He also exercised supreme judicial authority to judge the bodies and possessions of his feudal subjects. As protector of all three German Churches he had a voice in the election of new prelates. Some of these rights could only be exercised with the consent of the electors after 1711. Leopold I was also able to prevent the Empire from acting as a unit in diplomatic matters as was intended in the 1648 treaties; he simply assumed a right to negotiate on behalf of the Empire and presented the results to the *Reichstag* for ratification. As ruler of the Austrian lands he possessed diplomatic power: by means of subsidy treaties and alliances he could make his weight felt in Germany and he could offer some protection to the weak. The little German states and those close to the borders of Austria continued to look to the Emperor as a protector. The Emperor's influence was strong, especially in the south and west, among the smaller states throughout the Empire, particularly the Catholics, and among the imperial knights and counts, many of whom looked to Vienna for careers.

Even an interregnum following Ferdinand's death in 1657, when an imperial election was necessary because his second son, Leopold, had not previously been elected king of the Romans — his elder son, Ferdinand, who had, died in 1654 — did not lead to any substantial reduction in the Emperor's powers. During the long reign of Leopold I (1659–1705) imperial influence in Germany tended to stagnate, as the Emperor's efforts were devoted to consolidating Austrian power in the wars against Louis XIV's France and the Turks. Under Leopold Austria began a large-scale expansion eastwards. There was also a growing obsession with the future of the Spanish empire on the imminently awaited death of the sickly King Charles II of Spain (1665–1700). Leopold was very keen to possess Spain's Italian possessions. During this time Austria grew away from the Empire and neglected Germany, though there was a party in Vienna around the aulic chancellor Johann Paul Hocher, which continued to press the Emperor to take initiatives to restore his influence.

Imperial mercantilism (*Reichsmerkantilismus*) was one such scheme. In 1676 all French imports into the Empire were banned and in 1689 and 1702 imperial laws forbade all commerce with France. The bans were not enforced. In 1678 decisions were taken to float schemes for a common German economic policy and an imperial standing army. The idea of a common external tariff, associated with Christoph Royas y Spinola, Bishop of Wiener Neustadt, Peter Philip von Dernbach, Bishop of Bamberg, and the mercantilist writer Johann Becher, was revived. The yield from the tariff would be used to fund an imperial army. Of these plans only the much watered-down 1681 military constitution actually came into existence. Austrian propaganda in the *Reich* remained vigorous. An anonymous pamphlet of 1662 asked and answered a question: *What has Austria done for Germany? Austria has brought Germany to its Highest Flourishing.*

After the death of Leopold, his two sons, Joseph and Charles, held the imperial title in succession. Their reigns saw a conscious attempt to restore imperial influence in Germany, a process sometimes called the imperial reaction.[3] This reached its height during the reign of

Charles VI (1711–40), a man with an elevated conception of his imperial position, which he saw as far more than a collection of empty titles. He was determined to use his reserved powers to the full. His reign was in some ways a turning point as he was the last Emperor to make no real distinction between his position as Emperor and as ruler of the Habsburg lands. After 1740 there was a marked reversion to the situation of Leopold I's reign: the Habsburgs concentrated almost exclusively on Austria and its interests and abandoned attempts to control the Empire. They began to behave towards Germany like any other foreign power.

The imperial reaction began under Joseph I (1705–11). The wars against the French and the Turks in the later years of Leopold I's reign had revived imperial patriotism and the Emperor was able to benefit from this. For centuries this patriotism had become an increasingly insignificant and short-lived phenomenon with the rise of particularism, state egotism, but French policy helped to change this. French aggressiveness[4] in the 1670s and 1680s brought about a marked change of attitude among most German rulers; whereas previously they had regarded the Emperor as the main threat to peace and had looked to France for protection and for the promotion of their interests, for example in the League of the Rhine, they now saw the French as the main threat and looked to Vienna. States like Brandenburg, Münster and the Brunswick duchies, which had earlier operated a see-saw policy, moving between the French and the imperial alliance in pursuit of their immediate interests, moved back into the imperial orbit. German national sentiment grew as Germans became increasingly resentful of the trampling of the *Reich* by "the Christian Turks, the hereditary enemy of the German name". It was partly negative, focused against the hate-figure of Louis XIV, and partly positive in the form of growing attachment to the person of the Emperor.

In May 1674, during the Franco-Dutch War (1673–9), imperial war was declared against France, which had violated German neutrality. This was the first imperial war since Charles V's reign and the first of three in Leopold's reign. Peace was made between France and the Empire at Nijmegen in February 1679. Brandenburg, cheated of West Pomerania, in spite of its victory over the Swedes at Fehrbellin in 1675, became a secret ally of France. Louis XIV's *réunions* policy, under which the French, on the basis of documents "discovered" in archives, laid claim to and seized large areas of Germany as supposed feudal dependencies of territories belonging to the French crown in order to create a strong military frontier, aroused great hostility. In the 1680s and 1690s the French occupied large areas of Alsace and western Germany, including the city of Strasburg, which they had long coveted and which was seized by force in September 1681. When Louis XIV entered the city in October a large number of German princes were in his entourage. The loss of Strasburg was of great symbolic importance and its seizure was to fuel German nationalism in the nineteenth and twentieth centuries. Imperial propaganda also made much of it at the time, though it must be noted that the Habsburgs made similar use of some tenuous residual imperial rights to try to extend their political control in northern Italy and the south west of the *Reich*. Louis' persecution of the French Protestants after the revocation of the Edict of Nantes in 1685 also damaged his image in Germany.

The defensive League of Augsburg was set up in July 1686 and included the Emperor, Spain, Bavaria, Saxony, Sweden and the Circles of the south west. It was later enlarged when the Dutch and Britain joined. Imperial war was declared against France in 1688 and 1702. During the War of the League of Augsburg, also known as King William's War, the Nine Years' War and the War of the Palatinate Succession (1688–97) the French, again claiming German territory through the king's sister-in-law, the daughter of the elector palatine, invaded the western parts of the Empire. In the Palatinate they embarked on a campaign of deliberate incendiarism, in which hundreds of towns and villages were burned down. The damage was worse than that suffered during the Thirty Years' War. The reputation of France sank further. Southern Germany was again a theatre of war in the War of the Spanish Succession, during which the great majority of the German states fought against the French.

The Turkish siege of Vienna in 1683 gave a powerful boost to imperial patriotism. The lifting of the siege began a great offensive into Hungary and the Balkans, pushing the Turks back hundreds of miles. Under the terms of the peace treaties of Carlowitz (1699) and Passarowitz (1718) the Habsburgs gained substantial territories in the northern Balkans. These treaties and the treaties of Utrecht, Rastatt and Baden (1713–14), which concluded the Spanish Succession War, ended the threat from France and the Turks for a long time. The next threat to the stability of the Empire was to come from within Germany, from Prussia.

During this time loyalty to the Emperor could bring rewards: in 1697 it brought the House of Brunswick-Lüneburg an electoral crown.

Opposition to the Emperor could bring punishment. During Joseph's reign the electors of Bavaria and Cologne were placed under the ban of the Empire, involving the loss of their lands and titles, as a punishment for allying with Louis XIV. The tragedy of Bavaria was that, although it had substantial advantages, a compact state with an efficient centralized administration, it was too close to Austria and therefore did not have the freedom of action enjoyed by some other medium-sized states.[5]

Its rulers pursued a double policy to deal with the problem. They sought to have members of their house elected to as many ecclesiastical principalities as possible. Between 1583 and 1761 they were able to put a Wittelsbach on the throne of the electorate of Cologne, which was a base for further expansion. Clement Augustus, brother of the Elector of Bavaria, was Elector of Cologne between 1723 and 1761 and also held the bishoprics of Paderborn, Osnabrück, Hildesham and Münster. This policy was eventually ruined by biology: the Wittelsbachs did not produce enough male children. The second element in Bavarian policy was the French alliance. After 1670 the Bavarian Wittelsbachs were to remain the most loyal allies of France in the Empire for over a century. With French encouragement, they planned to take the imperial title: a Bavarian rival to the Habsburg candidate was first seriously considered as early as 1658. They derived little benefit from the French connexion and once came close to disaster because of it. In 1704 Bavaria was occupied by imperial troops, whose harsh behaviour provoked a peasant rising at Christmas 1705, put down with great brutality. The Wittelsbachs were restored to their titles and their ravaged lands in 1715 thanks to French intervention on their behalf.

During the Spanish Succession War Austria enjoyed a series of military successes thanks to the imperial commander Prince Eugene of Savoy, a brilliant general and diplomat. Austria made territorial gains in Italy and the Netherlands under the Treaty of Utrecht (1714) and in the Balkans under the Treaty of Passarowitz with the Turks (1718). The long French-inspired rebellion in Hungary was brought to an end in 1711 by the Treaty of Szatmar. By 1720 the Emperor's position in Germany was stronger than for ninety years. Habsburg power in Europe was at its apogee and Charles VI was stronger than Ferdinand II at the height of his success in the Thirty Years' War.

Personal factors also played a role in the imperial reaction. Joseph I suffered from the crown prince syndrome, the growing frustration of waiting during his father's long reign for his turn on the throne. He wished to imitate Louis XIV and make himself the Austrian Sun King. During his reign the sun symbol became part of the Habsburgs' iconography. Statues, pictures and medals were lavishly used for propaganda purposes, as they were by all rulers, to demonstrate the semi-divine status of the Emperor.

During the War of the Spanish Succession Charles VI had been a candidate for the Spanish throne supported, initially, by the anti-French coalition. It appears that his brief experience as King of Spain affected his attitudes. He was very aware of the dignity of his imperial titles. During his reign the memory of Charles V was consciously and deliberately cultivated. He went in for substantial building activity, for example extensions to the Hofburg Palace in Vienna. Baroque architecture reached its height under the Fischer von Erlach, father and son, and Johann Lukas von Hildebrandt. The Charles Church in Vienna made prominent use of the pillars of Hercules, a symbol of Habsburg power used by Charles V. Only a shortage of money prevented the building of a summer palace at Schönbrunn bigger than Versailles. At one time Charles planned to turn the monastery at Klosterneuburg near Vienna into the Austrian Escorial, a centre for the government of the whole Empire in imitation of Philip II's complex outside Madrid. He retained many Spaniards at his court to run the former Spanish possessions acquired by Austria at Utrecht.

Charles's reign was significant for two things, the Pragmatic Sanction and the imperial reaction. It was only in his later years that the Sanction acquired real significance. During Leopold's reign the last collateral Habsburg line, the Tyrolean, died out and all the Austrian Habsburg lands came together in his hands. They remained a collection of provinces united only by a single ruler and it was not clear what would happen to them if the male line died out. Dynastic stability was a factor of central importance in the states system of the time, as witnessed by the numerous wars of succession. The Pragmatic Sanction was drawn up in 1703. It was initially a secret family agreement declaring all the Austrian possessions an indivisible whole. This was significant: it has been described as the first codification of the Austrian state idea. It also designated the order of succession in the female line. In 1713 Charles altered it by a unilateral declaration to make any daughter he might have, in the absence of a son, heiress to everything in preference to his brother's daughters. The Sanction became an important item of European diplomacy when Charles' sons died as infants and his elder daughter, Maria Theresa, emerged as heiress. This arrangement was not accepted by all German or

European states and in the later years of Charles' reign a possible partition of the Austrian empire was beginning to obsess Europe, as had the fate of Spain in the later seventeenth century. It became a major aim of Charles' policy after 1730 to obtain guarantees of the Sanction from German and European states. Charles was not stupid. He did not place great faith in a piece of paper but hoped to link it to alliances, to make other powers dependent for their own security on the survival of a strong Austria. Prince Eugene is supposed to have said that a strong army and a full treasury would be a better guarantee. It is unlikely that Eugene would have said anything so obvious. Charles knew this well and made determined efforts to reform the administration and finances but he had a tendency to look for magic answers, such as commercial companies, rather than to carry out the thorough-going reform of the whole Austrian system, which was what was really needed. The financial administration of the state remained decentralized like the general administration.[6]

The reforms were not very successful and poor finances were to dog Austria. During the wars of Leopold I's reign very heavy state debts had been accumulated and Austria had become very dependent on Jewish financiers to arrange these. In 1703 one of the largest of these, the Oppenheim firm, collapsed, causing serious problems for the government. It is ironical that the successes of 1714–18 gave Austria great possessions but also gave her great commitments which she was barely capable of bearing. Charles VI also did little to advance the creation of a modern administration in his lands. He appreciated the individual traditions of his various possessions, Austrian, Bohemian, Hungarian, Netherlands and Italian. He made no attempt to set up a unified administration for his territories. The Estates survived with a major administrative role. Austria had a semi-amateur system of government and remained a half-formed absolutist state. Major reform and modernization were only undertaken after 1740 by Charles' daughter Maria Theresa. If the Sanction was the first codification of the Austrian state idea, the practice lagged sadly behind.

Charles' desire to obtain the *Reich's* support for the Sanction and to increase Austrian influence in Germany, using the reservoir of imperial powers still available, were motives behind the imperial reaction in addition to the personal ones already mentioned. Personalities also played an important role. While he was king of the Romans, heir apparent to the imperial title, Joseph I had gathered round him a group of younger men anxious to see a revival of

Austrian power in Germany, in the belief that Germany would not be neglected as Austria's "back yard". The main figures were Prince Eugene of Savoy and Frederick Charles von Schönborn, the imperial vice-chancellor. Both men were to occupy powerful positions when Charles VI became Emperor. Both favoured an extension of Austrian power in Germany, though for different reasons, Eugene purely in pursuit of Austrian state interests but Schönborn for more complex reasons.

Schönborn was a member of a family of small imperial counts, a class among whom imperial loyalty was traditionally strong, from Franconia, an area where imperial influence survived more persistently than in most parts of Germany. The family was consistently imperialist and its members had risen to high positions in the Church and the imperial diplomatic service through their loyalty. There were many other examples of families from similar backgrounds who rose to high office through service to the Habsburgs, for example the Metternichs from the Rhineland, but the Schönborns were the most successful. They were the main rivals of the Wittelsbachs for ecclesiastical preferments, using the growing family property holdings as security for loans to pay the necessary bribes.

Frederick Charles was appointed imperial vice-chancellor by his uncle, Lothar von Schönborn, who was Archbishop and Elector of Mainz. Schönborn was himself a Catholic priest and coadjutor (that is automatic heir) to the Bishop of Bamberg. The old-fashioned Borussian view saw him as an agent of political Catholicism but that was oversimple. Certainly he saw a serious threat to the survival of the Empire from the rising Protestant north German states, especially Hanover and Prussia, strengthened by their territorial gains from Sweden in the Great Northern War of 1700 to 1721, whose rulers he mocked as "theatre kings". Schönborn was afraid that the end of the Empire was close and he had a terrible vision of what would follow: the weak, including the small and ecclesiastical states, would fall prey to the strong. Germany would again become the battlefield of foreign powers and would be divided up among them and the more powerful German states. He did not see imperial power and the states' rights as exclusive but complementary: each was an essential element in the German constitution and, without Austria and the Emperor, he believed, there would be no Empire and no German liberty.

In 1709 he wrote a long report on the state of the Empire after taking over his office. He found imperial feeling at a low ebb: the Emperor lacked power, imperial jurisdiction was flouted and the imperial diet was crippled by petty squabbles. He suggested remedies to restore the loose ties of the Empire, urging his master Joseph I to exploit the reservoir of loyalty where it still existed, in the Circles of the south west and the Upper Rhine and among the Catholic and small states. A reactivation of imperial justice would, he argued, be a valuable instrument in this. He also urged the Emperor to construct an alliance system with those states who were still loyal. His aim was to build up an Austrian/imperial party in Germany.

Schönborn's office was in the gift of the arch-chancellor of the Empire, the Elector of Mainz and its holder acted as the elector's agent in Vienna as head of the imperial chancery (*Reichskanzlei*), the main administrative organ of the Empire. The power deriving from the position depended very much on the man who held it. By 1711 it was not what it had been, having been neglected under Leopold I and held by Austrians with no real interest in German affairs. As a result it had suffered a steady loss of power to the exclusively Austrian offices of state, especially the aulic chancery (*Hofkanzlei*) set up in 1620 by Ferdinand II. In Vienna Schönborn faced strong opposition from Austrian statesmen, who resented the intrusion of a German into what they regarded as the secrets of the House of Austria. Particularly strong opposition came from the head of the *Hofkanzlei*, Philip Ludwig von Sinzendorf. He pursued purely Austrian aims and saw the Holy Roman Empire as a barrier to Austrian progress. His policy was that Austria should abandon all imperial pretensions and seek allies among German states on exactly the same terms as other foreign powers and not try to exploit residual imperial powers, which were, in his view, worthless. Schönborn opposed this approach. He believed that if purely Austrian interests came to predominate in the *Reich*, this would only hasten its disintegration: Austria would be acting in exactly the same way as other states seeking to win something from the decline.

Schönborn was able to claw back some of the influence lost earlier by his office, including the establishment of a special weekly imperial conference (or cabinet meeting) and admission to the Inner Cabinet when imperial affairs were discussed. He was also able to persuade the Emperor that Germany could prove a valuable accession of power to the House of Austria if correctly exploited and that imperial authority could be used as an instrument of Habsburg dynastic power. In this he was pushing at an open door in view of Charles VI's own views. The many policies which Schönborn pursued contributed to the imperial reaction, which reached its height in the late 1720s.

It took various forms. Schönborn was well aware of the value of public relations. He hired scholars and writers to produce imperialist propaganda and sponsored the publication of collections of imperial laws. His main aim was to stop the growth of Prussian power, which he described as a gnawing worm in the bowels of the Empire. Prussia was seizing every chance to encroach on the rights and lands of its weaker neighbours, raising the threat of a new dictator in the Empire and a rival for the imperial crown. In particular he was anxious to keep Prussia out of southern Germany. In this he had one spectacular success: he was able to sabotage Prussian plans to buy the small Ansbach/Bayreuth territories in Franconia held by a cadet line of the Hohenzollern family. He also encouraged cases against Prussia in the imperial courts: at one time there were over forty cases pending against her. The imperial resident in Berlin had the unpleasant job of delivering imperial rebukes, some of which amazed contemporaries by their tone. Such rolling phrases of majesty had not been used against a senior prince of the Empire for a long time. A Prussian representative in Vienna warned his master that the Emperor would tolerate no infringement of his authority: Charles VI had ambitions to imitate Caesar Augustus and the grandeur of the first Roman Empire.

The main agency of the imperial reaction was the supreme judicial authority, exercised through the imperial aulic council (*Reichshofrat*), which was seen as the last remaining jewel in the imperial crown, the only institution which after 1648 gave the Emperor a realistic opportunity to increase his influence in the *Reich*. The council experienced the last major exercise of its power during the imperial reaction. Its rival, the chamber court (*Reichskammergericht*), was wholly paid for by the princes through special contributions and it suffered from a chronic financial starvation. A new ordinance for the chamber court was issued in 1654, including measures to speed up its procedures, but their effect was limited. By the eighteenth century it was inefficient and slow. Many stories circulated about it, all variations on the theme that periodically all the accumulated papers in the court were thrown up into the air and those which fell face up were dealt with. As a result of recent detailed research the court has been rehabilitated and its older essentially negative image must be modified in the light of this. Many litigants, especially the Protestant nobility of northern and western Germany, still thought it worthwhile to seek redress there. It was to experience a marked revival in the later eighteenth century.

The aulic council was established by the early eighteenth century as the highest tribunal of the Empire. Litigants had a choice between the two imperial tribunals and the aulic council experienced a substantial increase in its business from the late seventeenth century onwards. It had a very wide competence outside the Austrian lands. It was a civil court, the highest criminal court of appeal and the highest feudal tribunal with jurisdiction over the grant of privileges, declarations of majorities, the confirmation of succession arrangements, wills, contracts, adoptions, wardships and legitimizations. In the eighteenth century the Empire was still a collection of feudal territories with overlapping and competing jurisdictions, in which states with firm borders and unchallenged central authority were emerging only slowly. The jurisdiction of the aulic council was important in regulating the mechanism and keeping order.

One of the strengths of the aulic council was that it was entirely at the disposal of the Emperor: he appointed its members and paid their salaries and issued regulations for the court without reference to the German states. Successive Emperors firmly resisted all attempts by the princes to obtain a say in its management, personnel or competence. Judicial power was held to belong to the Emperor alone and it was the function of the aulic council to advise him on the exercise of it. Jurisdiction was shared with the *Reichstag*, in only one matter, the imposition of the ban of the Empire, when the imperial diet had to confirm a verdict of the aulic council. A committee of the *Reichstag*, the *Reichsdeputation*, was set up in 1654 to deal with the appeals against the verdicts of the imperial courts allowed under certain limited circumstances but this did not come into existence until the eighteenth century, when such appeals began to flood in. The council saw itself as a guardian of imperial rights and a strong *esprit de corps* developed under Charles VI. Charles also carried out a major reform of the aulic council and appointed talented lawyers as presidents.

The council was attacked by its enemies as an instrument of Habsburg despotism, religious and political, and there was a constant campaign by leading princes to place restrictions on it. A frequent accusation against it was that it was partial to Catholics. In the Westphalian treaties the Emperor had agreed to appoint a fixed number of Protestant members but this was not always done, often with the excuse that suitable candidates were not available or that Protestant councillors became converts to Catholicism. One commentator, Hippolitus a Lapide, a propagandist in Swedish pay and a bitter enemy of the House of Habsburg, in his *De Ratione Status in Imperio Romano Germanico* (1640) described it as "the most poisonous spring for the destruction of German liberty". These attacks came to a head under Joseph I and Charles VI and were made more violent by the perceived influence of Schönborn and the large number of converts to Catholicism in prominent positions in Vienna. 1711 saw the first imperial election for fifty years (Joseph I had been elected king of the Romans during his father's lifetime) and this gave the princes a chance to vent their long-accumulating grievances, especially against interference by the aulic council in the internal affairs of their states.

An increasing part of its business at this time was concerned with constitutional disputes in individual German states, of which there were many as the struggle to impose absolutist systems of government reached crisis point in many states. Paragraph 180 of the *Reichsabschied* of 1654 was a major cause of trouble. Under this all subjects were obliged to contribute financially to the costs of *necessary* military arrangements undertaken by their rulers as part of the defence system of the Empire, regardless of any contrary constitutional agreements. This was further extended in Leopold I's capitulation of election in 1658, which limited subjects' rights of appeal to the imperial courts and placed restrictions on the Estates. Under these provisions the princes had a mandate to impose taxes at will, arguing that they were privileged imperial taxes which subjects had to pay. The principle that subjects had to contribute to imperial taxes was established in the fifteenth century. In the 1670s and 1680s a group of absolutist rulers, known as the Extensionists (*Extendisten*), tried to obtain an extension of these provisions to dismantle the last remaining rights of subjects. This campaign was resisted by the Emperor and the aulic council on the grounds that the word *necessary* in paragraph 180 meant necessary for the defence of the Empire, not what the prince thought necessary.

Constitutional disputes flared up again in the early eighteenth century and the aulic council became involved in many of them. In the little state of Nassau-Siegen the council was responsible for the deposition of the ruling count, William Hyacinth, who was an insane despot. In East Frisia a civil war broke out in the 1720s over disputes between the prince and the Estates. The aulic council was deeply involved in attempts to deal with the problems. In the case of Mecklenburg-Schwerin a tyrannical ruler, Duke Charles Leopold, was deposed and an imperial provisional administration installed after 1719. Later the council played a major role during constitutional disputes in the substantial duchy of Württemberg. A large number of small states and cities had their form of government influenced by decisions of the *Reichshofrat*. Among the most striking examples are the city of Hamburg, which in 1712 was given a new constitution after decades of internal strife. Hamburg was also saved from Danish attempts to seize it. The *Reich*, however weak, could still exercise judicial authority. A complete victory of absolutism in Germany was prevented and the aulic council helped to keep alive, however weakly, an older tradition of popular participation in government. It also helped to keep alive in some parts of Germany the idea of German unity at a time when the individual states were taking control over more and more of the people's daily lives.

More important perhaps, during the imperial reaction in the 1720s the aulic council was able to help to contain a serious religious dispute in Germany. After 1648 religion slowly declined as a major factor in German politics and toleration spread, largely for pragmatic reasons. This was accompanied by the appearance of more spiritual trends in both Churches. In the Protestant Churches Pietism was a powerful movement from the later seventeenth century. Founded in the 1670s by Philipp Jakob Spener, a Lutheran minister in Frankfurt-am-Main and later in Berlin, this preached a tolerant and undogmatic Christianity based on individual or group contemplation combined with good works. It attracted a substantial following but was not all-conquering. This secularization of attitudes, which developed among rulers and intellectuals, was slow to break through among some sections of the clergy and the mass of the population. In states like Brandenburg-Prussia, where toleration was officially fostered for demographic and economic reasons, the mass of ordinary Lutherans, often tacitly encouraged by their pastors, looked askance at strangers of a different faith and made life difficult for them.

Many of the free cities, in which parity of faiths had been introduced in 1648, experienced constant religious friction. Religious dispute at the academic level was a German hobby, leading to the production of a huge theological literature. It was no coincidence that the Enlightenment in Germany was more concerned with religion than the movement elsewhere and often centred on questions of toleration rather than political matters. After the settlement of 1648, which, like that of 1555, contained too many compromises and too many points of potential friction, further intermixing of the religions continued. There was some cooling off in the face of a common enemy, France, but many Protestant princes continued to be afraid of a Catholic Emperor and looked to France for protection. Religion still mattered in the early eighteenth century and religious concerns were never far from the surface, resulting from a combination of sincerely held beliefs and defence of vested interests, for example the Protestant Succession in Britain, the special position of the German ecclesiastical princes, fears, probably baseless, of a Protestant Emperor among Catholics and the continuing close interconnection between religion and politics in German life.

In the early years of the eighteenth century there was a sharp revival of religious confrontation. The basic cause of the religious crisis of the 1720s was the so-called Ryswick Clause, article four of the Treaty of Ryswick (1697), which ended the War of the League of Augsburg. France occupied the Palatinate from 1688 until 1697 and during that period many Catholic churches were built or reopened in the electorate. The area was already the scene of a long-standing bitter dispute between Lutherans and Calvinists over incomes and property. Under the Ryswick Clause, these Catholic rights were to remain in existence after 1697. This left many potential flash-points, including a large number of church buildings where the *Simultaneum* operated, that is the sharing of a single building by different faiths. Serious trouble began in 1715: a Jesuit professor at Heidelberg wrote a pamphlet attacking Luther. The Palatinate Calvinist Church also brought out a new catechism dedicated to the elector, who had become a personal convert to Catholicism, containing very uncomplimentary remarks about the pope and pointed references to the links between Roman Catholicism and tyranny. In July 1715 an imperial decree was issued forbidding the publication or distribution in the Empire of any material containing attacks on other Christian sects. The troubles in the Palatinate simmered on until 1718: in that year the elector moved his residence back to Heidelberg, where he wanted to use the impressive Church of the Holy Spirit, the burial place of his predecessors, as his Catholic court chapel. The *Simultaneum* was already in operation there, with the Calvinists using the nave and the Catholics the choir. A wall had been built between them. The Calvinists refused to leave, even though they were offered a brand new church. Eventually the elector seized the church with troops and tore down the wall. This began the crisis.

The time was ripe for trouble. The bicentenary of the beginning of the Reformation fell in 1717, an event marked with lavish ceremonial in all parts of Protestant Germany.[7] As a result of a number of developments the German Protestants felt under threat. The conversion to Catholicism of the Elector of Saxony in 1697 and the inheritance of the Palatinate by a Catholic line of the house in 1685, were seen as a great loss, although in the case of Saxony the conversion was personal and not official. The early eighteenth century also saw a revival of religious persecution in a number of ecclesiastical states, in answer to which some Protestant rulers had taken reprisals against their Catholic populations, including Hanover and Prussia. The Palatinate crisis broke in the middle of this. Through the involvement of the Protestant organization in the imperial diet, the *corpus evangelicorum*, the dispute rapidly escalated until all the greater Protestant states were involved plus their foreign allies. The rapid involvement of foreign powers was a dangerous development. The *Reichstag* became paralysed by the dispute, which promoted the rise of extremists on both sides. Vicious pamphlet warfare developed and there was a serious threat of war. The Prussian government's reprisals against Prussian Catholics were very harsh and were encouraged by Hanover, which was playing a clever game, hoping to use the religious issue to drive wedges between the Emperor and Prussia.

The Emperor, as protector of the three German Churches, refused to take sides and referred the whole matter to the aulic council, which ordered all the parties involved to stop illegal actions. Prussia in 1720 received edicts which caused amazement. The King of Prussia was treated as a recalcitrant vassal and his offences were catalogued in detail, including the perversion of the imperial constitution, failure to pay contributions to the maintenance of imperial armies, attacks on his neighbours, forced recruiting in neighbouring states, the creation of a huge army which was a constant threat to his neighbours and a desire to make himself independent of the Empire, among others. These firm imperial actions played a major part in solving the religious crisis. Gradually the fire went out of the issue and the extremists became increasingly isolated. There was great fear of war, especially among the smaller states in both religious camps. Hanover and Prussia needed imperial support to enjoy their gains from the Northern War against Sweden and were concerned at the spread of Russian power in the Baltic. Eventually the persecutions faded away. The dispute lingered on into the 1730s but religion was losing its power to divide. It is significant that events like the expulsion of over 20 000 Protestants from Salzburg in 1731–2 were seen as relics of a Gothic past even by Catholics.

By 1730 the imperial reaction was over. The reasons included the decline of Schönborn's power in Vienna as Austrian interests reasserted themselves. In 1728 he became Bishop of Bamberg and Würzburg, which made necessary long absences from Vienna. As a result conditions in the imperial chancery became increasingly chaotic and there were accusations of massive corruption. In 1730 he offered the Emperor his New Plan, under which his own bishoprics were to form the core of an alliance and military system based on the ecclesiastical states. A chain of fortresses from the Austrian Netherlands to Austria would give the Emperor a base from which to restore his power in Germany. This was too expensive and anyway Austria had too many pressing commitments elsewhere to be able to devote effort to Germany. In 1734 Schönborn resigned as imperial vice-chancellor.

By then Austrian policy was increasingly concerned with the Pragmatic Sanction: purely Austrian interests were becoming paramount as the whole future of the Austrian state was coming into question. The late 1720s had seen the dangerous polarization of Europe into two alliance systems, with Spain, the Emperor and Russia allied against Britain, France and Prussia. Both groups were bidding for allies among the German rulers. In this dangerous situation the Emperor had to buy friends. The danger to the existence of Austria was becoming very real in the 1730s, when France again emerged actively in European affairs, having recovered from the damage she had suffered in the War of the Spanish Succession. During the Polish Succession War (1733–8) southern Germany was again a theatre of war and the Empire suffered further losses. France took Lorraine. The French revived their traditional policy of collecting clients among the German states, offering them the bait of a share of the Austrian lands in the forthcoming partition of the Habsburg state. This policy was especially successful with the Bavarian Wittelsbachs, who became the centre of a group of powers hoping to make territorial gains from a dismemberment of Austria, which would have left the Habsburgs only with Hungary. The electors of Bavaria and Saxony had claims to Austrian territory through their marriages to the daughters of Joseph I. France wanted the Austrian Netherlands, Spain coveted Naples and Sicily and Savoy had long desired the duchy of Milan.

The *Reichstag*, except the Elector of Bavaria, accepted the Sanction in 1732, after energetic Austrian diplomacy. This could be seen as the last triumph for Schönborn but it destroyed Charles VI's freedom of action. The Emperor had to bid for allies among the German princes as a petitioner in competition with other powers and he could not at the same time pose as head of the Empire and an impartial judge over them. It is interesting that from 1726 onwards Charles was signing treaties with German rulers as Archduke of Austria not as Emperor. This marked the symbolic end of the idea of the Empire above parties and was the beginning of the end for the imperial idea. Austria's prestige suffered badly during an unsuccessful war against Turkey (1737–9), in which it lost many of its earlier gains.

On the death of Charles VI in 1740 Frederick II of Prussia launched his invasion of Silesia. The Wittelsbachs achieved a long-held ambition when the Elector Charles Albert of Bavaria was chosen as Emperor in 1742, though he was little more than a puppet of the Prussians and French. The weakness of Austria meant that even traditional friends like Mainz felt compelled to vote for the Wittelsbach. Austria managed to survive thanks to the energy and skill of Maria Theresa. The main problem of the time was not the rise of Hanover and Prussia, as Schönborn believed, but the alienation of Austria from the Empire. The Pragmatic Sanction hastened this and ended the imperial reaction.

7 Dualism and Reform: Germany after the Seven Years' War

After 1740 there were clear signs of change in Germany. New ideas were beginning to spread even if there were very few new institutions. Certain basic characteristics and trends affecting the whole country can be isolated. As always there were exceptions to all generalizations.[1]

The Empire continued to provide a political framework for Germany but the political fragmentation of the country into a collection of virtually sovereign states continued and the Empire was losing what little unifying power it had possessed. There was a brief revival of interest in imperial institutions when Charles Albert, the Elector of Bavaria, was elected Emperor in 1742, but following his death in 1745 the title reverted to the Habsburgs in the person of Francis I, husband of Maria Theresa. By the reign of Joseph II (1765–90) the imperial title was seen as little more than an adjunct of Habsburg dynastic power, but still a significant one. While a young man, Joseph was instructed in the details of the imperial constitution by academic tutors, who emphasized its importance.

The growth of dualism, the emergence of Prussia as a second German great power alongside Austria, continued rapidly. This was significant as each saw the other, rather than as earlier a foreign state like Sweden or France, as the main enemy. German issues therefore became central to German politics. This was part of a general shift in the focus of European politics as a whole away from the Netherlands, the Baltic and the Rhine to the Franco-British competition for overseas empires and to Eastern Europe. Russia was a rising power while Poland was becoming an "empty area" to be exploited by its neighbours. That Germany did not become such a vacuum was because of the existence of the Empire and Austro-Prussian dualism.

The emergence of dualism was gradual. The first serious confrontation between the two German powers was in the imperial diet of 1653–4, when Prussia began to take over leadership of the Protestant anti-imperial party earlier held by Saxony and the Palatinate. In the 1670s and 1680s Brandenburg, like many other states, pursued a flexible foreign policy, switching between a French and imperial alliance as its interests dictated. Already before 1740 Vienna was coming to be seen as the centre of gravity of the Catholic and Berlin of the Protestant *Reich*.

A clear sign that dualism was established came in 1745 when Austria was forced to accept the Prussian seizure of Silesia. Frederick II's invasion of Silesia in December 1740 was a bold gamble which came off. He took advantage of the recent accession of the young and inexperienced Maria Theresa with the stated aim to make a name for himself and to end the "hermaphrodite" nature of his state between an electorate and a real kingdom. There was a very shadowy Prussian claim to Silesia but in reality it was simply a highly desirable strategically important province with a large mainly Protestant population of about a million, fertile soil and developed manufacturing, which lay conveniently on Prussia's borders.[2] During the ensuing War of the Austrian Succession (1741–8) Austria faced a hostile coalition of Prussia, France, Bavaria, Cologne, Sweden, Saxony, the Palatinate, Spain and Naples intent on dismembering her. The nadir of Austria's fortunes seemed to come in January 1742 when Charles Albert, Elector of Bavaria, already crowned King of Bohemia in December 1741, was elected Holy Roman Emperor Charles VII. This marked the attainment of a long-standing Wittelsbach ambition, for which Charles Albert had prepared by trying to make Munich a German cultural centre, even including an attempt to revive the Bavarian dialect of German as a standard high language.

Prussia and France had plans to enlarge Bavaria with Bohemia and a clutch of secularized bishoprics to give it a large territorial base to sustain a permanent possession of the imperial title. A meeting of some of the more important princes at Aschaffenburg in 1741 also put forward plans for a substantial reform of the imperial constitution involving a further major reduction in the Emperor's powers. Charles VII's career as Emperor was brief and sad. Bavaria was occupied by Austrian troops and he had to stay in Frankfurt. He died suddenly aged forty-seven in January 1745. A series of Austrian victories changed the German situation and Maria Theresa's husband, Francis Stephen of Lorraine, was elected Emperor Francis I, with Prussia and the Palatinate dissenting, in September 1745. Francis devoted most of his time to his duchy of Tuscany, which he had received in exchange for his native Lorraine, and Maria Theresa, the most able of the Habsburgs and a woman of strong moral convictions, was personally responsible for imperial policy. Much to her disgust, she was forced temporarily to accept her loss of Silesia by the Peace of Dresden in December 1745.

Prussia's possession of Silesia was challenged again in the Seven Years' War, in which Maria Theresa and her allies sought to eliminate Prussia as a European and even a German power. In spite of victories, Austria was unable to win back Silesia. An imperial army took the field, to be defeated by the Prussians at Rossbach in 1757. The army immediately became an object of ridicule in Germany though it was reorganized after Rossbach and, attached to the Austrian army, fought creditably in the later stages of the war. Prussia's possession of Silesia was again recognized by Austria at the Peace of Hubertusburg in February 1763. Significantly, the *Reich* was not involved in the negotiations leading to Hubertusburg; it was in the interests of neither of the German great powers to involve the other states.

The war left a damaging legacy: the imperial courts ceased temporarily to operate, the coinage was chaotic and religious friction was stirred up again. During the war both sides employed religious propaganda in order to influence German and foreign opinion. Prussia's accusations that Maria Theresa was mounting a crusade to eradicate Protestantism were given some credence. The Habsburgs regarded Roman Catholicism as a useful vehicle for their influence in Germany and Maria Theresa let it be known that her aim was not only to regain Silesia but also to punish wickedness and promote the Catholic faith. In his *Considerations on the Present State of Political Forces in Europe* (1738) Frederick argued that it was always the object of the imperial court to establish Habsburg despotism over the *Reich* and sweep away the democratic system which had prevailed in Germany since time immemorial. Frederick II portrayed himself as a new Gustavus Adolphus, protecting German Protestantism against the Counter-Reformation ambitions of the Habsburgs. When Maria Theresa attempted to have the ban of the Empire decreed against Frederick the Protestant princes in the *Reichstag* refused to consider this on the grounds that it was a religious matter. Frederick II was the first German for a long time to record substantial achievements and his reputation as a Protestant champion and a German hero grew with the development of pro-Frederick (*fritzisch*) sentiment even in the German states with which Prussia was at war.

After the war informal control of Germany was shared between Prussia and Austria. Both had major non-German interests and both behaved like foreign powers, as France had in the past, building up clientage blocs among the smaller German rulers. Neither was a wholly German state and neither looked to Germany as a main area for expansion. Both looked increasingly eastwards, where tempting gains seemed to beckon with the decay of the Turkish empire and Poland. In 1772 the first partition of Poland took place.

Prussia's ability to defeat Austria and retain Silesia was a result of the state-building activities of its rulers after the Thirty Years' War, in particular Frederick William the Great Elector (1640–88) and King Frederick William I (1713–40). The "Borussian" writers of the nineteenth century grossly distorted the significance of their work, portraying it as preparation for a Prussian leadership role in Germany, culminating in the unification of 1871. Although this was long ago discredited, an adulatory attitude towards Prussia can still be found in some German historiography in the later twentieth century. This can effectively conceal the true significance of the "rise" of Prussia; a succession of talented rulers pursued the same policies as most of the rulers of the larger states in Germany but pursued them with more consistency and ruthlessness than most. They concentrated in particular on the creation of a powerful army. After 1648 the possessions of the Hohenzollerns were scattered vulnerably across northern Germany from the Rhine to the Memel, creating a serious problem of defence. Territorial fragmentation, a factor which in the case of other states, for example the Palatinate, was a source of weakness became for Brandenburg-Prussia an incentive for state-building. As a result Brandenburg-Prussia's political weight in Germany and Europe grew rapidly and it became a model to be copied by others.

In the course of a century an authoritarian militaristic state was established in Prussia; the rationalization of the long-term damaging effects of this was another aspect of the Borussian legend. Prussian rulers were obsessed with the acquisition of extra land and population as the only genuine sources of strength for a state. Prussia had a great deal of empty land available. In the case of Prussia the will to become a great power was more important than the resources; eventually the exercise of will enabled the state to seize the extra resources it needed. In pursuit of this the Hohenzollerns were prepared to press all claims, however shadowy, for example in the case of Silesia, and adopted a predatory policy towards their neighbours. They also opened their state to useful refugees and followed a pragmatic policy of religious toleration for this purpose. Some 15 000 Huguenots came after the revocation of the Edict of Nantes in 1685 and about 20 000 Protestants from Salzburg in 1731. Internally ruthless efforts were devoted to the centralization of government and the husbanding of resources for military purposes. It is argued that a Calvinist spirit played an important role in all this. In 1613 the Elector John Sigismund became a convert to Calvinism but, because of the opposition of the nobility and people, he was unable to convert his state, which remained Lutheran. This personal conversion was important in several respects. It gave Brandenburg important international links, especially with the Dutch. Calvinism came to represent the "Prussian" idea. The Great Elector and Frederick William I employed a small Calvinist elite as their main agents; it was easy to maintain cohesion in a small group which formed a religious minority faced with the hostility of the traditional ruling class it was in the process of displacing. A small Calvinist Church developed covering the whole state and not, like the Lutheran establishment, rooted in the separate provinces. Toleration produced intellectual freedom and an openness in Brandenburg-Prussia not seen in most other German states. It became an early centre for the Pietist movement within Protestantism and the university at Halle, under the influence of the Pietist educationist August Hermann Francke, became the best in the Empire.

King Frederick William I was responsible for substantial achievements in building the state. Under him Brandenburg-Prussia acquired an army out of all proportion to its size and resources. He is said to have personified the Calvinist Pietist spirit most spectacularly. He reacted strongly against his father's expensive and showy court — the only permanent achievement of Elector Frederick III (1688–1713) had been the assumption in 1701 of the title of king — and installed a regime of thrift, discipline and hard work which came to be identified as archetypal Prussian virtues. He deliberately employed foreign or non-noble civil servants because the native nobility continued to oppose the changes he wished to introduce but, by a mixture of persuasion and compulsion, he was able to begin the conversion of the nobility into military and administrative servants of the state. Such service later became a jealously guarded badge of status among the Prussian aristocracy.

Frederick II (1740–86) was prepared to take risks which would have horrified his less imaginative father and he was not restrained by Frederick William's lingering imperial patriotism. His gamble of 1740 brought magnificent dividends. Silesia was the making of Brandenburg-Prussia. Frederick also made substantial gains from the first partition of Poland in 1772. He reversed his father's policy of employing non-nobles, convinced that the nobility had to be preserved as natural officers and administrators, and encouraged it by a range of measures, including a monopoly of certain land, cheap credit and substantial powers of local self-government. He also did not press his attempts to abolish serfdom on noble lands beyond persuasion. The unchallenged domination of Prussian society by the aristocracy was to have important effects later.

In addition to the quality of its rulers, the rise of Brandenburg-Prussia was due to other factors. A substantial measure of luck played a part: the Great Elector, Frederick William I and Frederick II had long reigns. The elder son of the Great Elector, Charles Emil, died in 1674, leaving a single heir. This avoided the possibility of a division of the Hohenzollern lands. They were fortunate that their potential rivals in the north were distracted from Germany and abandoned the expansionist policies they had earlier pursued there. Saxony was unfortunate in that two talented rulers, John George III (1680–91) and John George IV (1691–4) died prematurely. The next elector, Augustus, known as the Strong (1694–1733) was elected King of Poland in 1697. Thereafter it was the ambition of the Saxons to make themselves hereditary kings and to create a powerful state there. The Saxon-Polish union eventually brought economic benefits but did not enhance Saxony's power and after the Seven Years' War it abandoned foreign commitments and concentrated on internal rebuilding and reform. Brunswick-Lüneburg, another rising state in the late seventeenth century — its senior line acquired an electoral title in 1692 and the two main territories of the House of Welf, Lüneburg and Calenberg, were united as the electorate of Hanover in 1705 — was distracted from Germany by the acquisition of the British throne in 1714. After that Hanover was very much a side-show. Sweden's power in northern Germany was destroyed in the Great Northern War (1700–21). Other possible rivals, such as Denmark and Hesse-Cassel, lacked the opportunities and resources to challenge Brandenburg-Prussia.

As well as marking the arrival of Prussia as a great power, the Seven Years' War also roused general expectations of change in

Germany: a period of instability, which had lasted since 1740, seemed to have come to an end in 1763. Strangely for the "Age of Reason", there was in some quarters in the 1760s a millenarian atmosphere, with predictions of an imminent spiritual revolution, the greatest overturning since the Reformation, which would sweep away ignorance and allow the victory of Reason. The war was followed by a pause in the struggle between Prussia and Austria, which was only to become serious again in the late 1770s as a result of Joseph II's policies. 1764 saw the election and coronation of Joseph as king of the Romans. The failing health of his father, Francis I, was the main reason for the election. This event, attended by considerable pomp and ceremonial, was widely seen as a new beginning for the *Reich* and a symbol of its new unity. Joseph was the first king or Emperor elected by all the electors without dissent and no new restrictions were placed on him in his capitulation of election. These facts were commented on by some contemporaries as an optimistic sign for the future.

The Seven Years' War also contributed to political change in Germany, as a result of which the predominant form of government in Germany became enlightened or reforming absolutism. Under its influence many German states underwent substantial modernization. Prussia and Austria were able to recover from the devastation of the war and to consolidate their power. This in turn enabled the Holy Roman Empire to survive as the dualism of the two great powers guaranteed its existence. They were strong enough to prevent foreign domination of Germany but neither was strong enough to destroy the other.

There is continuing controversy about the nature of enlightened absolutism, whether any such thing ever existed and, if it did, the reasons for it. It was partly a result of the new ideas circulating in Europe from the late seventeenth century, with a much more optimistic view of man's capacity to change the world in which he lived in contrast to the essentially pessimistic assumptions which underlay much of classic absolutism. Man was seen as possessing an ability to change his fate and to be capable of progress and even perfection, which could be achieved by the application of Reason. The Enlightenment was a cosmopolitan international movement. It concerned itself primarily with cultural and philosophical questions. Initially its impact was intellectual rather than political but it did eventually have political results. It is a good illustration of the power of intellectual ideas to produce change in society though it would be dangerous to exaggerate the extent to which these new ideas overcame the resistance of vested interests, the stubbornness of popular religious enthusiasm and the innate conservatism of rural societies.

The alliance of absolutism and the Enlightenment was very much a marriage of convenience. Enlightened absolutism involved no change in the form of government — like "pure" absolutism it was based on the principle of everything for the people but nothing by the people — but, as new ideas spread, there were significant changes in perceptions of the objectives of the state or a reordering of priorities between the different tasks of government. Governments were now seen as having a duty to promote the happiness of their subjects as well as security and order. Concepts which had long been circulating among limited groups of intellectuals, such as the implied contract between ruler and ruled and the ruler's duty to promote the welfare and happiness of his subjects as a community, began to gain a wider following. These were not foreign imports into Germany but were rooted in the natural law teachings of Christian Thomasius (1655–1728) and Christian Wolff (1679–1754), both professors at Halle university. Wolff in particular developed social contract theory, from which he justified an extension of the power of the state: when man entered the contract, he gave up his freedom in return for justice, peace and order. Their explorations of the notions of the promotion of the common good and the happiness of mankind as duties of the state were also important in legitimizing authority. Also very influential were journals like Christoph Friedrich Nicolai's *Allgemeine deutsche Bibliothek*, founded in 1765. There was a "publications explosion" after 1770, a huge increase in the number of new journals being published, accompanied by a proliferation of reading circles and the like, a development often encouraged by the princes. In 1740 260 journals were founded, between 1770 and 1780 718 and between 1780 and 1790 1 225. Censorship in Germany was patchy and the press was often freest in the tiny states and the largest ones. There were oddities: Joseph II's government censored religious works of superstition but allowed the publication of free-thinking works. The journals were overwhelmingly philosophical and religious in content, catering for the two leading hobbies of educated Germans, and only marginally political.

Another important aspect of the German Enlightenment was the campaign of "popular enlightenment" (*Volksaufklärung*), which sought to overcome the social exclusivity of knowledge by making available the teachings of the Enlightenment to the adult common man, the

Volk, defined by contemporaries as those with a limited education, especially the rural population. From the mid-eighteenth century academic economists, the cameralists, became increasingly concerned with agricultural improvement and governments encouraged the formation of private societies to promote the new agriculture. The products of individuals, societies and governments offered advice and instruction on a fascinating variety of economic, social, veterinary, agricultural and health matters. What distinguished them from the mass of advice which rained down on the Germans from their governments was the undisguised intention to change mentalities, to teach the practical application of reason in daily life and to educate the people away from an unthinking acceptance of traditional attitudes and practices, which was seen as the badge of unenlightenment.[3]

There were also practical reasons for enlightened absolutism. After the Seven Years' War governments were faced with new and pressing problems, for which the old solutions were no longer effective. Marked economic expansion began again in the German states about 1740 with the onset of sustained population growth. The population of Europe as a whole began to rise from about 1750, there were inflationary pressures and governments were faced with the problem of meeting the higher costs of administration and warfare. Military considerations were as central to enlightened absolutism as they had been to traditional absolutism. The Seven Years' War, in its great length, world-wide nature and the size of the forces involved, caused huge losses in money and manpower. Prussia was especially hard-hit, losing at least 180 000 soldiers, largely a result of Frederick II's tactics of deliberately seeking confrontation with the enemy, and massive civilian losses.

The need for substantial internal reconstruction and another round of modernization and state-building was obvious. The inherent strains in absolutism were also becoming clear, especially the fact that it had achieved at best a partial modernization, administrative and military reform, but remained politically and socially conservative. This was a problem which was never resolved and there was always an ambivalence or even a lack of logic in enlightened government, a desire to change some things but not others. A second wave of modernization was needed and it was carried out in some German states.

The achievement of Frederick II in Prussia was not to change the basis of the Prussian state but to make the system work more efficiently and to try to apply reason to its working. It was the modification of his father's system which enabled Frederick and Prussia to survive the near-disasters of the Seven Years' War. Frederick was also responsible for important economic, judicial and educational reforms.[4] The years after 1763 saw a massive opening up of new land for cultivation by drainage, clearances and deforestation, with particularly beneficial results in the new land acquired in the first partition of Poland. Judicial torture was abolished in 1754, an example followed in other states, though some retained it into the nineteenth century. The use of cruel punishments, except for desertion from the army, also declined sharply. Frederick abolished serfdom on the royal domains but was unable to persuade the majority of the nobility to do the same on their lands. His attempt to deal with the financial problems of his state by means of the fiscal experiment of a general excise on the French model was not very successful and very unpopular. Of greater significance was his creation of the Prussian Giro Bank in 1765, which issued notes. It was to be twenty years before this was copied in Austria in the form of the Vienna Commercial Bank.

Frederick's codification of the civil law, the *Allgemeine Landrecht*, was also a significant reform and characteristic of enlightened absolutism. The first draft produced by Frederick's commission was ready in 1784. Its main framers, Carl Gottlieb Svarez and Ernst Ferdinand Klein, were strongly influenced by natural law theories and saw a law code as a substitute for a written constitution. It contained restrictions on royal powers but these were deleted from the final version published in 1794. During the drafting of the code Frederick consulted "public opinion" in the form of the noble-dominated Estates. As a result the code retained relics of the *Ständestaat* (society of rigidly defined orders) in the form of noble privileges. Such compromises between the progressive and the reactionary were common in many states. The code was not revolutionary but of great symbolic importance. It regulated relations between the government and the governed and laid down the rights of various social groups.

Prussia under Frederick II typified the partial modernization characteristic of enlightened absolutism. In general, reform at the top did not deeply affect the corporate structure of society and the old pre-absolutist institutional structures were not destroyed. Alexis de Tocqueville summed up the enlightened absolutist state well as "a modern head on a Gothic body". The state remained an alien corporation set over the people but not of them.

A similar process of reform was seen in Austria under Maria Theresa and Joseph II, who attempted to modernize the country after Austria came close to dismemberment in the Austrian Succession War.[5] Both were strongly influenced by the Prussian model. In the later years of Charles VI's reign Austria had gone to sleep and stagnated and there was an urgent need to catch up. Earlier reform had too often taken the form of tinkering and improvisation. Under the influence of Friedrich Wilhelm Haugwitz, a rational root-and-branch reform of the administrative, financial, judicial and military organization of the Habsburg lands was carried through. In the process Austria was converted into a state, not just a collection of provinces sharing the same ruler. The opposition of the Estates and other institutions of the old system was simply brushed aside. A second bout of reform and modernization followed the Seven Years' War. Joseph II tried to complete the process in a great rush, bringing several parts of his lands near to open revolt. A sharp reaction followed the death of Emperor Leopold II in 1792.

Perhaps in the past there has been too much concentration on the "great" German enlightened despots and not enough study of the smaller states. There was enormous variation within Germany but educated Germans came to regard enlightened despotism as their own particular and superior form of government, based as it was on reason not force. Some lesser German rulers also tried to put into effect the ideas of the Enlightenment. Most are not remembered by history but they were often able to achieve more than their better-known colleagues because they were not distracted by great power pretensions and could devote themselves more assiduously to internal affairs. States like Baden and Saxe-Weimar were, by the standards of the time, well-governed. After 1763 there were significant enlightened reforms in Saxony under the regent Maria Anthonia and the Elector Frederick Augustus III, who assumed power in 1768. The existence of the Empire helped: even though weak, it acted as an umbrella protecting the small states.[6] Even in the ecclesiastical states there was a new spirit of enlightened Catholicism, typified in the movement known as Febronianism, which advocated the formation of a reformed German national Church free of all papal control. One motive behind this appeal to the old tradition of "German liberty" by the German bishops was hostility to Joseph II's infringements of the rights of the Church in Austria.[7]

Enlightened absolutism also did nothing to strengthen national feeling. Its emphasis was exclusively on the prince and the state. The power of the individual state was further enhanced as it came to be seen as a source of progress as well as the preserver of order. The later eighteenth century also saw definite signs of a kind of local nationalism or patriotism appearing in Germany. The motivation behind these campaigns was the promotion of dynastic loyalty. The main concern of those in power was to preserve their position not to change Germany as a whole. Prussia was supremely a state: it had millions of non-Germans in its eastern provinces after the partitions of Poland but all subjects were equal in their subordination to the state and their right to enjoy the protection of the state and no distinctions were drawn on the basis of language or nationality. During Frederick II's reign the Prussian clergy were used to promote this and there are examples of the same policy at work elsewhere. Frederick's attitude to Germany was ambivalent. In his instructions for teachers in Prussian high schools he laid down that German history and politics were to be taught. In his *Ode to the Germans* (March 1760), however, he drew a clear distinction between Prussians and Germans and congratulated the former on their fortune in being able to leave a devastated Germany and find a better homeland for themselves. Well into the nineteenth century German writers used the word "nation" indiscriminately with reference to Germany or Prussia, Bavaria and so on.

There was no group or class in Germany strong enough to rival the princes as leaders. The old parliamentary Estates had either disappeared or had been emasculated. The Church, especially in Protestant states but also in many Catholic states, was virtually a department of state used to run the education system, teach obedience as a religious duty and spread the state's propaganda. The peasants, the overwhelming majority of the population, possessed only the negative power to resist change. The majority of peasants in the east were serfs. In the west many were facing growing economic difficulties. A sharp population rise produced growing land hunger and the period after 1770 saw the first major waves of emigration, especially to North America but also to Russia and south eastern Europe. There were also substantial internal migrations within Germany. There were signs of growing discontent against feudal relics, such as hunting rights, but there was no articulated or organized peasant movement. The majority of free cities were inward-looking and sleepy, ruled by conservative oligarchies anxious to keep political power within their own charmed circle. In most the economy was stagnant and dominated by the guilds. Only a few cities like Hamburg, Bremen and Frankfurt, which experienced economic expansion in the later eighteenth century, were prosperous and cosmopolitan, but they tended to look away from Germany into the Atlantic or France. Even in these more open cities power remained in the hands of a small elite and religious toleration was limited.[8] Localism remained very powerful. In spite of that, it was to be in the great commercial cities and some of the larger princely capitals that a new middle class began to emerge in the later eighteenth century.

Real power in Germany remained in the hands of the nobility and the rising and expanding class of officials. The administrations of many German states were in the hands of highly educated and trained bureaucrats, often strongly influenced by enlightened ideas. Administration was becoming increasingly professional. In 1770 a system of examinations for aspirant bureaucrats was introduced in Prussia, though it was not always strictly enforced because of Frederick II's preference for noble servants. In the later eighteenth century a strong *esprit de corps* grew up among the upper ranks of the administrators. They began to see themselves as members of a corporation, servants of the state rather than the prince, with a duty to defend the general welfare not only against vested interests but also against tyrannical rulers. Sometimes enlightened government is too closely identified with the person of the prince when in reality the impetus for progressive change came from reforming civil servants trying to push through reforms against the opposition of timid or conservative rulers or colleagues. In spite of absolutism, active politics were something which went on within the small ruling class and often involved real clashes of principle.

Although the Enlightenment did not provide a political blueprint, in later years of the eighteenth century, from about 1770, it began to take on a political tinge. By subjecting the contemporary situation to critical eyes, Enlightenment ideas opened the door to a movement for political change. Long-accepted institutions came to be questioned and measured for their usefulness or otherwise against criteria established by the Enlightenment, which asked the basic question: "Is it reasonable that. . .?" This test could be, and was, applied to monarchy, old privileges and customs, the mercantilist economic system, witch-trials, which continued into the 1770s, religious exclusiveness and the old colonial system, among others. There were also growing divisions of opinion about what exactly Enlightenment was.

In the German context religious issues were a major theme in the political debate. There were mounting attacks on irrational survivals in some free cities and ecclesiastical states, such as the use of the catechism to teach a political message, that it was sinful to disobey one's prince, to refuse to pay taxes or to neglect one's duties to social superiors. Many secular princes longed to get their hands on Church lands, which they saw as wastefully administered under the dead hand of the Church. There were among the ecclesiastical states some very glaring exceptions to enlightened despotism and attacks on clerical abuses did not all stem from self-interest. There were also more frequent attacks on religious exclusiveness and evidence of a more tolerant atmosphere in the later eighteenth century. Writers came out in favour of ending legal disabilities on the Jews. There were rationalist attacks on superstition in the Church, a questioning of the value of monasticism, campaigns against the Jesuits, culminating in the suppression of the order in 1774, and calls for tighter state controls on the Church.

Joseph II of Austria showed the way by his policies of religious toleration and various measures of modernization of the administration of the Church. In October 1781 he introduced religious toleration and subsequently introduced a series of measures which amounted to a nationalization of the Church. Joseph shared the view, common in Protestant Germany, that religious clergy were idle and useless and, by providing charity, encouraged idleness in the people at large. He closed a large number of monasteries and convents which had gone into sharp decline from the middle of the century. His attacks on the Church were very unpopular with the majority of the Austrian people, over whom the Church still had a powerful hold. Joseph's actions were especially significant. The Church had played a major role in the growth of the Austrian state from the sixteenth century. The carefully constructed system of baroque religious observance and imagery known as *Pietas Austriaca*, under which the Catholic Church and the dynasty mutually reinforced one another, was very important. This alliance was intensified by the wars against the Turks in the late seventeenth century, which were officially portrayed as crusades. Strict religious uniformity was enforced; only in Silesia, and the small portion of it left to Austria after 1745, was Protestantism tolerated. At the same time, the Habsburgs resisted outside interference with their control of the Church. Charles VI banned all appeals to Rome and the activities of the Church courts were severely restricted. Maria Theresa, although a pious Catholic, sharply reduced the clergy's influence on education and censorship and introduced limited religious toleration in Moravia. This was mirrored in other German states. For example, Bavaria banned further land transfers to the Church in 1764.

The institution of monarchy was also being questioned from both reactionary and progressive wings of opinion. Enlightened rulers were faced with hostility from a range of vested interests for carrying out too much reform and from progressives for carrying out too little. Some rulers saw the writing on the wall: perhaps the best-known example is the advice given by Joseph II in letters to his sister and her husband, the Queen and King of France. He warned them that they must either reform from above or there would be enforced reform from below. The concept of the monarch as first servant of state was available for use against unsatisfactory princes as new standards against which a ruler's performance could be measured emerged. The Duke of Württemberg Charles Eugene (1737–93) was attacked as a typical small-state despot because of his tyrannical treatment of his Estates in the early part of his reign. In the 1780s the rulers of Hesse-Cassel accumulated a huge fortune from their notorious trade in mercenaries, which made them an object of contempt, though they were not the only German rulers who engaged in this business. This also tended to overshadow the substantial achievements of the landgrave Frederick II in reconstructing his country after the devastation of the Seven Years' War.

Some commentators were concluding before the French Revolution that monarchy was dispensable if it did not make itself an instrument of reform. This was symbolized in literary attacks on tyranny, such as Schiller's *Don Carlos* (1787). Here the figure of Philip II of Spain, brutal, bigoted, suspicious and capricious, embodied everything which was wrong with tyrannical monarchy. Schiller's suggested solution was an enlightened prince relying on the guidance of an enlightened minister, Don Carlos and Posa.

Often the practical solutions suggested for bad government were, to say the least, naive: the ruler was to be carefully educated from birth. Bad princes were to be prevailed upon to abdicate and declare republics. The subjects of a bad ruler should pray hard for a better one next time. Other more realistic commentators favoured the creation of the *Rechtsstaat*, the state based on law, in which the powers of the government would be clearly defined in a written law code, which was actually happening in some German states.

A few rulers took the next logical step, abandoning monarchical absolutism once the people were held to be ready for responsible self-government. The best example is Joseph II's brother Peter Leopold,

Grand Duke of Tuscany, probably the greatest of the enlightened rulers but too little known. He was responsible for a large number of beneficial reforms in the Habsburg secundogeniture Tuscany, culminating in the proposal to set up the beginnings of a democratic system of government. This plan was vetoed by Joseph II, who feared the impact of the example in the Austrian lands. Peter Leopold became the Emperor Leopold II in 1790 but died two years later. His premature death was a severe blow to enlightened reform in Austria as there was a sharp reaction under his son and successor Francis II.

Some contemporary commentators believed that the logical next step, self-government, could be achieved through a modernized form of the old Estates. There was a minor renaissance of some of the German Estates in the late eighteenth century, with a revival of interest in constitutionalism, though most progressives condemned the Estates as totally reactionary, representing self-centred oligarchies and providing no foundation for democracy or Liberalism.[9]

Political debate was sharpened by serious economic and social problems which hit Germany after the Seven Years' War. During the war inflation was rampant in Prussia and other states and it was followed by the first severe depression since the first decade of the century. During this slump dozens of companies in the Netherlands and the German states, which had expanded rapidly during the war, went bankrupt. Another more severe economic depression came in the early 1770s. 1771 and 1772 saw serious harvest failures, leading to high mortality and unemployment.[10] This was the first serious subsistence crisis since 1708–12 and even well-organized states, which normally maintained full grain stores to meet emergencies, had problems, especially as some had sold grain to France to make a windfall profit before the full effects of the crisis were felt in Germany. The population was growing rapidly and strains in the economy were becoming very obvious. The population of Germany rose from an estimated twenty millions in 1750 to about twenty-four in 1800. In some parts, especially the Rhineland and the south west, overpopulation was becoming a serious problem. Prussia, which saw the fastest growth, was fortunate in having large areas of underpopulated land available. Other areas, such as Alpine Bavaria, saw no population growth, which would suggest that the rise was caused by specific local factors rather than general climatic, economic or medicinal change. The main cause was probably earlier marriage, made possible by the spread of manufacturing in rural areas, which gave country-dwellers alternative sources of income and freed them from traditional dependence on agriculture. The decline of the guilds, which had also artificially delayed the marriage of apprentices, also played a part.

If food supplies did become more secure because of climatic improvements and increased output, as some historians argue, it did not improve life for the majority of Germans but simply kept them alive to become chronically poor. The growth of a substantial underclass, in both town and country, was the subject of considerable contemporary comment. Pauperism again became a serious problem. It is estimated that after 1763 as many as a quarter of the population of Germany lived close to destitution. In spite of absolutism and the rain of *Polizeiordnungen* which had fallen on Germany, marginal groups were never eliminated from society. Mendicants and other dangerous classes, groups regarded as threatening and useless, like gypsies, itinerants and those without a fixed place in the social order, were becoming a growing menace in the countryside. The political division of the Empire made the apprehension of criminals who escaped from one jurisdiction to another very difficult. Only notorious criminals, for whose capture large rewards were offered, were likely to be caught. The widespread use of banishment, which amounted to social death, as a punishment added to the numbers of the dangerous classes. In towns and cities a growing number were in receipt of some form of poor relief. Work was seen as the best remedy for such problems and the period after the war saw a sharp increase in the number of workhouses and the like, where the indigent were confined.

At the same time new attitudes to the economy were beginning to appear with the spread of the theories of Adam Smith and the Physiocrats. These involved the revolutionary idea that, if each individual were free to pursue his own best interests, the whole of society would gain by the mysterious operation of the Hidden Hand. There was a dawning realization that poverty and other social ills were not caused by fecklessness but by flaws in the social system. The individual's ambition and desire to possess were reasonable and desirable and should be encouraged as a contribution to the common good. Economic progress was to be achieved by removing restraints on the economy. There were calls for the free movement of land, capital, labour and goods, all of which flew in the face of the prevailing economic and social system. The first translation of Smith's *Wealth of Nations* into German appeared in 1776 and his ideas quickly gathered a substantial following among academics. The basic ideas underlying the science of economic management began to change as leading exponents of cameralism, taught in most German universities, adopted the view that excessive state regulation of the economy was hindering rather than fostering its growth. The universities of Königsberg and Göttingen became centres for the diffusion of Smith's ideas and they began to exercise a growing influence on the generation of young men entering the German bureaucracies at this time. Political objectives remained predominant: states wanted to make more people work and people work more.

In practical terms the impact was limited. In order to be successful, a free market economy has certain prerequisites, productive agriculture and manufactures, a strong independent economic middle class and ample capital resources. Before the French Revolution such conditions were only to be found in a few areas of Germany, for example the northern Rhineland, where the old economic system was already breaking down. There was nothing resembling a German national economy at the time but rather a series of economic zones over and above individual states. The main problem was the high cost of transport but the fragmentation of the economy was a major cause of its weakness; barriers between and within states, especially in the form of toll stations, slowed down economic movement. There were at least thirty such barriers on the Rhine.

The economic picture in rural areas was also, with a few exceptions, bad. German agriculture was, in general, very inefficient as the great majority of those engaged in it were subsistence farmers. The backwardness of agriculture was a major barrier to modernization. The predominant crop, grain, was unsuitable to conditions in many parts of Germany but the peasants were very resistant to innovations. There was great reluctance to adopt new crops and techniques, though the famine of the early 1770s hastened acceptance of the potato. Rural economic individualism was very rare as there were few incentives or opportunities to improve cultivation even when urban markets were easily available. In areas where the peasants' tenure was favourable, such as the south west, land hunger and high rents and taxes made improvements difficult.

Some form of personal unfreedom was the predominant situation of the majority of the peasantry, though there were enormous variations from place to place and complex gradations of serfdom from hereditary *Leibeigenschaft*, the harshest form common in the eastern lands, through various forms of *Erbuntertänigkeit* (hereditary unfreedom) to little more than ceremonial relics in parts of the west. The institution of serfdom was coming in for attack for both economic and humanitarian motives. The system was portrayed as inefficient and wasteful of time, energy and enterprise. Many governments tried to carry through a conversion of services into money rents and to give peasants secure leases. There were problems everywhere arising from the peasants' deep conservatism, which led them to view all change with deep suspicion, and their lack of capital to invest in new methods. Unfortunately attempts to abolish serfdom also created problems. Governments often prevented reform by stopping landlords evicting their peasants in order to farm the land more efficiently. The state had a vested interest in restricting the mobility of the population to keep its taxpayers and recruits under control. Any proposed reform came up against the very difficult problem regarding the ultimate ownership of the serf's land: did it belong to the lord or the peasant? Attempts by enlightened monarchs like Frederick II and Maria Theresa to persuade lords to commute labour services into money rents by example had very limited success. Frederick abolished serfdom on royal domains and brought in a system of leases for the holders of royal lands under which the peasants were protected against abuse. Joseph II abolished serfdom in Austria in 1781, building on his mother's work, but this had to be withdrawn in 1790 by his successor as it was far too sweeping and revolutionary. A return to a voluntary approach had little real effect

The picture in manufacturing was little better. The guilds, with their power base in many free cities, represented a substantial force and could not easily be brushed aside. There were many strongly-worded attacks on their stultifying practices, especially after the temporary abolition of the powers of the French guilds in 1774. In Germany imperial legislation gave the states the right to reform the guilds and remove abuses, but few dared to challenge such a powerful vested interest and the guilds continued to play a major role in German manufacturing until the middle years of the nineteenth century.[11] Governments were also nervous about challenging the guilds because of the growing social tensions in many towns, usually caused by economic problems.

In some areas manufacturers migrated outside towns to escape guild restrictions. Such was the case in the north west, where vigorous textile and metal-working centres developed including Monschau in Jülich and Verviers in the Austrian Netherlands. A mixed system became common, with certain basic processes, for example spinning and weaving, carried on in peasant households under the putting out system and finishing processes in large centralized workshops. This proto-industrialization advanced rapidly in some areas; in 1789 over half the population of Berg was in non-agricultural employment.

The first mechanized factories were also operating before the French Revolution. There were large textile works, foundries and glassworks employing thousands in Berlin, Linz, Vienna, the Rhineland and Saxony but they were the exception. State-run industries remained very important to the economies of many states but few were strong enough to survive without state aid. The aim was that they would eventually become self-sufficient but this was rarely achieved. Too often governments did not allow their enterprises enough time to grow before beginning to raid their funds. Over-regulation was a constant problem, with civil servants interfering in enterprises following the fashionable economic nostrums of the time. Private consumption was very restricted. The state, usually the army, remained the main consumer of manufactured goods. Among private individuals only the nobility, the higher clergy and richer townspeople disposed of significant purchasing power. State-encouraged economic growth was not always a total failure and state enterprises, though they rarely reached the objectives set for them, may well have helped to alleviate some of the damaging effects of the economic backwardness of Germany. Some state initiatives were reasonably successful: Frederick II was responsible for significant improvements in the economy of Prussia, in particular in agriculture, which helped to sustain a larger population. He left a full treasury, a favourable trade balance and expanding output. The Austrian economy also improved under Maria Theresa and Joseph II: new lands were settled and commerce and manufactures were promoted, though Austria, like most German states, accumulated very large debts in the later eighteenth century.

If change in the German economy was slow, social change was speeding up in Germany after 1770 in the sense that the traditional distribution of economic, political and social power between the different social classes was coming under challenge. Social change is traditionally understood as *progressive* change, that is movement away from a closed and rigid social system towards a more open one in which social mobility is easier. The period saw challenges to the entrenched social position of the nobility and urban patriciates, which was not held to be reasonable. The nobles no longer played a vital role in society but still enjoyed privileges, usually including a monopoly of land designated as noble, tax exemptions, patrimonial jurisdiction and police powers over their peasant "subjects", ecclesiastical patronage, hunting rights, social predominance and guaranteed access to certain fields of employment. One problem was that nobility was still seen as the main source of status: too much wealth made in trade or public service was effectively sterilized by the purchase of titles and land to give noble status. The period saw the beginning of a challenge to this, as the middle classes grew in size and confidence and began to question the special rights of the nobles.

The old order, based on the notion of a division of society into well-defined Estates, was beginning to change well before the French Revolution although no well-defined new system, based on modern classes or individualism, had appeared to replace the older social order. Germany had entered a period of flux or transition, the outcome of which was unclear. The absolutist state, with its desire to simplify the social order and its downgrading of the old feudal relationships, was an important agent of this change. There were also new attitudes on the status of women and the role of the family.

The old *Ständestaat* was based on the concept of social inequality; the new idea of equality before the law was beginning to develop to challenge it. The growing self-confidence of a new middle class was measurable. There were enormous variations between state and state and town and town but certain trends were clear. There was a large "old" conservative middle class in the smaller towns and cities, with many of its members enjoying special privileged status, like the clergy and university staff and students, and a "new" progressive middle class alongside and often overlapping with it. A party of movement, of progressive opinions, was appearing. An early expression of this was found in the Patriotic societies, devoted to discussion and work for the good of the fatherland, which spread in the 1760s. Secret societies also played a part. The first German Free Masonic lodge was set up in Hamburg in 1737 to be followed by hundreds more. The reading circles which proliferated in the later eighteenth century were sometimes a cover for secret activities. The growth of these societies symbolized the development of a completely new form of voluntary association very different from the old institutions like the Estates, guilds and Churches, which had earlier determined peoples' view of their place in society but which were now becoming visibly weaker. They often went in for a great deal of rather silly ceremonial but they allowed mixing under circumstances of equality of nobles and non-nobles which boosted growing middle-class self-confidence. With the publications explosion, they contributed to the development of a middle-class consciousness (*bürgerliche Öffentlichkeit*), which envisaged a society of equal citizens rather than of *Stände*.

Central to the thinking of this group was the notion of mobility, social and physical, manifested in a desire to travel, something earlier restricted to a few. Status had to be earned and could not be possessed, like noble status, purely because of an accident of birth. The Patriot societies and other progressive associations were open to all those who were of a proper background and had the correct attitudes; once admitted, all members were held to be equal. A more favourable view of commerce and its practitioners began to appear in literature after a long period when the merchant was looked down on by members of the university-educated professional middle class. The concept of the citizen (*Staatsbürger*) with civic rights (*bürgerliche Rechte*) and the right to participate in the life of the state was well established. This right did not belong to all men but had to be earned by the possession of certain qualities and certain behaviour, increasingly identified with middle-class virtues and summed up in the word *Bildung* (education and cultivation).

Access to university education and the emergence of the concept of all-round education contributed to growing pride in middle-class achievement. Another factor was the rise of an all-German middle class, a group of mobile educated and professional people, including academics, students, officials, officers, diplomats, musicians and projectors, whose links with their *enges Vaterland* (narrow fatherland, the individual state in which they lived) weakened as they moved around the *Reich*. One feature of all this was a growing knowledge of and interest in the history of Germany and a better appreciation of how it had developed to its "monstrous" state.

A recent study of the French Revolution[12] has drawn attention to the great intensity and mobilizing power of a new form of patriotism which emerged in France after the Seven Years' War. This produced a new concept of citizenship which took precedence over regional, class or group loyalties, taught that all patriotic citizens had a duty to involve themselves in state affairs and began to breach the walls between the state and private spheres so typical of the *ancien régime*. While various factors produced a more restrained situation in Germany, it is clear that something similar existed there in the later eighteenth century. When the French Revolution broke out, many German intellectuals saw this as an attempt by the French to win for themselves by force what the Germans had already won by thought, in itself significant. By the beginning of the eighteenth century French fashions and habits had taken Germany by storm. This was true of all Europe but was especially strong in Germany and was commented on unfavourably by patriots. By the end of the century there were changes in German literature, a kind of intellectual revolution which led to a weakening of French influence. At first there was no national political content but this gradually changed. Although it was still very much a minority movement, the numbers of those who saw themselves as patriots or *Vaterlandsfreunde* were increasing.

The concept of the good citizen or patriot was political, social and moral: he was seen as having a duty to act as a model in his personal life, to involve himself in the community (*die gemeine Sache*) and to work for the common good of the fatherland, rising above the narrow class, occupational, religious or regional group to which he belonged. The Patriot movement represented a kind of political Third Way between the corporative state of Estates, regarded as reactionary, and the enlightened absolute monarchy and a middle culture between the frenchified courts and nobility and traditional regional *altständisch* culture. It was based on the involvement of the people, by which was understood the middle classes, in the state and in that lay the roots of popular sovereignty, democracy and modern nationalism.

If this was something recognizable as early nationalism, it was cultural rather than political, based on the notion of the linguistic spiritual *Kulturnation*, an "inner Germany", which would survive even if there was no *Staatsnation*, political unity. There was a growing movement to promote the use of the German language. Christian Thomasius used German rather than Latin in his lectures in the late seventeenth century, a revolutionary step at the time. Between 1774 and 1786 the German dictionary of J. C. Adelung was published in several volumes. One element in growing middle-class self-confidence was seen in a reaction against French fashions and resentment of the social predominance of the French language, which was seen as light and trivial. A mixture of class and national resentment was growing up.

In Germany the issue was complicated by the fact that every German had two states, the territorial state and the *Reich*. "Fatherland" could mean either of these or the German nation as an abstract cultural entity without borders. German patriotism was therefore innately ambivalent: it could lead to support for the untrammelled freedom of the individual states (*Staatssouveränität*) to liberate the reforming urges of progressive rulers, or for a revitalization of the imperial constitution as a barrier against the despotism of an unenlightened prince. A majority of the German patriots accepted that the essence of a good political system was one in which the only limits on freedom were those made necessary by the common good and in which there was some mechanism to restrain or moderate the exercise of power. This could include enlightened public opinion formed by a free press, written constitutions or law codes, creating the state based on law (*Rechtsstaat*), intermediate powers, such as parliamentary institutions and privileged corporations, or the imperial laws and tribunals. All could act as a barrier to tyranny.

Political debate in Germany became more lively under the impact of the American Revolution, between 1763 and 1783.[13] Some German thinkers were beginning to break out of Aristotelian concepts of the state and society as inseparable and were moving towards Liberal notions of the minimal state and self-regulating society, though it all remained in the realm of ideas. Up to that point the majority of progressive thinkers in Germany had admired the British constitution as a model. The American constitution was seen as the first practical application of things which had previously existed only in theory or were mistakenly believed to exist in England, such as the division of powers, popular sovereignty, a society without a nobility, equality before the law, the absence of an established Church, a federal system, a republic (a form of government which in Europe was known from Poland and Venice and was equated with weakness and decline), a written constitution and a free economy. America was far enough away from Europe to be romanticized. Not many commentators advocated the imitation of the American example in Germany, which was anyway seen as not needing a revolution but only more reform under its enlightened rulers.

Another effect of this quickening debate was that the new ideas were being answered by spokesmen for an articulate and intelligent conservatism, based on an organic view of the state and society and respect for traditions. J. J. Moser rejected enlightened absolutism as a false panacea for states (*Univeral-Staats-Medizin*), which would destroy traditional rights. These writers offered a defence of strong monarchy, the nobility and religious exclusiveness, among other things. Noble privilege was defended with the claim that the nobility was vital to the stability of the whole social order and, not being motivated by ambition and greed, provided the natural servants of the crown. This was a view strongly held by Frederick II.

The years after 1763 saw the foundations of the bodies of ideas which were to blossom in the nineteenth century into organized political Liberalism and Conservatism. The practical effects of the debate were limited and the changes which have been described affected only a tiny group at the top of German society. The great majority of Germans remained largely unaffected but there was a mounting atmosphere of expectation of change in the 1770s and 1780s.

The German question continued to concern the rest of Europe. French influence remained important and was accompanied by growing Russian influence, arising from intermarriage between the Romanoffs and German dynasties. In the years after the Treaty of Aix la Chapelle of 1748 Russia became an official guarantor of the imperial constitution, replacing Sweden in that role. Germany remained very much a side-show in European affairs. Internally it seemed to have settled down into a state of equilibrium, only occasionally troubled by small problems. Among these was the Württemberg constitutional dispute in the 1760s, which saw the last major intervention of the imperial aulic council in the internal affairs of a substantial state of the Empire. The Protestant constitutional establishment there was guaranteed by Hanover, Prussia and Denmark. In 1759 the prominent jurist and leader of the Estates, Johann Jakob Moser, was imprisoned by the duke, who was trying to bring in an absolutist system of government. In 1764 military force was used against the Estates when they protested against the duke's illegal taxation. After litigation the case was settled in favour of the Estates in 1770. Thereafter the Duke Charles Eugene became an enlightened ruler and promoted commerce and education. He abandoned military ambitions and was seen as a model ruler by the end of his reign.[14]

Another minor problem was the so-called Potato War (or War of the Bavarian Succession) 1778–9. This arose out of the succession problem in the Wittelsbach electorates, Bavaria and the Palatinate, which had run out of male heirs. The Bavarian male line died out in 1777 and its territory was inherited by the elector palatine, who also had no male heirs. Joseph II, who claimed a share of the inheritance as husband of the sister of the last Elector of Bavaria, was very eager to gain Bavarian territory. The whole thing could have been settled between Prussia and Austria to their mutual benefit but mistrust between them was too great. Eventually the whole inheritance passed to a cadet line of the Wittelsbachs. Frederick II was very nervous about the Austrian threat to Prussia and Joseph II's need to demonstrate his power. After a brief "war", in which the two armies avoided meeting one another, the whole matter was settled with French and Russian mediation by the Peace of Teschen in 1779.

Rivalry between Austria and Prussia deepened as a definite attempt to revive Austrian power in Germany to rival Prussia was launched. Habsburg candidates, including some of Maria Theresa's large brood of sixteen children, were elected to a number of important ecclesiastical positions. Joseph II's brother Maximilian Francis took over the sees of Cologne and Münster in 1784. Austria also revived an old scheme, to persuade the Elector of Bavaria to exchange his German possessions for the Austrian Netherlands. In addition to this Joseph had a comprehensive plan to extend Austria deep into southern Germany by exchanging Württemberg and Baden for Austria's Italian possessions, Tuscany and Modena. In the 1780s Joseph tried to revive lapsed imperial rights of presentation to benefices in imperial abbeys and foundations, of which there were almost 300 in the *Reich*, using the aulic council for this purpose. This did nothing to add to the Emperor's popularity in the German Catholic Church. Joseph also proposed a reform of the imperial courts, ignoring the rights of the princes in this matter. The reform was suspected to be a cover for attempts to ensure that the verdicts of the *Reichshofrat* were more uniformly in Austria's political interest and the suspicion was well-founded.

Such actions raised questions about the role of the Emperor. From the 1770s onwards there were calls for reform of the Holy Roman Empire, which even Germans were beginning to see as old-fashioned, but the demand was for a rationalization of the constitution not the abolition of the Empire or the creation of a united German state. National feeling expressed itself in calls for a strengthening of the *Reich* against the larger states, including Austria, which seemed ready to sacrifice the smaller states for their own narrow interests. The partition of Poland was seen as a dreadful warning of what could happen in the *Reich*. The large states were not interested in changing a system which suited their interests. One reason for this was growing fear of Austrian "tyranny" in the Empire, a fear encouraged by Prussian propaganda. This manifested itself in challenges to Austria's right to speak on behalf of the whole *Reich*. One expression of growing disquiet was a revival of the notion of *Drittes Deutschland*, the Third Germany, also known as trialism, the idea that the states which made up Germany without Austria and Prussia should come together in a closer arrangement to defend their independence against the two German great powers. The idea of the *Trias* was refloated in the 1780s by Baden, as a scheme of reform for the *Reich*. This proposed the division of Germany into three states, Austria, Prussia and a confederation of the rest. The period saw growing pressure for a long-overdue inspection of the *Reichskammergericht*, a sign of the desire of some of the smaller states to revive the institutions of the Empire as a means of saving it from the mounting egotism of the large states. In 1775 the *Reichskammergericht* was reformed to speed up its procedures and in 1782 extra judges were appointed, initiating a period of intense judicial activity with the backlog of old cases cleared up and a flood of new litigation.

The *Fürstenbund* (League of Princes), set up by Frederick II in 1785, had its origins in these developments. The League was designed to give Prussia German allies in case Austria tried to attack her after Frederick's death. It was also part of Frederick's scheme to create a Prussian sphere of influence in northern Germany, a security zone under Prussian control to guarantee the survival of the state under a weak ruler. The League was also a symptom of a growing constitutional crisis in the Empire. It began as a movement among some of the medium-sized princes to build a union of the Third Germany and it was only later taken over by Prussia for its own ends, when its original purpose was abandoned. Its stated aim was to preserve the status quo in the German constitution and article four of its act of association committed its members to seek a reform of the imperial supreme courts and to defend them against imperial encroachments. Frederick cynically used the defence of "German liberty" and anti-Catholicism as political weapons in his campaign. Prussia was able to portray the Bavarian exchange scheme as an attack on the *Reich* constitution. The League was joined by Hanover, Saxony, a number of small states and some ecclesiastical states alienated by Joseph II's attacks on the Catholic Church in Austria. Although Prussia was exploiting the Empire for its own purposes, there was a genuine hope among some of the smaller states that it would lead to real *Reichsreform*, calls for which were becoming more frequent.[15] The League was also a sign of reviving suspicion of the Emperor's intentions: Joseph II was seen as a violent and ambitious ruler, who used the Empire for Austrian purposes. The League made a partition of Germany between Prussia and Austria impossible as it amounted to a guarantee of the status quo, though this was not Prussia's intention. Frederick had the role of a national leader thrust upon him. The establishment of the *Fürstenbund* added to the constitutional debates and new questions were asked about the relationship of the Emperor and the Empire.

Disenchantment with the situation was typified in an anonymous pamphlet of 1787, which asked *Warum soll Deutschland einen Kaiser haben?* (Does Germany need an Emperor?) and concluded that the office was now redundant as the whole Empire was against the tide of the times. Such a view was unusual. Politically-informed Germans looking at their country in the later eighteenth century found much to bemoan but also much to praise. Typical was F. C. von Moser's anonymously published study of the German national spirit of 1765 (*Von dem deutschen National-Geist*), which contrasted the potential strength of Germany and the low esteem it enjoyed among its neighbours. Some reacted to the situation with resignation, others with a desire to change things; very few thought in terms of sweeping away the *Reich* and replacing it with something else. For one thing, it was difficult to define acceptable alternatives. There was a widespread view that Germans were singularly fortunate in the constitution of their country, which allowed a wide measure of freedom to the individual states and to individual Germans, while protecting certain basic rights against encroachments. Imperial law guaranteed to all subjects freedom to practise one of three legal religions somewhere in the Empire, freedom of movement within the Empire to all who were not tied to the soil, the right to inherit property anywhere in the Empire, the right to justice in properly conducted courts and the right to security of person and property under the law. Already in the second half of the eighteenth century the modern notion of freedom was beginning to grow up alongside the older tradition of liberties; in the eyes of many commentators the imperial constitution was flexible enough to accommodate and protect both. At the same time the old medieval universalist view, which had seen the *Reich* as the leading state of Christendom and the Emperor as its secular head, was passing away and was being replaced by a new universalism more in tune with the enlightened spirit of the age, a combination of patriotism and cosmopolitanism which saw the advancement of Germany as beneficial to the whole of humanity.

8 The End of the Empire: Germany and the French Revolution

There is still debate among historians whether the French Revolution modernized Germany or brought a period of progress to a sharp end. Before 1789 most of the German states were changing and, though generalization is as always dangerous, certain trends were visible. In many states major reforms had been achieved during the period of enlightened absolutism, resulting in marked improvements in the lives of subjects. Germany was still administratively progressive and economically and socially backward but things were changing. Economic individualism, secularization and social mobility were beginning to appear. Cultural developments were a significant sign of changing attitudes. There is no evidence of mass discontent with government in the majority of the German states but critical middle-class public opinion was becoming an important factor. This was reflected, for example, in attacks on the abuse of power by governments and in propaganda in favour of individual freedoms put forward by writers, though such ideas remained vague and unco-ordinated and there was still nothing resembling an organized opposition party with a coherent political programme.

In the years immediately before the revolution the pace of reform had begun to slow down in many states as opposition from vested interests grew. Important changes also took place in the two leading German states. With the death of Frederick II in 1786 Prussia entered a period of stagnation and in the last year of his reign Joseph II of Austria was facing rebellion in many of his provinces. All this sharpened debate within the ruling and educated classes about the nature and functions of government, in Germany as a whole and in the individual states.

Karl Friedrich Häberlin (1756–1808), an academic lawyer, a practitioner in the *Reichskammergericht* and a diplomat in the service of Brunswick, was a leading advocate of *Reichsreform*. He regarded the imperial courts as the last barrier against despotic government and praised the imperial system for giving Germans a measure of freedom and security, the like of which was only enjoyed by the English. August Ludwig von Schlözer (1735–1809), one of the fathers of German Liberalism, was a pioneer of political journalism in Germany as well as an academic historian and his journal *Statsanzeigen* had the largest circulation of any such publication in Germany. Otto Heinrich Freiherr von Gemmingen (1755–1836), a diplomat, playwright and author, while Badenese envoy in Vienna published a pamphlet *I am a German and want to remain a German (Ich bin ein Deutscher und will ein Deutscher bleiben)*. Wilhelm Ludwig Wekhrlin (1739–92) was a bold and active journalist of advanced views and publisher of a number of magazines, the most famous of which was *Das graue Ungeheuer*. In November 1783 Wilhelm von Edelsheim, chief minister of Baden, put forward a scheme for a union of the Third Germany, excluding the two great powers, plus an institutional reform of the *Reich*. One of the best-known advocates of *Reichsreform*, including a thorough-going modernization of the judicial system, was Karl Theodor von Dalberg, coadjutor of Konstanz and later the last Elector of Mainz.

It is interesting to hypothesize what would have happened had these trends continued. As it was, everything changed after the French Revolution. A French cartoon of 1793 showed the sans-culottes feeding the bread of liberty to various European rulers, including the Emperor, on the points of their bayonets. After 1789, as a result of their military victories, the French took over direct or indirect control of Germany and became the dictators of developments there. Germany experienced an imported revolution.

The years 1789 to 1814 were a very important transitional period in the history of Germany, which experienced rapid kaleidoscopic change.[1] This period saw sharp departures from existing developments and had important long-term effects which deeply influenced developments in the nineteenth century. It witnessed the destruction of the existing German political framework and, at the same time, developments which made it much more difficult to construct a new one. The main changes, in outline, were: the end of the Holy Roman Empire, a further strengthening of Austria, Prussia and the medium-sized states and a rapid modernization of government in many states. A distinct German nationalism emerged, strengthened by the rise of the Romantic Movement. There was also an acceleration in the growth of Liberalism, another important factor in nineteenth-century Germany.

The French Revolution did not burst on Germany from a clear sky. The soil was well prepared and a psychology of expectation was well established. There had been growing debate, at the intellectual level, on a variety of social, economic, political and religious topics from the 1770s onwards. Whereas the American Revolution had caused only a mild flutter, events on Germany's doorstep in the summer of 1789 clearly had a greater effect: they raised the temperature of the debate, although the immediate practical results were very small. Interest remained the preserve of a small group within German society. There was nothing approaching a mass revolutionary movement: in general mass movements were something conspicuously absent from German public life in the eighteenth century. The majority of Germans were apolitical, leading some to talk of a German "spectator psychology": they stood by and watched with interest but did not see the relevance of events in France to their own lives. They were *gedankenvoll aber tatenarm* ("full of theory but short of action"). In spite of superficial similarities between the two countries, there was no spontaneous revolution in any part of Germany.

The first reason must be sought in the character of revolutions.[2] Revolutions happen as the result of a combination of unusual circumstances and cannot be made to occur as an act of will, however much some people might want to bring about radical changes in society. A combination of predisposing factors is necessary. These include an economic crisis so severe as to approach what is called a universal crisis, the existence of a revolutionary class, mass discontent and acts of provocation by the government. A combination of these could turn urban demonstrations against food shortages or peasant riots into a revolution which causes political, economic and social power to migrate irreversibly from one group to another. The old ruling group is eliminated in one way or another and the material base of political power shifts.

In France the revolution originated as a revolt by the privileged nobility against their exclusion from political power and attempts by the royal government to reform the administration, especially the taxation system, as glaring faults had been revealed by the national bankruptcy following French involvement in the War of American Independence. The movement was taken up by elements in the middle class, excluded, in their eyes unfairly, from influence and office. This merged with a wave of urban and rural rioting arising from basic economic grievances, which produced mass pressure at the seat of government in Paris. The French government's response was inconsistent, a mixture of concession and repression. The discontented middle class, instead of trying to reform the existing system, saw an opportunity to overturn it and became a revolutionary class. In 1789 they began by establishing a constitutional monarchy, carried through a series of policies designed to modernize France and took the first steps in a great transfer of property. Once they were in power, divisions among revolutionaries led to growing extremism, the killing of the king, the establishment of a republic and the Terror.

Such developments were unthinkable in Germany, which consisted of hundreds of vested interests. The political, social and economic facts of life in each German state were different: well-run states, politically more advanced than France in 1789, bordered petty tyrannies. It is easier to decide why there was no revolution in, for example, Hesse-Cassel, than in Germany as a whole. Many German rulers were seen as the caring fathers of their people and were personally popular. Radicals like the journalist Christian Schubart might mock the worship of princes but his was an untypical voice. Above all Germany lacked a Paris: there was no similar great concentration of population and political power. Germany had a large number of capitals and centres, economic, political and cultural.

Social conditions were also quite different in the two countries. In most German states the aristocracy was entrenched in power as well as privilege. The states were usually based on an alliance of the crown, the nobles, the urban oligarchies and the bureaucracy. The last were motivated by a desire to improve their states not to revolutionize them. In most states there was still a relatively static society, more traditional and stable and less open to new ideas than that of France. The bulk of the middle class was more conservative and there was, in most cases, no bourgeoisie in the French sense. There was no revolutionary class prepared to give leadership and political direction to a large reservoir of inarticulate discontent, especially among the peasantry and among the poor in towns and cities. The peasants in western Germany were in general much better off than those in France. "Feudalism" survived only in the form of relics, which were in some cases actually beneficial to the peasants. Many states protected them against excessive exploitation and they had recourse to the imperial courts. They often had alternative sources of income. There was little middle-class landownership and the patriarchal relationship between lord and peasant survived. The peasants' position was much worse in the east but there they were usually too cowed to rebel.

There was in Germany a legacy of civic apathy, the product of absolutism and Lutheranism. In spite of changes taking place before the revolution life for most Germans was still organized by the state, the Church, the school, the guild and the extended family. There was a cultivation of negative virtues, such as stability, loyalty and obedience, rather than initiative and individualism. Habits of deference from those who traditionally obeyed towards those who traditionally ruled were deeply-rooted.

It is not surprising, therefore, that most ordinary Germans regarded events in France in the summer of 1789 with indifference. There was tremendous publicity in favour of the revolution, seen by most German intellectuals as a new dawn, a triumph of reason and the rights of man, the victory of liberty over tyranny, intolerance, injustice and oppression. Like the Reformation, whose great liberating work it continued, it was seen as universally relevant and not just a French event. In educated circles there was a general welcome for the written constitution, the abolition of clerical and noble privilege, equality before the law and a career open to talents: it was said, apparently without irony, that the French were trying to establish a state based on sound Prussian principles. Many intellectuals travelled to Paris to "drink at the well-springs of liberty." Louis XVI was now seen as an enlightened ruler on the German model. Revolution and reform initiated from the top were seen as alternative answers to deal with the same problems. Therefore a revolution was quite unnecessary in Germany. In the absence of other political outlets in Germany, enthusiasm for events in France acted as a kind of safety valve.

Of major German intellectuals only a few, including Goethe, opposed the revolution from the beginning. Support in Germany was further stirred up after 1790 by a well-organized French propaganda machine with centres in Strasburg, Basle and Vienna. It also spread through Masonic lodges and reading clubs. It would, however, be wrong to think that enthusiasm for the revolution in Germany was the work of foreign agitators, as German governments tended to do: the conspiracy theory was the easiest explanation of the revolution for conservatives to understand.

There were some more tangible echoes of the revolution in the spring and summer of 1789 and in 1790. There were several peasant and urban riots in various parts of Germany, especially in the

Rhineland. These outbreaks of violence were products of pre-existing problems. Imitation of events just over the border was a new outlet to express long-standing grievances against landlords, employers and governments. The economic troubles which had contributed to the revolutionary crisis in France also affected western Germany. There was agitation among the better-off peasants in areas where serfdom was only an irritating relic, especially the hunting rights retained by the lords. Such outbreaks were isolated and easily dealt with. After 1780 there was a sharp rise in grain, especially rye, prices, from which the free peasants benefited, though real incomes generally fell. The years 1790 to 1806 have been seen as the Golden Age of the Baltic, with huge grain exports and unprecedented prosperity. There was, therefore, less pressure for evictions, which had been a major cause of social grievance in previous decades. Emigration also acted as a safety valve for overpopulation in the west. In the towns there is some evidence that riots arose from economic grievances or from party squabbles within the oligarchies, in which one group used the mob against another.

In Aachen the guild artisans rioted against the introduction of new machines. There were isolated risings in other parts of Germany, usually arising out of local grievances: for example in the Tyrol there were anti-conscription riots and in Breslau and other centres in Silesia troubles caused by losses in the local linen industry because of English competition. The most extensive outbreaks were in Saxony, again arising out of local peasant grievances. The ringleaders used French revolutionary propaganda in their appeals but the troubles faded away when the Saxon government behaved sensibly and made concessions. Only in Austria did the situation approach the universality of crisis which preceded the revolution in France with a serious economic crisis, food shortages, war, unpopular military recruiting and political revolts.

Enthusiasm for the revolution among the majority of German intellectuals did not last long. The growing extremism of the revolutionaries, leading to poverty, civil war, attacks on religion and the Terror, understandably caused wide revulsion. The poet Schiller, given honorary French citizenship in the early days of the revolution, renounced it as an expression of his growing disgust at the violence in France. The French became the object of patronizing attitudes: they were considered to be incapable of fulfilling the promise of their own revolution. One result of this was an idealization of the early stages of the revolution, which, it was believed, had established a modernized state, an emancipated society and unparalleled national unity. In the early years of the nineteenth century German Liberals believed that the French had let their revolution slip into anarchy, by implication a mistake which Germans would not have made.

This disillusionment was increased by a change in French foreign policy. After initially declaring a break from the immoral diplomacy of the old regime, symbolized in the Partition of Poland, and denying any ambitions on the territory of its neighbours, the declaration of peace to the world, the French revolutionary government changed to a policy of seeking the natural frontiers of France, including the river Rhine, which would mean swallowing millions of Germans. The French also embarked on a policy of ideological expansion with promises of help for peoples struggling to be free. Friction between France and German states began from 1790 as the French started to interfere with the rights of the Empire in certain enclaves of German territory within the borders of France, including the extension to them of the abolition of feudalism enacted in France. The French were ready to pay compensation to those who lost as a result but it led to appeals to the Emperor for help from the German rulers involved. The French for their part became increasingly irritated at the activities of counter-revolutionary *émigrés* concentrated at Koblenz and Brussels. There was growing concern on the part of some German governments, seen in attempts to set up *cordons sanitaires* to keep out "the liberty influenza" by preventing the import of French revolutionary propaganda. Some speakers in the *Reichstag* in 1792 proposed a revival of the Circle associations as a means of guaranteeing the integrity of the Empire.

At first most German rulers had seen no threat from the revolution, which they believed was due to the incompetence of Louis XVI, who had not made concessions in time to save a fundamentally sound system of government. Gradually the conspiracy theory came to hold the centre of the stage: the revolution was seen as the work of wicked men and Freemasons. All those wanting change were tarred with the same brush, though the party of movement in Germany was very divided and fragmented. The name "Jacobin" was applied to all those who criticized the existing order. Progressive bureaucrats had to keep their heads down as a rain of repressive edicts fell on Germany. Other measures included the restoration of the death penalty, rigorous censorship, bans on meetings and tighter controls on the universities. Strict censorship was imposed in Prussia in 1794. 1790 also saw the beginning of a spate of conservative propaganda against the revolutionaries, including the use of sermons. There was a general clamp-down on Freemasons and Illuminati, a symptom of the powerful conviction that the revolution was the result of a Masonic plot. Austria also entered a period of reaction which was to last for fifty years. Ironically, the reforming Emperor Joseph II had created a secret police and other organs of repression to use against opponents of his reforms and reactionaries. These were turned against progressives under Francis II. This was seen clearly in the so-called Jacobin trials in Austria.[3]

The whole picture changed radically in April 1792, when the first revolutionary war began. The war arose from the French internal political situation, not from any desire by foreign tyrants to destroy the revolution. The French Revolution broke out when Eastern Europe was involved in the Russo-Turkish War, which began in 1787 and lasted until 1792, and the Russo-Swedish War in the Baltic from 1788 to 1790. As a result there no desire for a war in the West in Austria and Prussia.[4] There were deep divisions among the revolutionaries and political tensions in France were made worse by the rise of a powerful party of moderates, seriously worried by the extremism which the revolution had called forth. There was, apparently, a real danger of a counter-revolution. The moderate revolutionary Gironde party, under pressure from Left and Right, chose a policy of fireworks abroad instead of fireworks at home, a forward foreign policy to keep out of power the more extreme Mountain party and the royalists. They believed a war would "cleanse" the revolution and force traitors to reveal themselves. In April 1792 the National Assembly, in an atmosphere of super-heated patriotism, approved a declaration of war against the Emperor. The Gironde played on old-established anti-Austrian sentiment in France. The alliance with Austria, in existence since 1756, was seen as a cause of the decline of France and this sentiment had been increased by the frivolous behaviour of Queen Marie Antoinette, the sister of Joseph II and Leopold II.

In reality the French government had no war aims but dreamed up theories to justify its aggressive foreign policy, including the gaining of the so-called natural frontiers of France and the liberation of peoples groaning under tyranny. The second theory was embodied in the so-called liberty decree of 19 November 1792, which offered French aid to all peoples striving to recover their liberty. Very quickly the war became its own policy-maker. Its importance in French internal politics continued, as it increasingly determined policy, created economic and political crises, drove the revolution to extremes and made a military dictatorship more likely. Europe became increasingly terrified of a revived France, especially when the Jacobins came into power and embarked on a policy of ideological warfare. This led to a series of coalitions against the French. France engaged in the search for defensible frontiers, which led her to try to subordinate the whole continent.

The actions of the French helped to push together Prussia and Austria. The German states did not want war. Indeed, France and the West were not the main focus of attention for the leading states. Austria and Prussia continued to see one another as the main enemy. Prussian intervention in the Netherlands in 1788 to put down a rising against the Orange stadholder and in Liège in August 1789 in support of a rising against the bishop were anti-Austrian moves. Prussia was also an ally of the Turks. In 1789–90 Prussia had been planning to attack Austria and dismember her when she fell apart as a result of Joseph II's blundering. King Frederick William II yearned for territorial expansion to avoid living under the shadow of his uncle, Frederick II. Austria continued to pursue her own ambitions, including a revival of the Bavarian exchange scheme based on a plan to give the Wittelsbachs a new state made up of secularized ecclesiastical territories. From the summer of 1791 fear of France pushed the two into uneasy co-operation. They were encouraged to fight the French by Russia, which hoped in this way to divert their attention from the Balkans and Poland.

At first after the outbreak of war the allies drove back the French and seemed on the point of invading France but between September and November 1792 a great turning point came. Robespierre and the Jacobins came into power and initiated a much more efficient war effort with great ideological fervour. Great French victories were won at Valmy and Jemappes, after which they occupied the Austrian Netherlands and the Rhineland. A declaration of imperial war against the French was passed by the *Reichstag* in March 1793 but there was no great enthusiasm for it. Prussia in particular was anxious to withdraw from the war in order to digest her gains from the second partition of Poland.

Under Jacobin influence in the period 1792–5 French policy still at least paid lip service to ideals, seen in mottos such as "War on the chateaux, peace to the cottage" and attempts to win over the people of the occupied areas by, among other things, attacks on the old ruling groups, the establishment of revolutionary clubs and the planting of liberty trees.

1794 saw the fall of Robespierre in the Thermidorean reaction, after which power passed to the Directory, which established the policy to be continued by Napoleon after he seized power in France in 1799. This was essentially pragmatic and dropped all pretense of idealism, seen in a new motto, "War must feed war". This signalled a return to more traditional policies, the exploitation of Germany for the benefit of France, the creation of client states (called sister republics), the levying of requisitions and contributions in return for the French alliance and protection and, eventually, outright annexation. One reason for the change of French policy was disillusionment with the lack of enthusiasm for the French among the "liberated" peoples. As Robespierre said, "No one likes missionaries with bayonets." When the French first invaded the Rhineland in late 1792 the old regime collapsed and most of its leaders fled. There was no resistance and the overwhelming reaction of the people was indifference, a tribute to the success of absolutism in teaching obedience. Commissioners and commanders on the spot later reported strong anti-French feeling but this was ignored: French internal politics were the dominant factor in determining policy towards the occupied areas.

Important was the influence of Director Reubell, an Alsatian, who was very keen on the annexation of the Rhineland by France for defensive purposes and this was probably the ultimate aim of French policy from the beginning. The French tried to set up a puppet government, based on members of the Jacobin Club under the former librarian of the Archbishop of Mainz, Georg Forster, a man highly honoured because he had sailed around the world with the English explorer Captain Cook,[5] but it had little support except among French officers and pro-French intellectuals. Much attention has been paid to the German "Jacobins" by later German historians looking for the roots of twentieth-century political systems but their significance at the time was minimal. Men like Forster, Dorsch, a defrocked priest, Böhmer, former head of the Protestant grammar school in Worms, and Rheinhard, a teacher in France since 1787, were very untypical of the Rhineland population. A few industrialists in the Aachen region were pro-French, as they wanted to sell their goods into the French market. The brief Mainz Republic, 1792–3, was a provisional government run by Germans but it enjoyed no popular support at all and depended for its operation on French military power. After Forster himself visited France, he came back very disillusioned, saying "There is no virtue in the Revolution."

Although there was very little active resistance, there was a strong anti-French element in the officials of the former rulers, guild masters and priests and a large reservoir of sentimental loyalty to the old princes. During 1793, when the French were temporarily driven out of Rhineland, the old rulers flocked back to an ecstatic welcome from the people. When the French returned and took permanent possession in 1794, their attitude had changed. They now believed that the people had been so stultified by tyranny that they had to be forced to be free. This bred a strange attitude among the French towards the Germans, like that of colonial administrators towards "natives". Also, the main concern of the French after 1794 was to exploit the resources of the occupied areas for the benefit of the French war effort. Apart from this, one searches in vain for any coherent French policy towards Germany. The decision to annex the Rhineland was taken as early as 1793 but was not put into effect for years. Much of the policy was improvised by generals and commissioners on the spot. In 1794 the princes, higher clergy and nobility fled again. There was some resistance from the guilds, especially in Aachen and Cologne, and from the clergy. Many of the anti-clerical policies of the French were gratuitously provocative and helped to make them more unpopular with a pious population. In general the people were again totally quiet.[6]

After 1794 the French system was introduced in the Rhineland in a piecemeal fashion, including the abolition of the guilds, the full French legal, judicial and administrative systems and the abolition of feudalism in all its forms. This produced expectations of change elsewhere in the German states not occupied by the French. In Baden, for example, the commutation of labour services into rents had begun in 1785 but had stopped during the reaction of 1790. The Badenese peasants expected that the process would continue when their state became an ally of France and that the poor would gain big farms. This did not happen, as the French, after the failure of the Mainz Republic, preferred to run their satellite empire in co-operation with officials and representatives of the old regime. Increasingly, financial considerations became dominant as the French economy was in ruins by 1794. The revolutionary paper currency, the *assignat*, had lost value, causing rapid inflation. The Rhineland was a rich area and the French looked to it as a place where they could find solutions to their problems. They were increasingly willing to collaborate with the old order, the nobility and the old bureaucracies. This was especially true under the Napoleonic regime, which was very much an amalgam of the revolution and the old regime. In France Napoleon ruled through the so-called "notables", the richest men in each *département*.

The French occupation of the Rhineland also led to territorial changes in Germany east of the Rhine. In 1794 Prussia, anxious for peace, short of money, worried about a war on two fronts, against the French and against Polish rebels, and afraid of Austria and Russia combining against her, began negotiations with the French to pull out of the war. In April 1795, by the Treaty of Basle, Prussia and France came to a separate peace, under which the whole of Germany north of the Main river was neutralized. Prussia sought to justify the treaty by a vote of the *Reichstag* of 22 December 1794 calling for peace negotiations with the French, which the Austrian government chose to ignore. Prussia was already thinking in terms of a north German confederation of states under its leadership within the Empire. Prussia agreed at Basle to cede to France its lands west of the Rhine and it was promised compensation inside the rest of Germany for losses in the Rhineland, although these were a small part of the whole. As a result, Prussia was able to concentrate on her concerns in Eastern Europe. For ten years she remained passive and isolated. For ten years she effectively abdicated from participation in German affairs.

From the summer of 1796 into 1797 the south German states also began to come to separate terms with the French after their invasion of south Germany. The *Reichskrieg* ended. Germany became very much a side-show as the main theatre of war shifted to Italy, where Napoleon Bonaparte was making his name as a successful general commanding an army able to support itself without money from France. He was able to pursue an independent diplomacy without much reference to his supposed masters in Paris. In 1797 he negotiated a provisional settlement with the Austrians, finalized in October 1797 in the Peace of Campo Formio. By this Austria agreed to give up Belgium, Lombardy and, in a secret article, the Rhineland, in return for French permission to seize the republic of Venice. Again the principle was stated that German rulers who lost territory in the Rhineland were to be compensated in the rest of Germany. The details of this were to be worked out later.

Nine states were nominated by the imperial diet to represent the Empire in negotiations with the French and they were mandated to preserve the integrity of the *Reich*. A congress of ambassadors of these nine and other leading German states sat in Rastatt from December until April 1799 to do this but in reality it was a farce: from this point on the future of Germany was decided exclusively in Paris. Dualism was in abeyance as the only two German states strong enough to defeat France had either been defeated, Austria, or was neutral,

Prussia. Both had already entered secret agreements with France unknown to the other states. The lesser German states lined up to obtain territory which was now in the gift of the French. There was a lively trade in bribes in Paris, in the course of which the French foreign minister Talleyrand made a fortune.

The Rastatt conference finally collapsed when the French envoys were murdered by Austrian troops on 28 April 1799 but by then the War of the Second Coalition had already broken out. Napoleon came to power in France in November 1799 by a coup to prevent a restoration of the monarchy. He took over the German policy already established under the preceding regime, the Directory, the traditional French policy of sowing jealousy and division among the German rulers, dividing Austria from the rest, seeking an alliance with Prussia and strengthening the Third Germany to make it a satellite of France. He was very successful: he achieved more perfectly than before the aims of Louis XIV. As in the reign of Louis, many German princes fell over themselves to embrace the conquerer. French policy was increasingly based on buying the co-operation of the princes as the easiest way of achieving what they wanted. In the process Germany became a "great French prefecture": the French had access to German financial and human resources and was able to deny those resources to their enemies.

The Napoleonic period saw important changes and substantial if partial modernization in Germany — some historians write of a "Napoleonic revolution" or "the revolution of the princes" — but these developments were not the result of any coherent plan. The modernizing reforms which took place were incidental and a means of cementing Germany's colonial states. In addition, the French "settlement" took place in a period of continuous warfare, involving frequent political and geographical changes which gave the whole thing an air of impermanence. There was no period of prolonged peace and stability which might have made lasting changes possible. Certainly Napoleon had no intention of doing anything to foster German unity: he said that if the Germanic Body (a typical French belittling term for the Holy Roman Empire) did not exist, the French would have to create it expressly for their own purposes. His original aim was to preserve the *Reich* as the best way of reorganizing it in the French interest, for example by the creation of new electorates. The election of a Protestant Emperor was another possibility considered.

The main result of the Napoleonic reorganizations was a great territorial redistribution which led to the elimination of the majority of the ecclesiastical states, the free cities and the small states. Germany was reduced from something over three hundred to some forty states in a series of boundary changes presided over by the French, who used their power to tie German states more tightly to them. The main gainers were the south German states, especially Bavaria, Baden and Württemberg. The first major changes were rushed through at French dictation, the document known as the *Reichsdeputationshauptschluss* of 1803.

In December 1800 the last Austrian army in the field was defeated at Hohenlinden and in February 1801 France and Austria, on behalf of the Empire, signed the Peace of Lunéville. This confirmed the terms of Campo Formio, that France would annex the Left Bank of the Rhine and that the German states which lost territory would be compensated in the rest of the Empire. Austria also had to cede land in Italy but was allowed to annex the republic of Venice, Istria and Dalmatia to make this more palatable. Under the Peace of Amiens between France and Britain of March 1802 the House of Orange was to be compensated in Germany for its lost lands in the Netherlands. On 7 March 1801 the *Reichstag* accepted the terms of Lunéville and commissioned the Emperor to negotiate the details on behalf of the whole Empire. Francis refused. The Empire had to write its own death certificate. This led in October 1801 to a recommendation by the diet that an imperial deputation (*Reichsdeputation*), a committee of the diet, should be set up to work out the details. The Emperor agreed and the deputation, consisting of Mainz, Saxony, Prussia, Bohemia, Bavaria, Württemberg, Hesse-Cassel and the master of the Teutonic Order, met in August 1802. Its report, the *Reichsdeputationshauptschluss*, was published on 25 February 1803. Again the whole thing was a sham; all the decisions had been reached in advance in an agreement between France and Russia signed in June 1802 — the Russian imperial family was related to a number of German reigning houses and protected their interests — and between France and individual German states.

On paper the imperial deputation was to carry out a modernization and rationalization of the constitution and the internal boundaries of the *Reich*. In reality it simply legalized expropriation. At last rulers could legitimately seize territory they had long coveted. This showed that the Holy Roman Empire, even in its weakness, had been able to preserve Germany from a great dismemberment. The majority of free cities and small states were mediatized, simply absorbed by their neighbours. Attempts were made in the *Hauptschluss* to preserve existing rights in mediatized territories but there was effectively no mechanism to enforce this. The most spectacular feature of the 1803 settlement was the secularization of the ecclesiastical states. Only Mainz, the Teutonic Order and the Order of St John avoided this and in the case of Mainz it was only a postponement. The Trier and Cologne electorates disappeared and that of Mainz was transferred to Regensburg. Four new electorates, Baden, Württemberg, Hesse-Cassel and Salzburg, were created. Salzburg only lasted until 1805, when it was transferred to Würzburg.

Very few princes, the most prominent the Elector of Saxony, spoke out against the secularization. Most welcomed it as a marvellous opportunity. In the period before the French Revolution many German rulers had attacked the small states as bastions of misgovernment and corruption, which some were, but this was mainly an excuse for seizing them. Some, such as Prussia and Bavaria, did not wait until the discussions were complete and began seizing free cities and the land of knights and counts as early as 1791 and 1796. The secularization had been long prepared for in France and the Empire by propaganda campaigns against the supposed inadequacies of government in the ecclesiastical states, portrayed as centres of obscurantism. There were well-documented precedents for the whole procedure in the treaties of 1648, when secularization had similarly provided compensation. The majority of the governments at the same time began to seize Church property, Catholic and Protestant, both in newly acquired lands and in their former territories. This great dissolution of the monasteries led to a massive property transfer, the effects of which have not been sufficiently researched. In general it seems, initially at least, to have had damaging effects on education and the provision of charity. The position of the nobility in the ecclesiastical states also suffered as their traditional rights, for example in cathedral chapters, were lost.

The next major step came in 1806 with the establishment of the Confederation of the Rhine (*Rheinbund*), the abolition of the Holy Roman Empire, the creation of more French satellite states and the defeat of Prussia by the French. In 1805 a coalition of Austria and Russia was defeated at Austerlitz by France and her German allies, including Bavaria, Baden and Württemberg. The whole of non-Austrian Germany was either neutral or allied to France in this war. Under the Peace of Pressburg which followed, the clients of France made further gains involving more major territorial revisions. Prussia, Bavaria and other states were further enlarged. The south German states also proceeded to mediatize the imperial counts and knights. Although they kept their lands, they were no longer direct subjects of the Emperor. Bavaria also seized the free city of Augsburg. The other free cities were gobbled up later. The Confederation of the Rhine was established, a league of states under French protection.

Napoleon at first thought in terms of a small version of the Empire with common institutions, including a federal assembly, a constitution and a common law code but the German states were very hostile to this. Some, especially Bavaria, opposed the whole idea and wanted total sovereignty and independence. The idea of a constitution was raised several times during the life of the confederation but nothing ever came of it. Under several articles of the Act of Association France, as Protector of the Confederation, retained substantial rights of interference in the internal affairs of the member states. Finally the confederation came into existence on 12 July 1806 in the form of a perpetual alliance of sixteen sovereigns and France, which took over the defence and foreign policy of the whole alliance. A common army under total French control was established. In return for French protection all members provided men and money to the French war effort. Prussia, Austria, Denmark, Sweden and the north German states, accepted as a Prussian sphere of influence, were specifically excluded from the confederation. France wanted no rivals to her control.

After the defeat of Prussia in 1806 the French set up three artificial satellite states, the kingdom of Westphalia and the grand duchies of Frankfurt and Berg, ruled by Napoleon's brother Jerome, his brother-in-law Eugene Beauharnais and a French general, Murat. They joined the confederation, which was later expanded in the north until at its greatest it had thirty-seven members. As states joined the confederation, they left the Holy Roman Empire on the grounds that it could not protect its members and was no longer an effective bond, as its courts were useless and its diet paralysed. The abolition of the *Reich* was prepared for by a long propaganda campaign against it as a feudal Gothic survival. Its days were numbered when, in December 1804, Napoleon declared himself Emperor of the French. He had earlier dreamed of becoming Holy Roman Emperor himself. In 1803 he offered the title to the King of Prussia but he was not interested. Eventually a French ultimatum was issued to Francis II threatening war if he did not abandon the imperial title. On 6 August 1806 Francis II gave up his imperial crown and the Holy Roman Empire ended.

The end of the Empire did not produce a spectacular reaction in Germany. By then every reason for its continued existence had disappeared. A Nuremberg bookseller, Palm, published a pamphlet *Germany in her Deepest Humiliation*, as a result of which he was shot after a French court martial trial. Later he became a hero of German nationalism. This fact shows how little the Germans seemed to regret the end of the *Reich* which had lasted for over a thousand years.

The effects of the period of French control varied from area to area. After 1794 the Rhineland became effectively an integral part of France although the formal annexation came later. As a result the area experienced rapid modernization. Between 1801 and 1810 it enjoyed stability and prosperity. French rule became popular with the middle class and the area became a great nursery of Liberalism and free trade ideas in the nineteenth century.

The southern states, Bavaria, Baden and Württemberg, and the artificial states like Westphalia, Berg and Frankfurt experienced, in varying degrees, a period of so-called neo-absolutism or late absolutism. It was Napoleon's intention to make Westphalia a model of French good government, an example for the rest of Germany, but the demands of the French war effort took precedence here as elsewhere and its resources were regularly raided. The southern states had reform thrust on them. All faced two problems: they had to meet the very heavy commitments in men and money to France. As a result the indebtedness most had suffered before 1789 became much worse and radical financial and administrative reform became vital. They also had to absorb substantial new territories with widely different social, legal, economic and religious backgrounds. The easiest way of dealing with both was to scrap everything and impose a single new standard system for the whole new state. This produced, among other things, rapid modernizations of administrative and legal systems, the introduction of more efficient taxation involving new land surveys and the end of tax exemptions, the abolition of religious discrimination, the emancipation of the Jews and attacks on the power of the guilds. Bavaria, under its chief minister Montgelas, Württemberg and Baden experienced major reforms. Often French practices were adopted as the best available model, involving centralization of government, some form of the prefect system, judicial reforms and the introduction of clear and rational common legal systems.

The Code Napoleon of 1804, embodying equality before the law and freedom of the individual and of property, was a rational and easily exportable system and, in some form or another, it was widely adopted and in some parts of Germany it remained in force until 1900. The reforms were carried out by bureaucrats, sometimes only waiting for a chance to revive the work of enlightened despotism. Their efforts often came up against vested interests, such as the nobles, urban oligarchies and peasants, and change had to be tempered to accommodate political realities.[7] The abolition of "feudalism", for example, was not always welcome to the peasantry, who often lost benefits and found their feudal dues being converted into taxes. Shortage of capital continued to deprive most peasants of the benefits of emancipation. For example, in 1803 the Bavarian government gave peasants the right to buy out their landlords' rights but most were unable to do so. Only where governments made available long-term low-interest loans was a class of free small farmers created.

Some states, with French encouragement, introduced unitary constitutions on the French model as symbols and instruments of the unity of the newly constructed states. It would be a mistake to see this as a liberal step, though it laid the foundations for the growth of a Liberal constitutional movement later in the nineteenth century. The parliaments established under the new constitutions often became a platform for the older vested interests not for the people. Even in the French-ruled states like Westphalia there was no increase in popular participation in decision-making. German states were in a transitional phase; documents spoke interchangeably of *Bürger* (citizen) and *Untertan* (subject) without apparent awareness of any contradiction. The French period modernized the states and strengthened the power of the established authorities. The French period also legitimized the old order in another way. Grievances about new burdens of taxation, conscription and the economic problems arising from the Continental System (Napoleon's attempt to bring Britain to her knees by shutting Europe to British commerce) for example, could be shifted against the French rather than the native rulers. This led to a romanticization of the old order. Anti-French nationalism grew as a result but the chances of achieving German unity were reduced as the new states, enlarged under French patronage, were much stronger and more confident and self-sufficient. Disillusionment with the French Revolution also produced in many a turn to idealism and the pursuit of spiritual rather than material improvement, individual development rather than collective political action.

In terms of economic change the effects of the French period varied from place to place. It speeded up changes which had begun before

1789 and which were important preparatory steps for further economic modernization in the nineteenth century, including a weakening of the guilds, a releasing of land and capital and a freeing of labour. There was economic progress in some parts of Germany and changes in the nature of the economy and in the location of centres of economic activity. The period saw a decline of the Atlantic economy and, as new industries, textiles, coal and iron, became the basis of economic life, the rise of new inland centres in Belgium, north eastern France, Alsace, the Ruhr and northern Italy, the modern Golden Triangle of Europe. The industrial revolution was not to occur in Germany until the 1850s but some areas had entered the preparatory phase by 1815. The Rhineland in 1815 was further ahead of the rest of Germany than in 1789 after twenty years of French administration and it remained a centre of economic growth after 1815. Among certain groups in the Rhineland there was a strong desire to remain French in 1814–15 and the region kept French law until 1900. The middle class there was larger and enjoyed greater opportunities for economic activity than in most other parts of Germany. Elsewhere land and office remained much more attractive than enterprise. Napoleon's Continental System, introduced in 1806, might have had beneficial effects on the economies of the German states but it did not last long enough and resulted in a loss of British and other overseas markets for German goods and severe damage to German ports. It also operated as an instrument of French economic domination. An important result of the Continental System was the mechanization of the continental cotton industry, of which France was the main beneficiary.

The two leading German states, Prussia and Austria, also experienced change as a result of the French period. In both cases this arose indirectly. In the case of Austria the changes were very limited and took the form mainly of defensive reforms designed to modernize the army. One leading minister, Philip von Stadion, was in favour of more far-reaching reform but opposition was too powerful. The conservative anti-Josephine forces remained in power after the reaction of 1792, symbolized in the person of Metternich.

The Prussian Reform Movement (1806–19) was important, though again it is necessary to beware of the Borussian legend, the idea that during this period Prussia was equipping herself to lead and unify Germany. There was certainly nothing in Prussia's behaviour before 1806 to suggest this. Prussia withdrew from the French war in 1795 in order to concentrate on Poland, a sign of her growing concern with non-German interests. Her basic concern remained the same, to prevent any one power, Austria or France, from becoming too strong in Germany. The old view that Prussia stagnated totally after the death of Frederick II has been modified. The impetus for reform did not die away and enlightened ideas lived on in the bureaucracy. Between 1795 and 1806 Prussia experienced a prosperous and peaceful period, with a boom in grain exports and a flowering of culture. A code of written laws, the preparation of which had begun under Frederick II, was introduced. This marked the beginning of the *Rechtstaat* in Prussia. The relationships between the classes and between the government and the governed were regulated in great detail by the code. As in other states, there was some reaction after the French Revolution and the pace of reform slowed down. Many later leaders of the reform movement had to keep their heads down during this period. Prussia made substantial territorial gains as a client of France but her policy has, accurately, been described as "precarious and self-deluding non-alignment".

In November 1805 Prussia entered a secret agreement with Russia and came close to issuing an ultimatum to France demanding her withdrawal from Germany, Italy, the Netherlands and Switzerland. It was decided not to present it when news of the French victory at Austerlitz arrived. Instead she renewed her alliance with France and agreed to enforce a blockade against British imports, in return for which she was given Hanover. In October 1806 she woke up to the danger that France was becoming too strong and chose to attack her in alliance with Russia. The Prussian army had not been reformed since Frederick II had reconstructed it after the Seven Years' War. It was much inferior to the army of Frederick William I, which was responsible for the brilliant successes of the 1740s and 1750s. In particular there had been no changes to take account of the military revolution which had taken place in France after the revolution. On 14 October 1806 Prussia suffered a massive defeat at Jena. This was followed by a rapid French occupation of the country. In the subsequent peace settlement she had to sign away all her territory west of the Elbe, her Polish lands and her territory in south Germany. The most striking aspect of the whole affair was the total collapse of morale in Prussia after 1806, symbolized in the governor of Berlin's proclamation to the people in the name of the king after Jena, stating that the first duty of the citizen was to keep quiet (*Ruhe ist die erste Bürgerpflicht*). However well administered the state was, the majority of Prussians saw it as an alien corporation set over them. As in the

Rhineland in 1792–3, its defeat was not seen as a concern of the people.

This disaster gave the reformers a chance. They were able to capture the king's ear. The reform movement was not a result of popular demand, a factor singularly lacking in Prussia, and the whole thing was restricted to a small section of the ruling class, especially within Prussia's excellent civil service, which contained highly-educated and highly-motivated administrators. Its leaders were Stein, Hardenberg, Humboldt, Scharnhorst and Gneisenau.[8] They drew their ideas and aspirations from a variety of sources, including the Enlightenment, the early ideals of the French Revolution and Adam Smith's theories on free enterprise. There was a strong centre of support for the movement in Königsberg and east Prussia, where there were many Liberal nobles, a tradition of opposition to the crown and links to the wide world through trade. The reformers had been able to carry out reforms before 1806, including the freeing of the peasants on the royal domains and the new Polish lands, a reduction in noble privileges, cuts in internal tolls and a reduction of the restrictions on the transfer of land.

The basic desire of the reform movement was to take the logical next step from enlightened absolutism, that is to involve the people in the running of the state and in this way to interest them in its fate. This was seen as the only way of reviving Prussia faced with the great power of revolutionary France. Their stated aim, in the words of Stein's Nassau memorandum of June 1807, was to "reawaken a spirit of community, the employment of dormant or misapplied energies and unused knowledge, to create harmony between the views and desires of the nation (presumably Prussia) and those of the administrative authorities of the state, to bring about the revival of patriotism and the desire for national honour and independence." Some reformers combined with this a desire to create some kind of German union, though their ideas were vague. Most of the reformers evinced considerable devotion to the idea of a united Germany but they did not put forward concrete proposals as to how this was to be achieved. Most of the leaders were non-Prussians, though this was not unusual as there was a common market for men of talent in eighteenth-century Germany: Stein was an imperial count from the Rhineland, a member of a class and from an area where loyalty to the Holy Roman Empire remained strong in the late eighteenth century. Another major leader, Hardenberg, was a Prussian patriot, who pursued the policy of making north Germany a Prussian sphere of influence.

The reformers had a comprehensive scheme of change to transform Prussia, including the abolition of serfdom, full free enterprise, the end of guild powers and of restrictions on the transfer of land, equality of all before the law and major reforms in the army and government. They were unable to put these ideas into practice in full. The reasons for this failure were many: the reformers suffered from the inherent weaknesses of any movement seeking change in a despotic political system. The king was a weak and hopeless ally and they faced strong opposition from articulate and influential vested interests, especially the nobility.

The reform had a partial achievement: it carried through a renaissance and modernization of Prussia, which enabled it to over-come the stagnation which had followed the death of Frederick the Great in 1786. Prussia went on to join the coalition which defeated France in the years 1813–15. Noble privilege remained but it was no longer the monopoly of a small closed elite. The French period saw a further opening up of the land market. The economic crisis after the Seven Years' War produced many bankruptcies among noble estate owners and much land had come on to the market but non-noble purchasers could only buy it using subterfuges. The reform period removed artificial barriers to the transfer of land between the classes, leading to the emergence of a "modernized Junkerdom", a class of legally privileged large landowners sharing power with the bureaucracy. No strong landowning peasantry was created by the reform (and this had been one of its aims) and marked divisions between east and west remained. Urban self-government was intro-duced. Important reforms were also carried out in the army. Another major legacy of the reform period was a group of reforming civil servants who remained in post after the leaders of the movement had fallen. They had to be careful during the period of reaction which followed the defeat of Napoleon but they kept alive progressive ideas into the nineteenth century and were to be responsible for further measures of modernization in the 1820s and 1830s.

To sum up the results of the French period: as was the case with the Thirty Years' War, the period was not a great turning point or watershed. Like the Thirty Years' War it accelerated and intensified movements already begun before 1789, the modernization of states and of the German political structure. As a result of the changes of the period Germany, as under absolutism, experienced a further burst of partial modernization, especially in administration. But again there was no real social or political modernization. Germany entered the nineteenth century still bureaucratic in government and noble-dominated socially. In 1815 a new Germany was set up as a loose confederation of thirty-nine sovereign states with no ruler over them, a kind of streamlined or modernized Holy Roman Empire. Its vital function in maintaining the European balance of power was written into the Treaty of Vienna.

We have seen Germany develop from a medieval feudal monarchy to an informal federation, which ended in 1806, after which, until 1815, it was no more than a geographical expression. The basic problem throughout the period examined was to reconcile unity and diversity. A *modus vivendi* was found after 1648 but the end of the Holy Roman Empire in 1806 revived the problem. The period also saw the steady growth of foreign interference as Germany was a vital component of the European balance of power. A major feature was the rise of the state and the triumph of absolutism. This was reinforced in the eighteenth century by the Enlightenment, which also gave birth to modern Liberalism and Conservatism. This led to an idealization of the state and a lack of initiative and popular participation in decision-making. Germany remained politically retarded into the nineteenth and even the twentieth century. Economically Germany declined to become an economic backwater of Europe marked by a weak middle class and the social and psychological legacy of serfdom, especially in the east. A state with its physical and psychological centre of gravity in the east, Prussia, was to found a new *Reich*, very different from the first, in 1871.

Notes

Unless otherwise stated, the books are published in London.

Chapter 1. Introduction

1. See F. R. H. Du Boulay, *Germany in the Later Middle Ages* (1983) and J. Leuschner, *Germany in the late Middle Ages* (Amsterdam, 1981).
2. K. Leyser, "A recent view of the German College of Electors", in *Medium Aevum*, 23, 1954, 76–87, a review article.
3. M. Todd, *The Northern Barbarians* (Oxford, 1987): the Elbe was a distinct boundary between very different terrains even in the pre-historic period.

Chapter 2. Germany on the Eve of the Reformation

1. G. Strauss, *Manifestations of Discontent in Germany on the Eve of the Reformation: a collection of documents* (Bloomington, 1971) and (ed.), *Pre-Reformation Germany* (1972).
2. C. R. Friedrichs, "Capitalism, Mobility and Class Formation in the Early Modern German City", in P. Abrams (ed.), *Towns in Societies* (Cambridge, 1978) 187–213.
3. See F. L. Carsten, *Princes and Parliaments in Germany* (Oxford, 1959) for details.
4. See the first two chapters of A. G. Dickens, *The German Nation and Martin Luther* (1974) and N. Cohn, *The Pursuit of the Millenium: revolutionary millenarians and mystical anarchists of the Middle Ages* (3rd edn, 1970).

5. H. Baron, "Imperial reform and the Habsburgs 1486–1504", in *AmHR*, 44, 1939, 293–303, S. W. Rowan, "Imperial taxes and German Politics in the Fifteenth Century: An Outline", in *CEH*, 13, 1980, 203–17, S. W. Rowan, "A Reichstag in the Reform Era", in J. A. Vann and S. W. Rowan (eds), *The Old Reich* (Brussels, 1974).

Chapter 3. The Reformation in Germany

1. A. Friesen, *Reformation and Utopia* (Wiesbaden, 1974), R. Scribner, "Is there a Social History of the Reformation?" in *Social History*, 4, 1977, 483–505.
2. J. Atkinson, *Martin Luther and the Birth of Protestantism* (2nd edn, 1982).
3. G. Strauss, "Success and failure in the German Reformations", in *PandP*, 67, 1975, 30–63, on the deep attachment of the German people to superstitious and irrational religious practices.
4. T. A. Brady, *Turning Swiss: cities and empire 1450–1550* (Cambridge, 1985).
5. G. Strauss, *Nuremberg in the Sixteenth Century* (revised edn, Bloomington, 1976), S. E. Ozment, *The Reformation in the Cities* (New Haven, 1975), B. Moeller, *Imperial Cities and the Reformation* (Philadelphia, 1972), T. A. Brady, *Turning Swiss: cities and empire 1450–1550* (Cambridge, 1985), H. Baron, "Religion and politics in the German imperial cities during the Reformation", in *EHR*, 52, 1937, 405–27, 614–33, L. G. Duggan, *Bishop and chapter* (Rutgers, 1978), R. Po-chia Hsia, *Society and Religion in Münster 1535–1618* (New Haven, 1984).
6. It has recently been argued by P. S. Fichtner, *Protestantism and Primogeniture in Early Modern Germany* (New Haven, 1989) that in one respect the Reformation set back the consolidation of the states because Protestantism taught the duty of fathers to care equally for all their children. This led to a revival of the practice of dividing territories to create appanages for younger sons.
7. G. H. Williams, *The Radical Reformation* (1962), C. P. Clasen, *Anabaptism. A Social History* (Ithaca/London, 1972), M. A. Mullett, *Radical Religious Movements in Early Modern Europe* (1980).
8. R. Scribner and G. Benecke (eds), *The German Peasant War of 1525: New viewpoints* (1979). See also T. Scott, "The Peasants' War: a

Historiographical Review", in *HJ*, 22, 1979, 693–720, 953–74, P. Blickle, "Peasant revolts in the German Empire in the late Middle Ages", in *Social History*. 4, 1979, 223–39.

9. K. Brandi, *The Emperor Charles V* (1939), R. Tyler, *The Emperor Charles V* (1956), J. M. Headley, *The Emperor and his Chancellor* (Cambridge, 1983), H. Koenigsberger, *The Habsburgs and Europe 1516–1660 (Ithaca, 1971).*

10. The Saxon Wettin lands were divided in 1485, with the Ernestine line taking the electorate with its capital at Wittenberg, and the Albertine Thuringia.

11. A. J. La Vopa, *Grace, Talent and Merit. Poor Students, clerical careers and professional ideology in eighteenth-century Germany* (Cambridge, 1988).

Chapter 4. Peace and Polarization: Germany 1555–1618

1. H. J. Cohn, *Government in Reformation Europe* (1971), M. Raeff, *The Well-Ordered Police State* (London/New Haven, 1983).

2. F. L. Carsten, *The Origins of Prussia* (Oxford, 1954) and *A History of the Prussian Junkers* (Aldershot, 1989). R. Brenner, "Agrarian Class Structure and Economic Development in Pre-Industrial Europe", in *PandP*, 70, 1976, 30-75, a major article which began a debate on the differences between the nature of peasant communities east and west of the Elbe river. H. Wunder responded with reference to conditions in Germany in *PandP*, 78, 1978, 47–55. There is further material in T. H. Aston and C. H. E. Philpin (eds), *The Brenner Debate* (Cambridge, 1987).

3. See the excellent study by R. J. W. Evans, *Rudolph II and His World* (Oxford, 1973).

4. G. Benecke, *Society and Politics in Germany 1500–1750* (1974).

5. J. Whaley, *Religious Toleration and Social Change in Hamburg 1529–1819* (Cambridge, 1985), G. L. Soliday, *A Community in Conflict: Frankfurt Society in the Seventeenth and Early Eighteenth Centuries* (Hanover, New Hampshire, 1974).

6. J. de Vries, *The Economy of Europe in an Age of Crisis 1600–1750* (Cambridge, 1976).

7. R. Po-chia Hsia, *The Myth of Ritual Murder. Jews and Magic in Reformation Germany* (New Haven, 1988).

8. D. W. Sabean, *Power in the Blood: popular culture and village discourse in early modern Germany* (Cambridge, 1984).

9. J. H. Franklin, *Bodin and the Rise of Absolutist Theory* (Cambridge, 1973).
10. M. Raeff, *The Well-Ordered Police State* (London/New Haven, 1983).
11. J. I. Israel, *The Dutch Republic and the Hispanic World 1606–1661* (Oxford, 1982). There is an important series of articles by P. Brightwell: "The Spanish system and the twelve years' Truce", in *EHR*, 89, 1974, 270–92, "The Spanish Origins of the Thirty Years' War", in *ESR*, 9, 1979, 409–31, "Spain and Bohemia: The Decision to Intervene 1619" and "Spain, Bohemia and Europe 1619–21", in *ESR*, 12, 1982, 117–41 and 371–99. R. A. Stradling, *Europe and the Decline of Spain* (1981).
12. G. Parker, *The Army of Flanders and the Spanish Road 1567–1659* (1972).
13. R. Chudoba, *Spain and the Empire 1519–1643* (Chicago, 1952).

Chapter 5. The Thirty Years' War and its Consequences

1. G. Parker (ed.), *The Thirty Years' War* (revised edn, 1987), P. Limm, *The Thirty Years' War* (1984), T. K. Rabb, *The Thirty Years' War* (2nd edn, 1981), H. Langer, *The Thirty Years' War* (New York, 1980), G. Benecke, *Germany in the Thirty Years' War* (1978).
2. There is no modern biography of Wallenstein in English. Golo Mann, *Wallenstein* (5th edn, Frankfurt, 1971) is in German.
3. T. K. Rabb, *The Struggle for Stability in Early Modern Europe* (New York, 1975), P. Clark (ed.), *The European Crisis of the 1590's* (1985), G. Parker and L. M. Smith (eds), *The General Crisis of the Seventeenth Century* (1978), T. H. Aston (ed.), *Crisis in Europe 1560–1660* (1965).
4. P. Goubert, *Louis XIV and Twenty Million Frenchmen* (1970).
5. J. Van Horn Melton, *Absolutism and the Eighteenth-Century Origins of Compulsory Schooling in Prussia and Austria* (Cambridge, 1988).
6. C. Wilson, *Mercantilism* (1958), D. C. Coleman, *Revisions in Mercantilism* (1969).
7. C. R. Friedrichs, *Urban Society in an Age of War: Nördlingen 1580–1720* (Princeton, 1979).
8. S. H. Steinberg, "The Thirty Years' War. A New Interpretation", in *History*, 32, 1947, 89–102.
9. E. Sagarra, *A Social History of Germany 1648–1914* (1977), H. Kamen, *The Iron Century. Social Change in Europe 1550–1660* (1971).

Chapter 6.   Absolutism and Particularism: Germany after 1648

1. J. Black, *The Rise of the European Powers 1679–1793* (1990).
2. J. Vann and S. Rowan (eds), *The Old Reich* (Brussels, 1974).
3. M. Hughes, *Law and Politics in Eighteenth-Century Germany* (Woodbridge, 1988).
4. R. Place, "The Self-Deception of the Strong. France on the Eve of the War of the League of Augsburg", in *French Historical Studies*, 6, 1970, 459–73.
5. J. Black, "The Problem of the Small State: Bavaria and Britain in the Second Quarter of the Eighteenth Century", in *EHQ*, 19, 1989, 5–36.
6. J. W. Stoye, "Emperor Charles VI: the Early Years of the Reign", in *TRHS*, 5th series, 12, 1962, 63–84.
7. J. Whaley, *Religious Toleration and Social Change in Hamburg 1529–1819* (Cambridge, 1985).

Chapter 7.   Dualism and Reform: Germany after the Seven Years' War

1. T. C. W. Blanning, *Reform and Revolution in Mainz* (Cambridge, 1974), J. Gagliardo, *Reich and Nation: the Holy Roman Empire as Idea and Reality 1763–1806* (Bloomington/London, 1980), K. Epstein, *The Genesis of German Conservatism* (Princeton, 1966), C. J. Friedrich, "The Continental Tradition of Training Administrators in Law and Jurisprudence", in *JMH*, 11, 1939, 129–48.
2. W. Hubatsch, *Frederick the Great of Prussia* (1975), D. B. Horn, *Frederick the Great and the Rise of Prussia* (1964), G. Ritter, *Frederick the Great: a historical profile* (1968), G. P. Gooch, *Frederick the Great* (1947).
3. A. Ward, *Book Production, Fiction and the German Reading Public 1740–1800* (Oxford, 1974), J. Van Horn Melton, "From Enlightenment to Revolution", in *CEH*, 12, 1979, 103–23.
4. See H. Rosenberg, *Bureaucracy, aristocracy and autocracy: the Prussian experience* 1660–1815 (Cambridge, Mass., 1958).
5. E. Crankshaw, *Maria Theresa* (1969), C. A. Macartney, *Maria Theresa and the House of Austria* (1969), G. P. Gooch, *Maria Theresa and Other Studies* (1951), D. Beales, *Joseph II*, vol. I, "In the shadow of Maria Theresa, 1741–1780" (Cambridge, 1987).

6. Helen Liebel, *Enlightened Bureaucracy versus Enlightened Despotism in Baden* (Philadelphia, 1965), C. W. Ingrao, *The Hessian Mercenary State* (Cambridge, 1987).

7. Febronius was the pseudonym of Johann Nikolaus von Hontheim, suffragen Bishop of Trier.

8. Mack Walker, *German Home Towns: community, state and general estate 1648–1871* (Ithaca, 1971).

9. R. R. Palmer, *The World of the French Revolution* (1971) and J. Godechot, *France and the Atlantic Revolution of the Eighteenth Century* (New York, 1971).

10. Wright, *Serf, Sovereign and Seigneur* (Minneapolis, 1966).

11. H. Kisch, "Growth Deterrents of a Medieval Heritage: The Aachen-area Woollen Trades before 1790", in *JEcH*, 24, 1964, 517–37.

12. S. Schama, *Citizens* (1989).

13. G. Parry, "Enlightened government and its critics in eighteenth-century Germany", in *HJ*, 6, 1963, 178–92.

14. There is useful material on this in Mack Walker, *Johann Jakob Moser and the Holy Roman Empire of the German Nation* (Chapel Hill, 1980).

15. H. Gross, *Empire and Sovereignty. A History of the Public Law Literature in the Holy Roman Empire* (Chicago/London, 1973).

Chapter 8.   The End of the Empire: Germany and the French Revolution

1. G. P. Gooch, *Germany and the French Revolution* (1920), J. M. Diefendorf, *Businessmen and Politics in the Rhineland 1789–1834* (Princeton, 1980), M. Hughes, *Nationalism and Society. Germany 1800–1945* (1988), chapter 3, G. A. Craig, "German Intellectuals and Politics 1789–1815. The Case of Heinrich von Kleist", in *CEH*, 2, 1969, 3–21.

2. R. R. Palmer, *The World of the French Revolution* (1971), J. Godechot, *France and the Atlantic Revolution of the Eighteenth Century 1770–1799* (New York, 1971), G. Best (ed.), *The Permanent Revolution. The French Revolution and its Legacy* (1988).

3. E. Wangermann, *From Joseph II to the Jacobin Trials* (1959).

4. T. C. W. Blanning, *The Origins of the French Revolutionary Wars* (1986).

5. G. A. Craig, "Engagement and Neutrality in Germany: The Case of Georg Forster", in *JMH*, 41, 1969, 1–16.
6. T. C. W. Blanning, *The French Revolution in Germany* (Oxford, 1983).
7. Mack Walker, "Napoleonic Germany and the Hometown Communities", in *CEH*, 2, 1969, 99–113.
8. G. S. Ford, *Stein and the Era of Reform in Prussia* (Princeton, 1922), W. M. Simon, *The Failure of the Prussian Reform Movement 1807–1819* (Ithaca, 1955), M. W. Gray, *Prussia in Transition* (Philadelphia, 1986).

Suggestions for Further Reading

Unless otherwise stated, books are published in London. Only works in English are listed. Readers who wish to consult works in German are recommended to look at the relevant volumes in the excellent series published by the Siedler Verlag, Berlin, "Das Reich und die Deutschen" and "Die Deutschen und ihre Nation". They are up-to-date and have full bibliographies:

H. Bookmann, *Stauferzeit und spätes Mittelalter. Deutschland 1125–1517* (1987).
H. Schilling, *Aufbruch und Krise. Deutschland 1517–1648* (1988).
H. Schilling, *Höfe und Allianzen. Deutschland 1648–1763* (1989).
H. Möller, *Fürstenstaat oder Bürgernation. Deutschland 1763–1815* (1989).

General Works

Macmillan History of Europe:
T. Munck, *Seventeenth Century Europe 1598–1700* (1990).
J. Black, *Eighteenth Century Europe 1700–1789* (1990).
Longmans General History of Europe:
D. Hay, *Europe in the Fourteenth and Fifteenth Centuries* (2nd edn, 1989).
H. G. Koenigsberger (et al.), *Europe in the Sixteenth Century* (2nd edn, 1989).
D. H. Pennington, *Europe in the Seventeenth Century* (2nd edn, 1989).
H. S. Offler, "Aspects of Government in the Late Medieval Empire" in J. R. Hale (et al., eds), *Europe in the Later Middle Ages* (1965).
J. Hale, *War and Society in Renaissance Europe* (1985).
D. Waley, *Later Medieval Europe: from St. Louis to Luther* (revised edn, 1975).

B. Guenee, *States and Rulers in Later Medieval Europe* (1985).

M. Jones (ed.), *Gentry and Lesser Nobility in Late Medieval Europe* (1986).

H. Trevor-Roper, *Renaissance Essays* (1985. Including essays on Maximilian I as an art patron and the outbreak of the Thirty Years' War).

H. G. Koenigsberger, *Early Modern Europe 1500–1789* (1987).

G. R. Elton, *Reformation Europe 1517–1559* (1963).

C. Wilson, *The Transformation of Europe 1558–1648* (1976).

J. H. Elliott, *Europe Divided 1559–1598* (1968).

G. Parker, *Europe in Crisis 1598–1648* (Glasgow, 1979).

J. Stoye, *Europe Unfolding 1648–1688* (1969).

G. N. Clark, *War and Society in the Seventeenth Century* (Cambridge, 1958).

J. Black, *The Rise of the European Powers 1679–1793* (1990).

J. Miller (ed.), *Absolutism in Seventeenth-Century Europe* (1990).

O. Hufton, *Europe: Privilege and Protest 1730–89* (1980).

W. Doyle, *The Old European Order 1660–1800* (Oxford 1978).

G. Rudé, *Revolutionary Europe 1783–1815* (1964).

G. Best, *War and society in Revolutionary Europe 1770–1870* (1982).

H. Kellenbenz, *The Rise of the European Economy* (1976).

J. de Vries, *The Economy of Europe in an Age of Crisis 1600–1750* (Cambridge, 1976).

——*European Urbanization 1500–1800* (1984).

P. Kriedte, *Peasants, Landlords and Merchant Capitalists. Europe and the World Economy* (Leamington Spa, 1983).

R. Ehrenberg, *Capital and Finance in the Age of the Renaissance* (1928).

C. Lis and H. Soly, *Poverty and Capitalism in Pre-Industrial Europe* (Hassocks, 1982).

S. Woolf, *The Poor in Western Europe* (1986).

Y-M. Bercé, *Revolt and revolution in early modern Europe* (1987. Study of the violence endemic in early modern societies.)

R. Mackenney, *The City State 1500–1700* (1989).

General Works on Germany

G. Barraclough, *The Origins of Modern Germany* (revised edn, 1988). (Still very valuable survey of German history from Charlemagne to Adolf Hitler).

J. B. Gillingham, *The Kingdom of Germany in the High Middle Ages* (Historical Association pamphlet, 1971).

H. Fuhrmann, *Germany in the High Middle Ages 1050–1250* (Cambridge, 1986).

A. Haverkamp, *Medieval Germany 1056–1273* (Oxford 1988).

F. R. H. Du Boulay, *Germany in the Later Middle Ages* (1983).

H. Holborn, *A History of Modern Germany*, vol. I, The Reformation (1959), vol. II, 1648–1840 (1965).

C. T. Atkinson, *A History of Germany 1715–1815* (1908, old but useful for the wealth of factual detail. Often described by its author as "the charnel house" after a reviewer said it failed to breathe life into the dry bones of eighteenth-century German history).

R. Vierhaus, *Germany in the Age of Absolutism* (Cambridge, 1989). (A translation of a well-reviewed German survey of the period 1648–1763, first published in 1978.)

G. Benecke, *Society and Politics in Germany 1500–1750* (1974. Not quite what the title suggests, mainly a detailed study of the small territory of Lippe, but an important step in the revision of traditional views of the Holy Roman Empire).

F. Heer, *The Holy Roman Empire* (1968. Glossy, descriptive and rather sentimental survey).

J. W. Zophy (ed.), *The Holy Roman Empire: A Dictionary Handbook* (1980).

JMH, 58, 1986, Supplement, "Politics and Society in the Holy Roman Empire 1500–1806" (a collection of important essays).

J. J. Sheehan, *German History 1770–1866* (Oxford, 1990).

F. L. Carsten, *Princes and Parliaments in Germany* (Oxford, 1959).

——*Essays in German History* (1985).

——*The Origins of Prussia* (Oxford, 1954).

——*A History of the Prussian Junkers* (1989).

E. Sagarra, *A Social History of Germany 1648–1914* (1977).

P-C. Witt (ed.), *Wealth and Taxation in Central Europe* (Leamington Spa, 1987).

C. McClelland, *State, Society and University in Germany 1700–1914* (Cambridge, 1980).

R. Aris, *A History of Political Thought in Germany from 1789 to 1815* (1936).

F. Hertz, *The Development of the German Public Mind* (1962).

M. Geisberg, *The German Single-Leaf Woodcut 1500–1550*, 4 vols, 1973.

D. Alexander, *The German Single-Leaf Woodcut 1550–1600*, 3 vols, 1975.

——*The German Single-Leaf Woodcut 1600–1700*, 2 vols, 1977.

J. R. Paas, *The German Political Broadsheet 1600–1700*, vol. I, 1600–1617 (Wiesbaden, 1985). (Part of a projected ten-volume work.)

A. Nitschke, "German politics and medieval history", in *JContH*, 3/2, 1968, 75–92 and W. Ullmann, "Reflections on the Medieval Empire", in *TRHS*, 5th series, 14, 89–108. (Two articles examining the distortions in earlier treatments of medieval history in Germany.)

Germany on the Eve of the Reformation

G. Strauss, *Manifestations of Discontent in Germany on the Eve of the Reformation: a collection of documents* (Bloomington, 1971).
——(ed.), *Pre-Reformation Germany* (1972. A valuable collection including essays on the medieval background and the imperial reform movement).
S. W. Rowan, "The Common Penny 1495–9", in *CEH*, 10, 1977, 148–64.
C. Tilly (ed.), *The Formation of National States in eastern Europe* (Princeton, 1975).
G. Benecke, *Maximilian I* (1982).
H. J. Cohn, *The government of the Rhine Palatinate in the fifteenth century* (Oxford, 1965. A pioneering work on modernization of administration in one German state).
P. Dollinger, *The German Hansa* (1970).

The Reformation

G. Hoffmeister (ed.), *The Renaissance and the Reformation in Germany* (1977). (Collected essays.)
R. Po-chia Hsia (ed.), *The German People and the Reformation* (1988).
F. Lau and E. Bizer, *A History of the Reformation* (1968).
P. Chaunu (ed.), *The Reformation* (Gloucester, 1989). (A collection of essays by sixteen international historians covering all aspects of the Reformation.)
H. Daniel-Rops, *The Protestant Reformation* (1961).
M. A. Mullett, *Luther* (1986).
K. Randell, *Luther and the German Reformation* (1989).
A. G. Dickens, *The German Nation and Martin Luther* (1974).
——*Reformation and Society in Sixteenth-Century Europe* (1966).
——*Martin Luther and the Reformation* (1967).
R. Bainton, *Here I Stand. A Life of Martin Luther* (1950).

E. G. Rupp, *The Righteousness of God: Luther Studies* (1953).

R. W. Scribner, *The German Reformation* (1986).

——*For the Sake of Simple Folk* (Cambridge, 1981).

J. Atkinson, *The Trial of Luther* (1971).

——*Martin Luther and the Birth of Protestantism* (2nd edn, 1982).

G. Strauss, *Nuremberg in the Sixteenth Century* (revised edn, Bloomington, 1976).

——*Law, Resistance and the State: the opposition to Roman Law in the Reformation* (Princeton, 1986).

——"Protestant dogma and city government. The case of Nuremberg", in *PandP*, 36, 1967, 38–58.

——"Success and failure in the German Reformation", in *PandP*, 67, 1975, 30–63.

R. Po-chia Hsia, *Social Discipline in the Reformation. Central Europe 1550–1750* (1989).

T. A. Brady, *Ruling Class, Regime and Reformation at Strasburg 1520–55* (Leiden, 1978).

J. M. Estes, *Christian Magistrate and State Church* (Buffalo, 1982. A study of Johannes Brenz, the main reformer of Württemberg).

T. Scott, *Freiburg and the Breisgau* (Oxford, 1987).

——"Community and Conflict in Early Modern Germany", in *EHQ*, 16, 1986, 209–16. (A review article.)

L. J. Abray, *The People's Reformation. Magistrates, Clergy and Commons 1500–1598* (Oxford, 1985. A study of Strasbourg).

L. Roper, *The Holy Household. Women and Morals in Reformation Augsburg* (Oxford, 1989).

The following collection of essays and articles are valuable:

A. G. Dickens, *Reformation Studies* (1983). (Some on Germany but most dealing with England.)

F. H. Littell (ed.), *Reformation Studies* (1962).

E. I. Kouri and T. Scott, *Politics and Society in Reformation Europe* (1987).

K. von Greyerz (ed.), *Religion, Politics and Social Protest: Three Studies in Early Modern Germany* (1984).

K. von Greyerz (ed.), *Religion and Society in Early Modern Europe 1500–1800* (1984).

R. W. Scribner, *Popular Culture and Popular Movements in Reformation Germany* (1987).

J. D. Tracy (ed.), *Luther and the Modern State in Germany* (Kirksville, 1986).

* * *

H. A. Oberman, "The nationalist conscription of Martin Luther". in C. Lindberg (ed.), *Piety, Politics and Ethics* (Kirksville, 1984).
H. Robinson-Hammerstein (ed.), *The Transmission of Ideas in the Lutheran Reformation* (Dublin, 1988). (A collection of essays on the various means by which the Reformation message spread.)
E. L. Eisenstein, *The Printing Press as an Agent of Change*, 2 vols (Cambridge, 1979).
P. A. Russell, *Lay theology in the Reformation: Popular pamphleteers in South West Germany 1521-5* (Cambridge, 1986).
C. Andersson, "Popular Imagery in German Reformation Broadsheets", in G. P. Tyson and S. S. Wagonheim (eds), *Print and Culture in the Renaissance* (1986).
G. Strauss, *Luther's House of Learning. The indoctrination of the young in the German Reformation* (Baltimore, 1978).

* * *

S. E. Ozment, *The Reformation in the Cities* (New Haven, 1975).
B. Moeller, *Imperial Cities and the Reformation* (Philadelphia, 1972).
T. A. Brady, *Turning Swiss: cities and empire 1450-1550* (Cambridge, 1985).
H. Baron, "Religion and politics in the German imperial cities during the Reformation", in *EHR*, 52, 1937, 405-27, 614-33.
L. G. Duggan, *Bishop and chapter* (Rutgers, 1978). (A study of the bishopric of Speyer to 1552.)
R. Po-chia Hsia, *Society and Religion in Münster 1535-1618* (New Haven, 1984).
J. Kitch (ed.), *Capitalism and the Reformation* (1967).
H. J. Cohn (ed.), *Government in Reformation Europe* (1971).
P. S. Fichtner, *Protestantism and Primogeniture in Early Modern Germany* (New Haven, 1989).

* * *

G. H. Williams, *The Radical Reformation* (1962).
C. P. Clasen, *Anabaptism. A Social History* (Ithaca/London, 1972).

M. A. Mullett, *Radical Religious Movements in Early Modern Europe* (1980).

R. E. McLaughlin, *Caspar Schwenckfeld. Reluctant Radical* (New Haven, 1986).

C. A. Pater, *Karlstadt as the Father of the Baptist Movement* (Buffalo, 1984).

S. C. Karant-Nunn, *Zwickau in Transition 1500–47* (Columbus, 1988).

T. Scott, *Thomas Müntzer. Theology and Revolution in the German Reformation* (Cambridge, 1989).

*   *   *

R. W. Scribner and G. Benecke (eds), *The German Peasant War 1525: new viewpoints* (1979).

P. Blickle, "Peasant revolts in the German Empire in the late Middle Ages", in *Social History*, 4, 1979, 223–39.

*   *   *

B. P. Levack, *The Witch-Hunt in Early Modern Europe* (1987).

G. Scarre, *Witchcraft and Magic in 16th and 17th Century Europe* (Basingstoke, 1987).

R. Po-chia Hsia, *The Myth of Ritual Murder. Jews and Magic in Reformation Germany* (New Haven, 1988).

*   *   *

K. Brandi, *The Emperor Charles V* (1939).

R. Tyler, *The Emperor Charles V* (1956).

J. M. Headley, *The Emperor and his Chancellor* (Cambridge, 1983).

H. G. Koenigsberger, *The Habsburgs and Europe 1516–1660* (Ithaca, 1971).

S. Fischer-Galati, *Ottoman Imperialism and German Protestantism 1521–55* (Oxford, 1959).

R. A. Kann, *A History of the Habsburg Empire 1526–1918* (Berkeley, 1977).

K. J. Dillon, *King and Estates in the Bohemian Lands 1526–64* (Brussels, 1976. A detailed analysis of Ferdinand's policies in Bohemia, showing his skill in extending royal power in the face of considerable opposition).

Germany 1555–1618

H. Kamen, *The Iron Century* (1971).

——*European Society 1500–1700* (1984).

P. Clark (ed.), *The European Crisis of the 1590's* (1985), esp. H. Schilling, "The situation in German towns".

G. Parker and L. M. Smith (eds), *The General Crisis of the Seventeenth Century* (1978).

T. H. Aston (ed.), *Crisis in Europe 1560–1660* (1965).

O. Subtelny, *Domination in Eastern Europe. Native Nobilities and Foreign Absolutism* (Gloucester, 1986. Includes material on extension of Habsburg power in south-eastern Europe.)

C. H. Carter, *The Secret Diplomacy of the Habsburgs 1598–1625* (New York, 1964).

R. Bireley, *Religion and Politics in the Age of the Counter-Reformation* (Chapel Hill, 1981. A balanced study of Ferdinand II).

M. Prestwich (ed.), *International Calvinism* (Oxford, 1985).

M. Greengrass, *Conscience and Society: Calvinism in Early Modern Europe 1560–1635* (1988).

——*Continental Calvinism* (1989).

R. J. W. Evans, *The Making of the Habsburg Monarchy 1550–1700* (Oxford, 1979).

——*Rudolf II and His World: a study in intellectual history 1576–1612* (Oxford, 1973).

H. Rebel, *Peasant Classes* (Princeton, 1982: a detailed study of the peasantry in the Austrian archduchies between 1511 and 1636).

T. Robisheaux, *Rural Society and the Search for Order in Early Modern Germany* (Cambridge, 1989). (A detailed study of villages in the small territory of Hohenlohe in the later sixteenth century, a neglected period.).

G. Parker, *The Army of Flanders and the Spanish Road 1567–1659* (1972).

——*The Military Revolution* (Cambridge, 1988).

C. V. Wedgewood, *The Thirty Years' War* (1938)

S. H. Steinberg, *The Thirty Years' War and the Conflict for European Hegemony* (2nd edn, 1977).

——"The Thirty Years War. A New Interpretation", in *History*, 32, 1947, 89–102.

G. Pagès, *The Thirty Years' War* (1970. A translation of the original French edition of 1939.)

P. Limm, *The Thirty Years' War* (1984).

T. K. Rabb, *The Thirty Years' War* (2nd edn, 1981).

H. Langer, *The Thirty Years' War* (New York, 1980).

G. Benecke, *Germany in the Thirty Years' War* (1978. Documents).

J. V. Polisensky, *The Thirty Years' War* (1971. Translation from the Czech).

——*War and Society in Europe 1618–48* (Cambridge, 1978).

——"The Thirty Years' War", in *PandP*, 6, 1954, 31–43.

——"The Thirty Years' War and the Crises and Revolutions of Seventeenth-Century Europe", in *PandP*, 39, 1968, 34–43.

G. Parker (ed.), *The Thirty Years' War* (revised edn, 1987. A very valuable up-to-date survey of all aspects of the conflict by experts).

R. A. Stradling, "Olivares and the origins of the Franco-Spanish war 1627–1635", in *EHR*, 101, 1986, 68–94.

J. I. Israel, "A Conflict of Empires: Spain and the Netherlands 1618–1648", in *PandP*, 76, 1977, 34–74.

M. Roberts, "The political objectives of Gustavus Adolphus in Germany 1630–2", in *TRHS*, 5th series, 7, 1957, 19–46.

* * *

W. Coupe, "Political and religious cartoons of the Thirty Years' War", in *Journal of the Warburg and Courtauld Institutes*, 25, 1962, 65–86.

The Consequences of Thirty Years' War

J. H. Shennan, *Liberty and Order in Early Modern Europe. The Subject and the State 1650–1800* (1986). (A study of the rise of the modern state. It draws the bulk of its illustrations from France and Russia but includes material on central Europe and makes general points which are valid for Germany).

——*The Origins of the Modern European State 1450–1725* (1974).

T. K. Rabb, *The Struggle for Stability in Early Modern Europe* (New York, 1975).

——"The Effects of the Thirty Years' war on the German Economy", in *JMH*, 34, 1962, 40–51.

H. Kamen, "The Economic and Social Consequences of the Thirty Years' War", in *PandP*, 39, 1968, 44–61.

G. Benecke, "The Problem of Death and Destruction in Germany in the Thirty Years War", in *ESR*, 2, 1972, 239–53.

* * *

R. J. W. Evans, "Culture and Anarchy in the Empire 1540–1680", in *CEH*, 18, 1985, 14–30.

M. Raeff, *The Well-Ordered Police State* (London/New Haven, 1983. The author, earlier a specialist in Russian history, compares the growth of the state in Germany and the Russia of Peter the Great).

S. Stern, *The Court Jew. A Contribution to the History of Absolutism in Europe* (New York, 1985).

D. Ludloff, "Industrial Development in 16th and 17th century Germany", *PandP*, 12, 1957, 58–73.

C. R. Friedrichs, *Urban Society in an Age of War: Nördlingen 1580–1720* (Princeton, 1979).

H. Powell, *Trammels of Tradition: Aspects of German life and culture in the 17th century and their impact on the contemporary literature* (Tübingen, 1988).

J. Whaley, *Religious Toleration and Social Change in Hamburg 1529–1819* (Cambridge, 1985).

G. L. Soliday, *A Community in Conflict: Frankfurt Society in the Seventeenth and Early Eighteenth Centuries* (Hanover, New Hampshire, 1974).

M. Fulbrook, *Piety and Politics. Religion and the Rise of Absolutism in England, Württemberg and Prussia* (Cambridge, 1983).

Post-1648 Germany

J. Vann and S. Rowan (eds), *The Old Reich* (Brussels, 1974: a collection of essays on different aspects of the Empire, itself an important stage in its "rehabilitation").

G. Strauss, "The Holy Roman Empire revisited", in *CEH*, 11, 1978, 290–301. (A review article.)

H. Gross, *Empire and Sovereignty. A History of the Public Law Literature in the Holy Roman Empire* (Chicago/London, 1973).

*   *   *

H. W. Koch, *A History of Prussia* (1978).

E. J. Feuchtwanger, *Prussia: Myth and Reality* (1970).

R. von Thadden, *Prussia: The History of a Lost State* (Cambridge, 1987).

F. Schevill, *The Great Elector* (Chicago, 1947).

R. A. Dorwart, *The Prussian Welfare State before 1740* (Cambridge Mass., 1971).

——*The Administrative Reforms of Frederick William I of Prussia* (Cambridge Mass., 1953).

J. P. Spielman, *Leopold I of Austria* (1977).

L. and M. Frey, *The Question of Empire: Leopold I and the War of Spanish Succession 1701–5* (New York, 1983. A factual uncontroversial survey).

J. W. Stoye, *The Siege of Vienna* (1964).

C. W. Ingrao, *In Quest and Crisis. Emperor Joseph I and the Habsburg Monarchy* (West Lafayette, 1974. A rather negative view of Joseph's policies in the Empire).

R. H. Thompson, *Lothar Franz von Schönborn and the diplomacy of the electorate of Mainz* (The Hague 1974. A detailed study of the activity of the Archbishop of Mainz in German and European politics. Such studies are rare in English).

J. A. Vann, *The Swabian Kreis. Institutional Growth in the Holy Roman Empire 1648–1715* (Brussels, 1975).

——*The Making of a State. Württemberg 1593–1793* (Ithaca, 1985).

M. Hughes, *Law and Politics in Eighteenth-Century Germany* (Woodbridge, 1988).

R. Hatton, *George I, Elector and King* (1978).

Germany after the Seven Years' War

K. Epstein, *The Genesis of German Conservatism* (Princeton, 1966. An off-putting title for an excellent survey of the impact of enlightened ideas in Germany).

G. Parry, "Enlightened government and its critics in eighteenth-century Germany", in *HJ*, 6, 1963, 178–92.

C. B. A. Behrens, *Society, Government and Enlightenment: The Experiences of 18th century France and Prussia* (1985).

R. Porter, *The Enlightenment* (1989).

H. P. Liebel, "The Bourgeoisie in South-West Germany 1500–1789: a rising class?" in *International Review of Social History*, 10, 1965.

*   *   *

C. A. Macartney, *The Habsburg and Hohenzollern Dynasties in the seventeenth and eighteenth centuries* (1970).

H. M. Scott (ed.), *Enlightened Absolutism* (1989).

J. G. Gagliardo, *Reich and Nation: the Holy Roman Empire as Idea and Reality 1763–1806* (Bloomington/London, 1980).

——*Enlightened Despotism* (1968).

S. Andrews (ed.), *Enlightened Despotism* (1967).

M. Walker, *Johann Jakob Moser and the Holy Roman Empire of the German Nation* (Chapel Hill, 1980).

H. Liebel, *Enlightened Bureaucracy versus Enlightened despotism in Baden 1750–92* (Philadelphia, 1965).

H. Strakosch, *State Absolutism and the Rule of Law: the struggle for the codification of civil law in Austria 1753–1811* (Sydney, 1967).

J. Stroup, *The Struggle for Identity in the Clerical Estate* (Leiden, 1984. A study of enlightened clergy in Hanover and Brunswick and their opposition to absolutism).

C. McClelland, "The Aristocracy and University reform in Eighteenth-Century Germany", in L. Stone (ed.), *Schooling and Society. Studies in the History of Education* (Baltimore, 1976).

*   *   *

G. Ritter, *Frederick the Great: a historical profile* (1968).

G. P. Gooch, *Frederick the Great. The ruler, the writer, the man* (1947).

C. Duffy, *Frederick the Great. A Military Life* (1985).

H. Rosenberg, *Bureaucracy, aristocracy and autocracy: the Prussian experience 1660–1815* (Cambridge Mass., 1958).

W. O. Henderson, *Studies in the economic policy of Frederick the Great* (1963).

——*The state and industrial reform in Prussia 1740–1870* (Liverpool, 1958).

*   *   *

G. P. Gooch, *Maria Theresa and Other Studies* (1951).

E. Crankshaw, *Maria Theresa* (1969).

C. A. Macartney, *Maria Theresa and the House of Austria* (1969).

D. Beales, *Joseph II*, vol. 1, "In the shadow of Maria Theresa, 1741–1780" (Cambridge, 1986).

P. G. M. Dickson, *Finance and Government under Maria Theresa 1740–1780* (2 vols, Oxford, 1987). (An exhaustive analysis, very technical in places.)

T. C. W. Blanning, *Joseph II and Enlightened Despotism* (1970).

S. K. Padover, *The Revolutionary Emperor: Joseph II* (1934).

P. P. Bernard, *The Limits of Enlightenment: Joseph II and the Law* (Urbana/London, 1979).

P. P. Bernard, *Joseph II and Bavaria. Two Eighteenth-Century Attempts at German Unification* (The Hague, 1965. Apart from the bizarre subtitle, a straightforward account of Joseph's Bavarian exchange scheme).

*   *   *

W. E. Wright, *Serf, Sovereign and Seigneur. Agrarian reform in Eighteenth-Century Bohemia* (Minneapolis, 1966).

R. Okey, *Eastern Europe 1740–1980* (1982).

K. Roider, "Origins of Wars in the Balkans 1600–1792", in J. Black (ed.), *The Origins of War in Early Modern Europe* (Edinburgh, 1987).

A. Klima, "Industrial developments in Bohemia 1648–1781", in *PandP*, 11, 1956–7, 87–97.

F. Spencer, "An eighteenth-century account of German Emigration to the American colonies", in *JMH*, 28, 1956, 55–9.

W. H. Bruford, *Germany in the Eighteenth Century: the social background of the literary revival* (Cambridge, 1935).

A. Menhennet, *Order and Freedom. Literature and Society in Germany from 1720 to 1805* (1973).

C. McClelland, *State, Society and University in Germany 1700–1914* (Cambridge, 1980).

J. Van Horn Melton, *Absolutism and the Eighteenth-Century Origins of Compulsory Schooling in Prussia and Austria* (Cambridge, 1988. Shows how government plans to use education as an instrument of social control did not always work out).

A. J. La Vopa, *Prussian School Teachers 1763–1848* (Chapel Hill, 1980).

——*Grace, Talent and Merit* (Cambridge, 1988. A study of poor students, usually the sons of Protestant clergymen, who obtained university scholarships in the eighteenth century, illustrating Pietism and the Enlightenment).

J. Gagliardo, *From Pariah to Patriot: The changing image of the German Peasant 1770–1840* (Lexington, 1969).

J. W. Van Cleve, *The Merchant in German Literature of the Enlightenment* (Chapel Hill, 1986).

T. C. W. Blanning, *Reform and Revolution in Mainz 1743–1803* (Cambridge, 1974).

C. W. Ingrao, *The Hessian Mercenary State 1760–85* (Cambridge, 1987).

A. Fauchier-Magnan, *The Small German Courts in the Eighteenth Century* (1958. A translation from the French, a general survey drawing examples from the Württemberg courts).

G. W. Pedlow, *The Survival of the Hessian Nobility 1770–1870* (Princeton, 1987). (A study of the way in which the nobility of Hesse-Cassel successfully adapted to change and retained their privileged position.)

The Impact of the French Revolution

R. R. Palmer, *The World of the French Revolution* (1971).

J. Godechot, *France and the Atlantic Revolution of the Eighteenth Century 1770–1799* (New York, 1971).

G. Best (ed.), *The Permanent Revolution. The French Revolution and its Legacy* (1988).

T. C. W. Blanning, *The French Revolution in Germany. Occupation and Resistance in the Rhineland 1792–1802* (Oxford, 1983).

——*The Origins of the French Revolutionary Wars* (1986).

S. S. Biro, *The German Policy of Revolutionary France.*, 2 vols (Cambridge Mass., 1957. A full, factual, rather dull and sometimes inaccurate survey).

F. Venturi, *The End of the Old Regime in Europe 1768–76* (Princeton, 1989).

H. T. Mason and W. Doyle (eds), *The Impact of the French Revolution on European Consciousness* (1989).

G. D. Holman, *Jean-Francois Reubell* (The Hague, 1971). (A biography of the member of the Directory and leading exponent of annexationist policies.)

G. P. Gooch, *Germany and the French Revolution* (1920).

——"Germany's Debt to the French Revolution", in *Studies in German History* (1948).

A. Ramm, *Germany 1789–1919: A Political History* (1967).

*   *   *

F. Wangermann, *From Joseph II to the Jacobin Trials. Government policy and public opinion in the Hapsburg dominions in the period of the French Revolution* (1959).

C. A. Macartney, *The Habsburg Empire 1790–1918* (1968).

*   *   *

G. S. Ford, *Stein and the Era of Reform in Prussia* (Princeton, 1922).

G. A. Craig, *The Politics of the Prussian Army 1640–1945* (1964).

G. Ritter, *The Sword and the Sceptre.*, vol. I, "The Prussian Tradition 1740–1890" (Coral Gables, 1969).

P. W. Schroeder, "The Collapse of the Second Coalition", in *JMH*, 59, 1987, 244–90. (This contains useful material on Austrian policy in Germany.)

F. Crouzet (et al., eds), *Essays in European Economic History 1789–1914* (1969. Contains: G. Adelmann, "Structural Change in the Rhenish Linen and Cotton Trades at the Outset of Industrialization".

F. Crouzet, "Wars, Blockade and Economic Change in Europe 1792–1815", in *JEcH*, 24, 1964, 567–88.

H. Freudenberger, "State intervention as an obstacle to economic growth in the Habsburg monarchy", in *JEcH*, 27, 1967, 493–509.

*   *   *

O. Connelly, *Napoleon's Satellite Kingdoms* (London/New York, 1965).

W. M. Simon, *The Failure of the Prussian Reform Movement 1807–1819* (Ithaca, 1955).

J. M. Diefendorf, *Businessmen and Politics in the Rhineland 1789–1834* (Princeton, 1980).

*   *   *

F. L. Ford, "The Revolutionary-Napoleonic Era: How much of a watershed?" in *AmHR*, 69, 1963–4, 18–29.

Central European History, 22/2, 1989: special issue "The French Revolution in Germany and Austria".

Index

Frederick William I, King of Prussia, 119, 142, 143
Frederick William II, King of Prussia, 175
Freemasons, 159, 171, 174
French Revolution, x, 50, 153, 156, 159, 160, 167 ff.
Fuggers of Augsburg, 12, 13, 36, 74

German language, 7, 38, 112, 140, 161
Germans, eastward migration of, 8
Godly law (*göttliches Recht*), 47
Graz, Treaty of (1617), 84
Gregorian calendar, 66
Grundherrschaft, 9
guilds, 12, 75, 110, 121, 151, 155, 157, 159, 172, 177, 185
Gutsherrschaft, 9, 111
gypsies, 76

Habsburgs, 1, 7, 85, 120
Hamburg, 107, 108, 134, 150
Hanover (Brunswick–Lüneburg), 93, 96, 102, 114, 120, 125, 136, 138, 144, 165
Hanseatic League, 8, 11, 13
Henneberg, Berchtold von, 25
Henry VII, Emperor, 2
Henry II, King of France, 59
Herny IV, King of France, 80
Herrenhausen, Treaty of (1725), 119
Hesse, 40, 65, 92, 115, 120, 144, 153
Hohenstaufens, 2
Hubertusburg, Peace of (1763), 141
Huguenots, 109, 110, 125, 143
humanism, 37, 39
Hungary, 1, 23, 24, 29, 62, 114
Hussites, 6, 15, 19, 33, 36

Ice Age, Little, 75
Innsbruck, 23
Interregnum, Great, 2
Investiture Contest, 3, 5
Italy, 3, 5, 19, 23, 83

Jacobins, 173, 175, 176
Jena, battle of (1806), 186
Jesuits, 67

Jews, 13, 94, 128, 152
Joseph I, Emperor, 123, 124, 126 f., 137
Joseph II, Emperor, 139, 145, 149, 152, 153, 157, 158, 163, 164, 165, 167, 174, 175
Junkers, 9, 65, 111, 112, 188

knights, free imperial, 15 f., 33, 40, 45, 120, 123
Kues, Nicholas of, 21

League, Catholic, 78, 84, 87, 91
leagues, urban, 7, 22
Leopold I, Emperor, 121, 122, 123 f., 128, 130
Leopold II, Emperor (Grand Duke Peter Leopold of Tuscany), 149, 153–4
Liberalism, 162, 169, 189
liberty, Germanic (*teutsche Libertät*), 26, 94, 115, 129, 149, 165
Lippe, 68
Louis XIV, King of France, 98, 101, 119, 123, 124, 126, 127, 179
Luther, Martin, 29, 30, 33 ff., 50
Lutheranism, 15
Luxembourg, House of, 6, 7

Main, river, 7
Mainz, 36, 53, 99, 115, 129, 138, 176, 181
Majesty, Letter of, 82, 86
Maria Theresa, Empress, 127, 128, 138, 139, 140, 149, 152, 157, 158, 163–4
Matthias, Emperor, 81 f., 83, 86
Maximilian I, Emperor, 1, 19, 20, 21, 22 ff., 28 f.
Maximilian II, Emperor, 63, 83
Maximilian I, Duke of Bavaria, 83, 84, 88, 89
Mecklenburg, 8, 90, 91, 109, 110, 133
Mediterranean, 11
Melanchthon, Philip, 34, 60
Memmingen, Twelve Articles of, 48
mercantilism, 75, 103, 108, 112, 123, 151
middle classes, 16, 110, 159, 160